RENEGADE HERO

RENEGADE HERO

The true story of RAF pilot Terry Peet and his
clandestine mercy flying with the CIA

by Michael Hingston

Pen & Sword
AVIATION

First published in Great Britain in 2011 by
Pen and Sword Aviation
An imprint of
Pen and Sword Books Ltd
47 Church Street
Barnsley
South Yorkshire
S70 2AS

Copyright © Michael Hingston 2011

ISBN 978 1 84884 530 5

Printed and bound by CPI UK

Pen and Sword Books Ltd incorporates the imprints of
Pen and Sword Aviation, Pen and Sword Maritime, Pen and Sword Military,
Wharncliffe Local History, Pen and Sword Select, Pen and Sword Military
Classics and Leo Cooper.

For a complete list of Pen and Sword titles please contact
PEN AND SWORD BOOKS LIMITED
47 Church Street, Barnsley, South Yorkshire, S70 2AS, England
E-mail: enquiries@pen-and-sword.co.uk
Website: www.pen-and-sword.co.uk

Contents

Maps

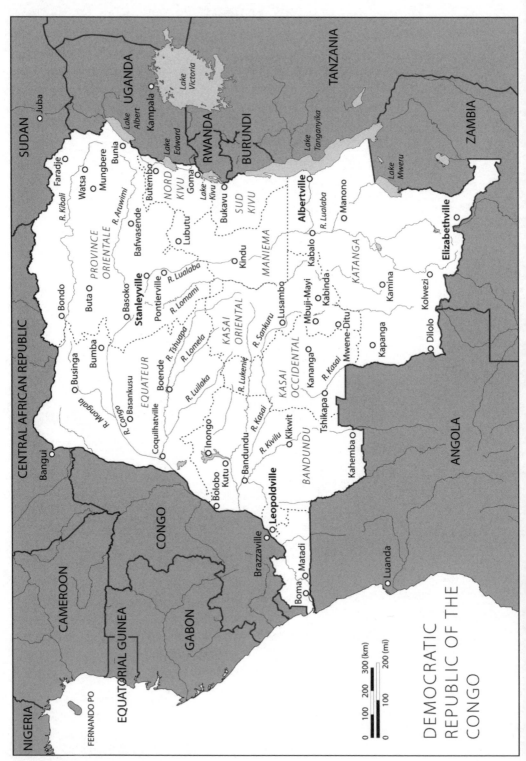

The principal towns are shown with the colonial names they bore at the time of Terry Peet's arrival in 1965. (Alan Hunns – alan@hunnsgraphics.demon.co.uk)

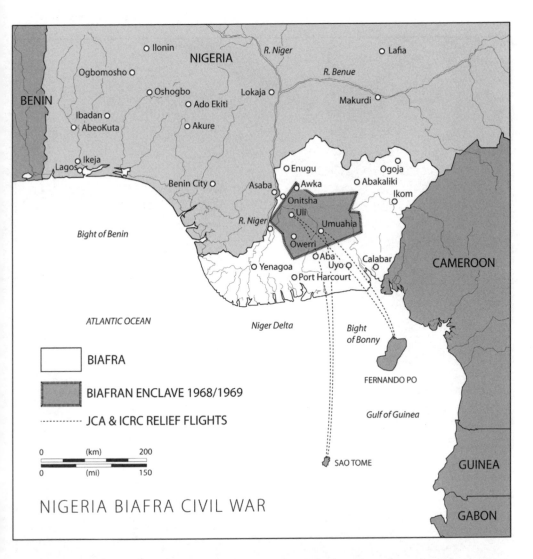

The Biafran enclave was shrinking during the period and the boundary shown is approximate. Uli was the principal airstrip for relief flights although Umuhaia was among a number of other strips used briefly at different periods. The UNICEF helicopter relief flights under Terry Peet's control were principally between Calabar and Uyo in what was then Federally held Biafra.

(Alan Hunns – alan@hunnsgraphics.demon.co.uk)

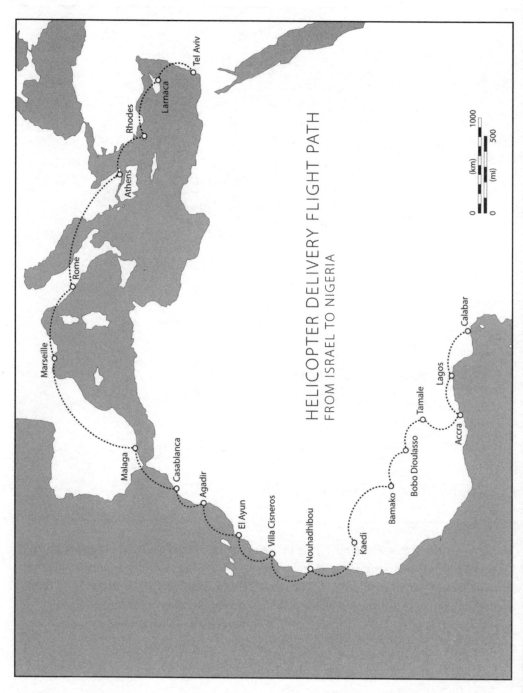

HELICOPTER DELIVERY FLIGHT PATH
FROM ISRAEL TO NIGERIA

The flight path for the epic delivery of helicopters from Israel for the UNICEF Calabar-based relief operation. The diversion to Accra from Tamale followed the arrest of Terry Peet and his colleagues on their arrival in Ghana. (Alan Hunns – alan@hunnsgraphics.demon.co.uk)

Acknowledgements

I am deeply indebted to a great many people without whose help writing this story about Terry Peet would have been impossible. In particular my thanks go to his second wife, Joan Peet (née Milner), for sharing her diary recordings and many intimate memories, as well as to his late mother, Annie 'Nance' Peet, and brother, Barry Peet, for their candid recollections.

For the early chapters about Terry's exploits in the Far East I relied heavily on invaluable input from his former commanding officer in Malaya and Borneo, Wing Commander Derek Eley. My thanks also go to other former RAF colleagues, Lofty Marshall and Mike Bailey, and to Mrs Royston Garwood, the widow of his commanding officer at RAF Tern Hill.

Former mercenary aircrew colleagues Bob Brannon, Ares Klootwyk, Eugenio Papotti, Kevin Bell and Pelle Ornas provided much of the background to events in the Congo, for which I am grateful. In addition my special thanks go to the late Dr William T Close, father of the celebrated five-times Oscar-nominated Hollywood actress Glenn Close. During sixteen years working in the Congo, most of them as President Mobutu's personal physician, he renovated the capital's hospital and played a key role in combating the deadly Ebola epidemic. He came to know Terry well and coined the phrase 'gentleman warrior' to describe him.

Although I was unable to interview Leighton Mishou, Terry's principal CIA contact in the Congo, since he was incapacitated by a stroke and in a veterans' hospital where he later died, I am hugely indebted to his wife, Jane Mishou, and daughter Catherine Sines. They allowed me unrestricted access to his unpublished memoir full of valuable, first-hand information about Operation *WITHRUSH*. My gratitude is also due to the late Larry Devlin, the former Congo CIA station chief who put me right on facts about the operation and added his own insights before he, too, died in December 2008.

Colonel Julian Brooke-Fox helped with information about his father's role as the British military attaché in Leopoldville and I was also assisted by Terry Laurendine who worked at the US embassy there and *Madame* Francine Troger, Dr Close's former chief nursing assistant.

For Terry's audacious exploit ferrying helicopters to Nigeria from Israel and the subsequent account of his involvement in the UNICEF-sponsored relief effort during the Biafran War, my thanks go to Bob Billings, Dennis Clarcq, Terry Crawley, Margaret Clark and Mary Price, sister of the late Robert Robards, who organized the helicopter-borne aid flights. In addition, Ares Klootwyk provided candid recollections of the role played by mercenary pilots in attempting to interdict what remains the largest emergency airlift since the immediate post-war 'Berlin Crisis' in 1948.

Graham Salt and Matthew Hogan helped with the task of searching for relevant documents at the UK National Archives in Kew, London, and US National Archives and Records Administration, in Washington. Dermot O'Shea Hoare spent many hours trawling newspapers for me at the British Library. In New York, Monika Tcakova, Paola Casini and Upasana Young helped with searching the UN and UNICEF archives. I was also assisted by Mark Frost of the Dover Museum and Kate Wilson at the Parliamentary Archives. I thank them all.

I am also indebted to Gilbert Blades of Chapman Wilkins, lawyers specializing in military law and courts martial, for helping me with the final chapter and to Clive Richards of the Air Force Historical Branch, Ministry of Defence, and staff at Officers' Records, RAF Innsworth. There were also other people who asked to remain anonymous who helped me in valuable ways. They know who they are and I thank them.

In the course of researching and writing the story I disrupted countless of Terry's evenings with telephone interviews and am grateful to his long-suffering wife, Marie, for her understanding. I am also profoundly indebted to my wife, Julia, and to my friends for their unwavering enthusiasm and support throughout.

Finally, I want to thank my agent, John King of Brandon Associates, and Ting Baker, my editor at Pen & Sword Books.

Preface

Cold War helicopter ace Terry Peet lived for flying. He was a 'go anywhere, do anything', Royal Air Force pilot with a reputation for 'sheer guts'. The more challenging the mission, the more eagerly Terry volunteered to undertake it. Whether ferrying troops to remote jungle landing zones or snatching casualties from makeshift clearings surrounded by 200-feet high trees, he willingly pushed himself and his primitive Sycamore helicopter to the limit. Nothing excited him more than the heady smell of octane and accompanying burst of flame and smoke as the Sycamore's engine whirred to life carrying him airborne. Alone in the cockpit, his hands deftly tweaking the aircraft's controls, the debonair young flight lieutenant knew no fear. During two years in the hot spots of Malaya and Borneo he repeatedly cheated death and earned a Queen's Commendation for Valuable Services in the Air. His nerve and skill saved him from one emergency that, according to his commanding officer at the time, 'would have killed anyone else'. With rotary flight still in comparative infancy, his career looked promising. Then suddenly he disappeared without trace, apparently drowned tragically while on a recreational scuba dive off the North Wales coast. Six years later he dramatically reappeared in a back-from-the-dead drama worthy of fiction. The media hailed him enthusiastically as a 'renegade hero' and 'flying Pimpernel' when the story of his mysterious disappearance and subsequent extraordinary double life unfolded.

The courageous, lifesaving exploits of this Nottinghamshire miner's son first came to my attention late one evening at the end of the first week in October 1971. I was working as a reporter at *The Birmingham Post*, the morning newspaper serving Britain's second city, when the night editor walked across to my desk and handed me a single sheet of paper.

'Here, see what you can make of this,' he said, passing me a page torn from one of the teleprinters in the centre of the expansive, open-plan newsroom that we shared with a sister, evening newspaper. I read the one-paragraph, news agency flash under the heading 'Airman "back from the dead"'. Flight Lieutenant Terence Peet from RAF Tern Hill, who was believed to have drowned off Anglesey in October 1965, had been apprehended and was being returned to the UK under close arrest. That was it.

Three weeks later I went to RAF Innsworth in Gloucestershire to cover the proceedings of Peet's court martial for desertion. I recall being struck by the handsome, clean-cut, uniformed figure of the thirty-six-year-old defendant. He pleaded guilty and asked for clemency on the grounds that he was driven to stage his death by a combination of factors. His marriage had failed, he was afraid of being grounded because of having high blood pressure and he felt compelled to use his skill as a helicopter pilot to help save the lives of nuns and missionaries who were being butchered in the former Belgian Congo. We were told that after disappearing, he went to Africa where he saved more than five hundred lives over a two-year period and became President Mobutu's personal pilot. Afterwards, he went to Nigeria and headed a United Nations Children's Emergency Fund (UNICEF) helicopter airlift to feed starving refugees during the bloody Biafran War, saving many more lives.

This was a *Boy's Own* -style tale of derring-do and by any standard a sensational story. It provided me with a front-page lead under the banner headline: 'RAF gaols pilot who "deserted to save lives in the Congo"''. Most of Britain's national newspapers ran prominent reports under similar headlines. Peet was then forgotten. This no doubt suited the Ministry of Defence and the RAF, who must have known very well the potential for embarrassing questions if all the facts about his desertion had come out at his trial. Although I had no reason to suspect anything at the time, I later learned the murky truth. Both America's Central Intelligence Agency and Britain's Secret Intelligence Service were implicated in the affair and the RAF's behaviour was questionable.

From what I could tell, Peet was a classic example of a working class boy made good. Yet we were asked to believe that on his own initiative he had thrown his remarkable achievements away to risk his life in the pursuit of an ideological cause in equatorial Africa where he had no connections. What is more, he had callously abandoned a wife and two young children and caused his whole family deep distress to pursue this cause. It made no sense. Observing him from where I sat on the Press bench only a few feet distant, he did not have the appearance of a hard-hearted man. Nor did I see the characteristic smirk of a maverick or contemptuous grin of someone with complete disregard for his uniform. The more I thought about the case afterwards, the more I became increasingly convinced that there had to be something more than an unhappy marriage and ideological whim to explain his action. I decided to try and find out. Three years after his court martial I traced him to Hawaii, where he was then living.

In an exchange of letters he revealed in confidence that he had been recruited by the CIA for a clandestine air force involved in paramilitary operations in the former Belgian Congo. He was told that his departure from the RAF had to be 'covert'. The summary presented in court crucially omitted this. It also failed to disclose that his employment as a mercenary, or 'contract pilot' to use the CIA's more inoffensive terminology, received the tacit approval of British intelligence. Moreover, a claim that the RAF had not seen or heard anything of him following his disappearance in Anglesey was completely untrue.

When I originally corresponded with him back in 1974, the events concerned were still too recent for him to go public and that was how we left it. We lost touch and for me the exploits of the 'airman who came back from the dead' became an oft-repeated dinner party yarn. That remained the case until 2004 when I decided to try and find Terry again and resurrect the idea of telling his story. As luck had it, I had kept my correspondence with him. This included an eleven-page document summarizing what he claimed had happened nearly forty years earlier, still in the manila envelope he originally posted to me from Hawaii. I rooted it out and started to make enquiries, eventually leading me to an elderly aunt of his who agreed to forward my contact details to him. Some weeks later a one-line email popped up on my computer screen.

'I understand you're looking for me. Terry Peet.' We were back in touch.

He was living in France and I wrote telling him that I wanted to revive my original idea of writing a book about what he had done and why. Over the subsequent weeks and months we exchanged occasional messages until he finally agreed to tell me the whole story, keeping nothing back. I flew to Toulouse and rented a car to drive and meet him at his home in the Dordogne. The last time I had seen him was in court at RAF Innsworth but I recognized him immediately when he pulled up outside my hotel in a dilapidated blue Citroën and hauled his ample bulk out of the driver's seat. He was dressed in a rather scruffy, faded tracksuit with open sandals but despite the extra girth and fuller face of a man in his early seventies, I could still picture the good-looking, young officer in air-force blue in my mind's eye.

'I hope I haven't kept you waiting too long,' he apologized, sticking his hand out.

'Only about thirty years,' I quipped.

He was short of breath and suffering from a niggling heart condition that a cardiac specialist warned him needed surgery but which he at the time dismissed as a minor irritation. From his affable welcome, I sensed we were going to get on well as he drove me to his newly built home at Le Boulet near Souillac. He pulled up a couple of chairs on the terrace and brought out a bottle of pastis with two glasses and a jug of water.

'I take it you drink this stuff?' he correctly assumed, pouring a generous slug into my tumbler and turning it milky white with a splash of water and then doing the same for himself.

We talked for hours until the September sun turned watery and the evening chill drove us indoors. Eventually, he took me to a small *auberge* for dinner, where he was greeted with the enthusiastic intimacy of a close family friend. As I soon discovered, this would be the case wherever we went, always accompanied by a shaggy-haired mongrel called Iggy that Terry rescued and coaxed back to life after finding him half-dead on the road. 'I'd like you to know that he's a highly bred *berger du Boulet*,' he chuckled, after telling me how he found the near-lifeless, rain-soaked bundle of fur on the way home one day.

'Ah, Terri,' the proprietor of a small bar exclaimed, embracing him warmly when we went out for lunch the next day. *'Tu vas bien ?'* Terry grinned mischievously and answered immediately in his idiomatic French. 'Yes I'm fine but I'm not supposed to be drinking,' gesturing to his heart. 'So we'd better have a bottle of wine!' The bar exploded in laughter and Terry chortled. He has a wonderful and, at times, wicked sense of humour and it is easy to understand why he is so well liked. Almost every assessment of him during his brief RAF career drew attention to his engaging personality. It is something that binds people to him even when he has done things that would normally deserve their rejection. He is a complex, larger-than-life character, by his own admission no saint; in many ways even an anti-hero. Yet he was no ordinary mercenary and, as this book reveals, would probably never have done what he did but for an unusual combination of circumstances and a chance meeting that provided the impetus.

Leafing through his flight log with him was like unlocking the secrets of a coded diary as he translated the seemingly mundane recordings, often nothing more than single words like 'casevac' or an obscure place name, into one hair-raising reminiscence after another, each of them always as understated by him as the entries on the page. After a couple of days he suggested continuing our conversation in the car while he took me on a tour of the local sights. He was in the middle of telling me about flying the former Palestinian president, Yasser Arafat, around in an aircraft loaned to him by the Saudi royal family as we approached Rocamadour, the gravity-defying medieval jewel that clings precariously to sheer limestone walls rising six hundred feet above the Alzou in the Causse de Gramat.

'I usually stop the car and put Beethoven on to go round this corner,' he announced. But he did not have the disc with him and we drove on in silence.

'This is as far as the Moors got,' he told me, confessing a weakness for history. 'It's pretty impressive, isn't it?'

Later, we followed the signs to an old mill that he admitted he had always wanted to visit, eventually arriving at a forest clearing where the road ended. Another sign informed us that the mill was two kilometres away by foot, at the bottom of a valley, which sloped steeply from where we were parked. The rocky path was carpeted with autumnal leaves and hazy sunlight shafted through the gaps in the semi-clad branches.

'Are you sure you want to do this?' I challenged, conscious that the return hike might be too much for his ailing heart.

'You sound like bloody General Walker in Borneo when we had to walk out from a jungle landing zone. The bugger was twice my age but kept stopping to turn round and ask if *I* was okay,' he rejoined. The mill was being restored and after a short stop to marvel at what it must have taken to build three centuries earlier, we headed back. The return climb was punctuated by repeated rest breaks with Terry gasping for air and me feeling awkward because I could sense his discomfort at having a witness. I realized then that nothing was going to stop him accomplishing this mission once he had set his mind on it. From boyhood Terry has always needed to prove himself. The trek to the mill was another challenge: in his condition, another example of his appetite for attempting near-impossible feats. He could just as easily have been back in the pilot's seat trying to land a Sycamore in a space not much larger than its own length between trees 200-feet high in Malaya; or making repeated, risky night flights in a dangerously overloaded 'bubble' Bell helicopter to rescue nuns facing rape and murder at the hands of Simba rebels in the Congo; or struggling with inadequate resources to feed starving refugees ensnared in Nigeria's brutal civil war.

This book is the product of many, many hours interviewing Terry and recording his first-hand testimony on which it is largely based with corroborative material wherever possible. For this I have relied on extensive searches of UK and US Government and United Nations archives and interviewed or received material from members of his family; former RAF and CIA colleagues; contemporary mercenary pilots; aid workers, and other people who worked alongside him or were close to him during the six years of his secret missing life, including the young, hippy girl who met him the day after his 'drowning' and later became his second wife. She remembers being impressed by his good manners on their first encounter. Always the gentleman – that is how she and most of his compatriots think of him and why one of them neatly summed him up to me simply as a 'gentleman warrior'. Yet the newspaper label 'renegade hero' is probably more apt.

Michael Hingston
Castera-Verduzan, France

Chapter One
Mind Twisting Times

Moelfre is a melancholic-looking cluster of old fishermen's cottages and houses nestling round a nondescript hillock on a windswept, treeless promontory jutting from the east coast of Anglesey in North Wales. Although the official visitors' guide trumpets enthusiastically that it 'looks like every child's idea of a seaside village', the truth is more prosaic. The small collection of buildings on the bare rise that gives the village its name is unremarkable except for the uniform dreariness of the grey, stone and pebble-dash walls and dark, slate roofs. Even the shingle beach is grey. On more days than not, so too are the sky and sea. What aesthetic attraction the village has lies in its accidental harmony with the austere surroundings of this stretch of shipwreck coast. With an eye to tourism, today's inhabitants have added cheering splashes of brilliant whitewash here and there and immortalized their most famous son – a renowned lifeboat coxswain – in a striking, life-size bronze. The stocky, sou'wester-clad figure of Dic Evans,[1] twice winner of the Royal National Lifeboat Institution's prestigious gold medal for courageous rescues, faces resolutely across the sea towards the Dee Estuary and Liverpool Bay, conjuring dramatic images of gale-lashed heroism. But before these efforts at prettification and attraction, Moelfre more typically looked cold and unwelcoming. This was certainly the case on an autumnal day in 1965 when the ink-black waters offshore, mirrored leaden, brooding clouds overhead. For Flight Lieutenant Terry Peet, it was the perfect place to die.

Aged thirty, this tall, athletic and charismatic Nottinghamshire miner's son was not an obvious candidate for suicide. Blessed with classic good looks, he stood a shade less than six feet in height and was thick set with a mop of brown hair, smiling brown eyes and a firm, square jaw. In uniform he could make women swoon. No less attractive than his appearance, were his manners. Terry was the sort of man who automatically opened car doors for ladies and unfailingly jumped to his feet when a woman entered or left the room. He never swore in their presence and eschewed hard-drinking, heavy-smoking machismo. In fact, he never smoked. By dint of sheer determination he had overcome his humble, working-class origins, successfully rising through the ranks from the lower deck as a boy sailor in the Royal Navy to the comparatively exalted heights of the officers' mess in the Royal Air Force. With the British class system then under pressure but still alive and well, this was a creditable achievement. Better still, he had distinguished himself in his first operational posting as a helicopter pilot in Malaya and Borneo and been rewarded with a Queen's Commendation for Valuable Service in the Air. To the casual observer then, he was what the *Worksop Guardian*, his hometown newspaper, might have described as the quintessential 'local boy made good' with a promising career beckoning. Added to that, he had apparently done well for himself romantically. His wife of six years was a dark-haired, blue-eyed Scottish beauty from a well-to-do family who had borne him two exceptionally pretty daughters. Outwardly at least, he seemed to have everything going for him.

Wing Commander Derek Eley, one of his former commanding officers in the Far East and the man responsible for recommending him for the Queen's Commendation, remembers him well. In his words Peet was 'a splendid fellow – very nice chap and damned good helicopter pilot'. He vividly recalls that in the jungle in Malaya and Borneo, he always exhibited an irrepressible thirst for assignments.

> He'd be standing there volunteering when none of the others was interested because it was peeing with rain or a very dodgy place to get in and out of, or a bank holiday or what have you. He was a sort of fearless, enthusiastic character who I think put a lot of people to shame. I put him up for his gong for saving himself and the aircraft when he had a tail rotor failure. Now that's serious. Anybody else would've been killed.

This sort of lavish praise is not handed out lightly as a rule and certainly not by men of Eley's experience. Significantly, it is not just the product of a glossy recollection, kindly coloured by nostalgia either. Eley formally recognized Terry's 'drive, initiative and sheer guts' in a written confidential assessment back in 1964.

Given this track record it would have been perfectly natural for Terry to feel pleased with life and optimistic about his prospects. Yet this was not the case. What he convincingly portrayed outwardly as a happy marriage was in truth, for him at least, a loveless sham. The resulting tension and verbal warring ate away at him as lethally as a visceral illness. He knew that he should end the marriage. That would have been the difficult but honest thing to do. However, owning up to the failure, coupled with the grim prospect of an acrimonious divorce, was more than he could face. Day by day he asked himself what it was that had gone wrong between himself and the former nurse called Joan McKay with whom he became hopelessly infatuated after meeting her at a dance. At the time she was working at Edinburgh Royal Infirmary. He was coming to the end of an upper yardman's course at the nearby Royal Naval station at Lochinvar in the earnest hope of qualifying as a Fleet Air Arm pilot.

Terry was young and virile but he was also a hopeless romantic, inclined to turn every encounter to love. This was especially true with Joan, who he saw as everything he wanted in a woman – beguilingly attractive, intelligent with a canny sense of humour and middle class as well. Wooing her became such an ardent objective that he flunked his exams, sacrificing his chance of a Royal Navy commission, something he had spent seven years working towards. The effect on him was traumatic. For the second time in his life he felt a crippling sense of personal failure, just as he had after throwing away the coveted prize of a grammar school education by being expelled for running away. At least then he had had an understandable excuse. He absconded to escape constant bullying. But the pursuit of a lustful craving for a girl to the exclusion of all else, especially the studying that would have brought him the career reward he so badly wanted, was not so easily forgiven. Terry knew this. He felt utterly ashamed of himself and struggled to find the courage to tell his parents, who he knew would be devastatingly disappointed. Letting them down filled him with disgrace.

His only consolation was that the time he invested in his impassioned courtship of Joan succeeded in winning her. They were married on 28 March 1959 in his home town of Worksop. According to Terry's mother, Joan's parents disapproved of the match and warned her that her son would live to regret it. That ominous prophecy seemed unlikely as the happy couple started married life together. Joan was the pillar around which Terry started to rebuild his life. Severely chastened by his failure to gain admission to the RN, he immediately focused on retrieving his self respect by passing an RAF selection board for trainee pilots. One of his naval tutors assured him that the air force was less choosy about its officers than the navy and he had a good chance of being able to transfer. He loved the navy but not enough to spend the rest of his career as a telegraphist chief petty officer. So after seven unblemished years with the Senior Service he left to join the air force as an officer air cadet, or as he sardonically recalls, 'the lowest of the bloody low'. He knew perfectly well that Joan could not be held in any way responsible for his failure to make it to the naval wardroom. All the same, in later years he could not look at her without being reminded of his failure. Whether this lay at the root of their subsequent marital breakdown or simply aggravated other underlying problems is debatable but it was undoubtedly a factor. So too was Terry's eye for other women and their unfailing attraction to his seductive, effortless charm, although he does not readily admit it.

Shortly after successfully earning his wings and being posted to Malaya as a flying officer, Joan joined him there. She arrived with two-year-old Erica and new-born Nicola. It should have been the start of a tropical idyll. They were allocated a spacious, luxury apartment complete with servants on the beautiful island of Penang, where Joan could enjoy leisurely days at the beach while Terry was in his element choppering around the jungle. However, like many marriages that go irreconcilably wrong, what began as small rifts in the relationship quickly developed into chasms and their union was over in everything except name well before they returned to the UK three years later. Terry could probably have continued to cope with this intense romantic chagrin if he had still enjoyed the euphoria of an adventure-filled role in the air. Instead, after the daily excitement of adrenalin-driven flying in the combat zones of Malaya and Borneo, he found himself literally going round in circles as a basic training instructor, making repetitive circuits over rural Shropshire. For him, this was the equivalent of trying to run a high-octane engine on low-grade paraffin.

Towards the end of his tour in the Far East, with over a thousand hours of operational helicopter flying under his belt, Terry had listed his preferences for subsequent postings as secondment to a US helicopter unit or assignment to either the Metropolitan Communications or Queen's Flights. Ironically it was Eley, then the squadron leader in charge of 110 Squadron operating out of the Royal Australian Air Force base at Butterworth in Malaya, where Terry was stationed, who recommended an 'instructional tour as good experience for his first two preferences'. In hindsight he concedes that this was probably a mistake. 'The interesting part about instructing, the variable if you like, is the difference in the people you teach and the need to vary the approach. I don't think that was enough for Terry. He needed something more challenging where he could prove himself. He was always trying to prove himself.' Eley's recommendation was meant as an accolade of sorts, a recognition of Terry's flying skill. Terry saw it as a rebuff, a soft posting where his career would stagnate.

At the time Central Flying School's helicopter training unit was based at RAF Tern Hill, near Market Drayton, a small English town famous for being the birthplace of Clive of India and the reputed home of gingerbread. Ideally located on a spacious plateau surrounded by acres of gently undulating meadows and woodland, the school was responsible for elementary training of helicopter pilots in Sycamore Mk 14s and more advanced training, using larger Whirlwind Mk 10s. Terry was allocated to the elementary training section using the Sycamores in which he had so distinguished himself in Malaya. Tern Hill was given up by the RAF in 1974, when some of the housing was sold off and the rest retained for use by the Army as Clive Barracks, later targeted by IRA bombers in a high-profile, unsuccessful attack. However, the airfield's two 1,000-yard runways continued to be used as an overspill for the tri-services helicopter establishment at nearby RAF Shawbury. This is still the case today. On most days passers-by are treated to a ballet-like spectacle of helicopters going through various manoeuvres: taking off, hovering, landing, taking off again to fly sideways then backwards, stopping abruptly and pirouetting on the spot then dipping their noses into forward flight for a quick circuit before returning to perform another choreographic sequence. Fascinated onlookers watch from the car park of the *Stormy Petrel* pub near the intersection of the trunk roads passing the base, just as they did more than forty years ago when helicopters were still a comparative novelty and Terry arrived in January 1965 to start his instructor's course.

He was assigned Flight Lieutenant Dave Pendlebury, the acknowledged ace of the base, as his teacher. They had done their original flying training on helicopters together but Terry recalls that Pendlebury 'was so bloody good that they kept him back as an instructor'. He was regarded with a certain amount of disdain owing to his lack of any operational experience. Nonetheless, Pendlebury's flying skill was never in question and he succeeded in getting Terry through the instructor course. He deserves some credit for this since Terry accepts that he was a reluctant pupil. Moreover, instructing in a Sycamore meant overcoming a unique difficulty. The aircraft enjoyed the distinction of being the first British-designed helicopter to fly. Its extensive use in the latter years of the Malayan Emergency and early stages of the Indonesian Confrontation helped to revolutionize concepts of air support for ground operations, changing established dogma in the Air Ministry about the superiority of fixed wing aircraft. Yet the Sycamore suffered a serious design flaw – the configuration of its controls. Helicopters have two hand-operated control levers – one called the collective and the other the cyclic. Instead of having separate, identical controls for each of its two cockpit seats, the Sycamore was designed with a single, centrally mounted collective lever, an idiosyncrasy that during its twenty years of service confounded many pilots and contributed to a number of accidents.

The collective lever is L-shaped with a twist, motor-cycle-style throttle at the top. Pulling the lever up or pushing it down while twisting the throttle to increase or decrease power controls the pitch and speed of the rotor blades collectively, and governs upward and downward flight. The cyclic lever changes the angle of attack of the rotor blades at different points of rotation and moving it forwards, backwards or right and left controls directional flight. In Terry's words, 'the best way to think about it is to imagine a spinning saucer. Pulling the collective up or pushing it down, makes the saucer respond vertically. Moving the cyclic tilts the saucer in the direction of flight.' During flight both levers and throttle usually require constant adjustment. This means that the pilot has his hands full as well as having to work a foot pedal to control the pitch of the tail rotor, which is essentially the aircraft's rudder and provides the anti-torque necessary to stop the fuselage spinning under the main rotor. Unlike fixed-wing pilots, who fly from the left-hand seat, helicopter pilots normally sit in the right-hand seat, operating the collective with their left hand and the cyclic with their right hand. But as an instructor you had to be able to fly from the left-hand seat as well. With the dual controls common in most aircraft this presents no problem but the Sycamore's central collective made the transition a feat of ambidextrous expertise.

Terry confirms that mastering this act of mind-twisting was like changing driving seats in a car and having to press the brake with your clutch foot and the clutch with your brake foot 'only a lot more complicated'. Progressing through the instructor's course, candidates flew together, taking it in turns to fly from the left-hand seat and 'trying not to kill each other'. Just getting off the ground successfully when flying from the 'wrong' seat was a potential hazard because the Sycamore had a tendency to fall forwards and roll to the left on take-off. This had to be corrected by moving the cyclic lever back and to the right while pulling up the collective and opening the throttle. Trained pilots did it instinctively from the right-hand seat but had to think about it hard when they reversed hands to fly from the left-hand seat. A moment's hesitation could have catastrophic consequences.

Just over two months after arriving at Tern Hill, Terry conquered the art of twisting his brain as he changed seats and successfully qualified as an instructor. His marks were average, falling disappointingly short of the consummate flying ability he had frequently demonstrated in the difficult jungle terrain of Malaya and Borneo. In a confidential assessment, his commanding officer, Squadron Leader Royston Garwood, revealingly wrote of him: 'He has a rather casual manner and if he has any enthusiasm for the job he does not show it.' Garwood's assessment accurately reflected Terry's disenchantment with his new role. With his marriage on the rocks, the lack of any real excitement at work simply intensified his unhappiness. He desperately wanted to do something that would make him feel good about himself. The knowledge that there were hot spots all over the world where he believed he could put his skill to better use and really prove his worth rankled with him. Within weeks of qualifying as an instructor, he started angling for a new posting. When the RAF's then head of flight training, Air Commodore H A C Bird-Wilson, visited the station to present him with his Queen's Commendation, Terry collared Bird-Wilson's female ADC in the mess and, turning on his characteristic charm, sweetened her up as much as he could.

'You could do something useful for me,' he eventually told her. 'Get me another foreign posting as soon as possible.'

'Yes, I could do that,' she smiled back noncommittally.

Of course, she never did anything of the sort. Nevertheless, Terry kept trying to secure another operational posting, volunteering for just about anything that came along.

Understandably, his acute frustration with his relatively undemanding capacity as an instructor was intensified by his marital unhappiness. He felt unfulfilled, both as a teacher and husband. His sense of worthlessness was heightened further by international events that angered him, or as he puts it more colourfully, 'got right up my nose'. On and off for more than a year, Terry had been reading graphic newspaper reports about the brutal slaughter of nuns, missionaries and white settlers in the former Belgian Congo by communist-backed rebels. As he saw it, Britain was sitting on the sidelines in the face of these atrocities in the newly independent Democratic Republic of Congo, yet contemplating the use of force in suppressing ambitions for white supremacy in Rhodesia (today's Zimbabwe), where British settlers feared a similar outcome to African majority rule. An RAF squadron had even been deployed to Zambia, neighbouring Rhodesia, and airmen threatened with courts martial if they defied a ban on playing cricket against a white Rhodesian eleven. What made all this particularly galling for Terry was that he had learned to fly with a Rhodesian named Parker, who remained a good friend. He recollects a lot of bad feeling in the country over the British Government's stance and vividly remembers being in a pub in London with Parker at the height of the political tension leading to Rhodesian premier Ian Smith's unilateral declaration of independence (UDI).

'I'm sorry, you can't buy a drink in here mate,' the licensee announced when he realized that Parker was Rhodesian. Incensed, Terry and Parker made to walk out when the landlord broke into a huge grin and added, 'They're on the house for you!' So far as Terry was concerned, Rhodesians were British kith and kin and any idea that he might go to war against them was preposterous. On the other hand, his experience in Malaya performing casualty evacuations told him that there was an obvious role for helicopters performing rescue work in the Congo conflict and he would gladly have participated in that.

Looking back more than forty years on, he acknowledges that this was naïve idealism that ignored the political realities of the day. However, at the time he believed it sincerely and his lack of self worth was reinforced by the knowledge that while he supervised trainees doing circuits over peaceful Shropshire, innocent people were dying for want of rescue in equatorial Africa. According to Terry, this combination of profound personal, professional and political disillusion bordering on despair was what brought him to an emotional wit's end. His mind was being twisted by a lot more than changing seats in the Sycamore.

Notes

1   Evans succeeded his uncle as coxswain in 1954 and retired in 1970. He died in 2001 aged ninety-six and the memorial bronze was unveiled by HRH The Prince of Wales in 2004.

Chapter Two
Disappearing Act

Despite his disappointment with his new posting, Terry tried to give instructing his best shot. He recalls some interesting students, among them squadron leaders on fixed wing aircraft who then realized that helicopters were the up and coming thing and not the backwater that they had previously been regarded. Today, the essential role of helicopters in warfare is taken for granted. As transports, helicopters provide vital speed and mobility for ground troop deployments with the tactical advantage of surprise. As gunships, they offer crucial air cover. And as ambulances they evacuate the wounded rapidly from inaccessible and remote areas. In the current Afghanistan conflict, British troops call them their 'guardian angels'. And their importance was exemplified by the political furore over the British Army chief's complaint that operations in Afghanistan were seriously impaired and troops exposed to unnecessary additional risks by an acute shortage of helicopters. In Colombia the success of US-backed Government forces against the FARC (Revolutionary Armed Forces of Colombia, translated from the Spanish – *Fuerzas Armadas Revolucionarias de Colombia*) guerrilla movement can be almost entirely ascribed to the widespread use of helicopters. However, back in 1965 the once scornfully dismissive attitude to helicopters in the RAF hierarchy was only just beginning what would become a rapid change of attitude. Terry remembers the arrival at Tern Hill of the first-ever batch of graduates from the RAF College at Cranwell, who were being sent straight to helicopter squadrons rather than fixed wing ones as the boffins in the Air Ministry finally recognized the vital role of helicopters in modern warfare. He was responsible for training one of those first Cranwell cadets, a man named Palmer. At about the same time two American helicopters paid a surprise visit to Tern Hill.

Lessons about the value of helicopters learned by Britain in stemming the Far East insurgencies were not lost on the Americans. They had already used them to great effect during the Korean War and were about to make them iconic symbols of the rapidly escalating conflict in Vietnam.

Helicopter gunships were yet to evolve but in the summer of 1965 the US military was evaluating three competing aircraft for what they termed LOHs (light observation helicopters). For some reason, that July two examples of one of the contending designs dropped in at Tern Hill. On their arrival Terry was called to the CO's office and informed that he was to fly with the visiting lead pilot, a man named Captain Leach. Terry gave Leach a quick demonstration flight in one of the Sycamores, paying particular attention to Leach's request to be shown the specialized techniques of limited area manoeuvring, absolutely essential in conducting jungle warfare operations. Leach then invited Terry to fly one of the visiting helicopters. From what Leach told him, he was the only RAF pilot who had been allowed to do this because the cockpit was crammed with US technology that was still classified.

'You handle these things pretty well,' Leach remarked when they landed. Terry instinctively knew that Leach was checking him out, but he had no idea why or what for, and to this day does not know whether it was connected with the dramatic turn of events that followed shortly afterwards.

He remembers the incident because it was one of the rare breaks in the monotony of daily instructing. His flight log for the period graphically highlights the humdrum routine, listing page after page of repetitive exercises in which the only things that change apart from the aircraft identification and exercise numbers are the names of the students like Palmer. The students were men by the name of Taylor and McCracken, when in late August or early September, almost nine months after he arrived at Tern Hill, the outcome of a chance meeting promised to resolve the suffocating sense of futility that then dominated Terry's life. During a break in flying one morning, he wandered over to the control tower. As he started up the stairs he encountered a senior officer who he knew from the Far East. The officer cannot be named because Terry undertook never to divulge his identity and even now insists on maintaining his silence. What he has disclosed is that the officer was middle ranking and Terry knew him well enough to open up completely to him. At the officer's suggestion they chatted privately in an office in the tower normally occupied by Squadron Leader Garwood, who was not present. Terry poured out all his marital woes, his desperate boredom with instructing and his longing for another operational posting. He said that he had been badgering continually for an overseas transfer without any success.

Apparently, Terry's confidante listened sympathetically without saying much in response. This changed when Terry started talking about events in the Congo and his fervent conviction that in the jungle terrain there a few helicopters flown by pilots with his experience could play a crucial role in saving lives. The officer then stopped him in mid-flow.

'Look,' he interrupted firmly, 'I think I can help you do something in the Congo if that's what you really want. But before I go any further I have to have your word that you will treat anything I say to you in complete confidence and promise me that whatever happens, you will never reveal my name in connection with this.'

'You can count on that,' Terry willingly agreed, seduced by the intrigue and acutely conscious that middle-ranking officers rarely risked doing anything without an eye to their own promotion prospects.

'Okay then, try calling this number,' the officer suggested, quickly copying a telephone number from his pocket book onto a scrap of paper. 'These people need experienced helicopter pilots and may be able to offer you something interesting. Remember though, once you call the number you're on your own and if you ever say that the information came from me I will, of course, deny it. This conversation has never taken place. Is that absolutely clear?'

When Terry rang the Liverpool number from a call box in the entrance to the officers' mess later the same day, he had no idea what to expect. A woman answered the telephone. She simply confirmed the number rather than providing a name. Terry introduced himself and repeated what he had heard about a requirement for helicopter pilots. He does not remember how the rest of the conversation went but at the end of it he was given another telephone number to ring, this time in Nottingham. He pushed more coins into the old push-button A and B payphone and repeated the earlier conversation to the person who answered. He remembers being annoyed because he was then given a London number to call. 'I thought I was being given the run around and frankly I was a bit pissed off. I nearly left it at that because I was running out of change for the 'phone.' His irritation quickly subsided when he dialled the London number and an American male voice at the other end quickly answered identifying it as the office of Anstalt WIGMO. Not only was the respondent expecting his call, but he also knew exactly who Terry was. 'I found that reassuring and assumed that the officer friend who gave me the original number to call must have advised them that they'd be hearing from me.'

Anstalt WIGMO was a Liechtenstein-registered front for a secret Central Intelligence Agency paramilitary air force in the former Belgian Congo. Outwardly, it gave the appearance of being a civilian-operated aircraft maintenance company. Anstalt is the generic name for a Liechtenstein company and WIGMO was said to be an acronym for Western International Ground Maintenance Organization. In truth, it could just as easily have been a whimsical word made from the initials of its shadowy, Florida-based, CIA-funded owners, William Guest and George Monteiro. Whatever the truth, it was also by happy coincidence part of the company's London address in Wigmore Mews. Terry did not know any of this at the time. His respondent confirmed that WIGMO had an urgent need for helicopter pilots with his kind of experience and that there was a job for him flying rescue and reconnaissance missions in the Congo if he wanted it. Hard as it is to believe, no terms were requested by him or volunteered by the WIGMO representative. However, there was one stipulation. Before being taken on by WIGMO Terry would have to exit the RAF.

> I was left in no doubt that my departure had to be covert because openly recruiting me would present diplomatic problems. What I was told was something to the effect that Her Majesty's Government could not be seen to be implicated and I had to be deniable by the US Government. How I disappeared was left to me but it needed to be without trace.

Once he had successfully done this he was to report immediately to WIGMO's mews address in London where he would receive further instructions. That was all.

Although he could not be sure, he was reasonably confident that he was talking to the CIA. Moreover, he genuinely believed that his informant's involvement in giving him the telephone number meant that the British authorities were aware of what was being proposed but could not be seen to be. This belief was reinforced by the fact that the WIGMO representative told him on the telephone that he would be 'cleared all the way' and had nothing to worry about.

> I couldn't imagine that a serving officer in the RAF could be involved in helping to recruit me for the Americans unless he'd had the unofficial nod from the powers that be. Looking back now, I accept that I was incredibly naïve to place so much faith in this belief.

In his defence, Terry was caught at an emotionally vulnerable time when he was naturally inclined to believe what he wanted to hear rather than being rational. Joining WIGMO promised escape from the wreckage of his marriage and tedium of his job and the opportunity to do something worthwhile by helping people in danger and need. It would save him from the pain of an ugly confrontation with Joan and the admission of another failure to his parents. The more he thought about it, the more he convinced himself that he had been selected for a secret mission and that in itself was a thrilling incentive for a man in his disconsolate state of mind.

The excitement of what beckoned, however, was tempered by nagging guilt over walking out on his daughters, then aged six and four, and the distress he knew he would cause the rest of his family, especially his parents. For several days he did nothing except go over the pros and cons of what had been proposed. Around mid-September though, after a lot of soul searching, he finally made up his mind that Flight Lieutenant Terence Peet, official number AF/4230629, recent recipient of a Queen's Commendation, would cease to exist.

After making the decision to accept WIGMO's offer, how to vanish 'without trace' became Terry's principal preoccupation. His imagination went into overdrive as he considered the possibilities. Very quickly he determined that he had to appear to die rather than simply disappear. Whatever his differences with his wife, he did not want her and the children or the rest of his family left in limbo. Similarly, he did not want to be a fugitive. 'Dying' would ensure that the RAF would not pursue him. The challenge then became how to stage his death convincingly enough to allow him to make his escape and start his new life? He says the answer came to him in one of those eureka-like, revelatory flashes of inspiration that have the appearance of genius at the time but are blindingly obvious in hindsight. Terry was taking a pilot through repeats of simple exercises in the twenty-six exercise, basic training schedule. He knew them so well that he could have flown them blindfolded and inevitably his thoughts dwelt on the urgent business of ending his existence. Then the ruse of a diving accident dawned on him with the glaring clarity of a Malayan sunrise. It made perfect sense. Terry was an accomplished scuba diver and ran the squadron diving club. He was due to organize a dive on the famed wreck of the steam clipper *Royal Charter* off Anglesey and could use this as the pretext for doing a reconnaissance alone. The remains of the ship lay in the murky waters of Port Eleth, a small bay on the north side of Moelfre, where she was dashed to pieces by hurricane-force winds with the loss of 454 lives and tons of gold bullion in 1859.

Within the next couple of days Terry formulated the details of how to accomplish his apparent death by accidental drowning. He dismissed any notions of a mock suicide even though it might have been easier to make that look authentic. No, even in death he had his pride to consider. A whingeing suicide note was not his style. He made a mental action-list, including small but important requirements such as cancelling his life insurance policies so that there could never be any accusation of attempted fraud. He drove to a travel agency in nearby Market Drayton and picked up some timetables for the Holyhead to Dublin ferry service. His plan was to leave them behind to be found in order to obscure his trail to London if anything went wrong and he ended up being pursued. He tried to think of everything, anxious to eliminate any possible hitches. At the time he felt pleased with his thoroughness but in retrospect admits that 'it was all rather amateurish' and not likely to fool any but the most casual investigators.

With Squadron Leader Garwood's permission for his absence to undertake the *Royal Charter* reconnaissance, he booked himself 'out' in the station duty roster for the rest of the week from Wednesday 29 September, the day he had chosen to be his last. In the run up he made a point of calling at the *Robin Hood* pub near the base for a few drinks and letting some of his co-instructors know that he was heading to Anglesey to go diving. If everything went to plan he would not be missed at Tern Hill until the following Monday morning at the earliest and by then he expected to be out of the country with enough evidence left at Moelfre to suggest he had suffered a fatal accident while diving. Even if the alarm was raised earlier, he reasoned there would be no grounds to suspect anything other than his tragic death by drowning.

At around 7.30 on the Wednesday morning he left his wife asleep in bed. He had told her he was going diving the night before so there was no reason to disturb her. Anyway, he had nothing more to say to her. He quickly packed a few belongings into a parachute bag, including his passport, flying suit, flying helmet and flight log, which he now accepts were hardly the sort of things that a man going on a diving recce in Wales would normally have taken with him. Then he tip-toed into the girls' room and kissed them goodbye. He found this the hardest moment of his disappearing act but claims that he never really believed that he was saying goodbye for ever. Terry was good at convincing himself of the improbable and as he looked fondly at the sleeping forms of Erica and Nicola, he assured himself that one day they would learn that he was still alive and be reunited with him. The WIGMO contact had intimated during their telephone conversation that he could be joined by his family in due course if that was what he wished and conditions permitted. In truth, of course, as Terry readily admits, that was 'pie in the sky' but at the time it made saying goodbye bearable.

He pushed the front door of the house firmly shut behind him with a feeling of finality. There could be no second thoughts; once that door was shut there was no going back and he was very focused on what had to be done next. That meant driving to RAF Shawbury, eight miles away on the A53 towards Shrewsbury, to pick up the necessary scuba gear. Terry was well known there because apart from the squadron diving club he also ran its athletics programme and the Shawbury station boasted an indoor athletics facility, where he was a frequent visitor. With the help of the storekeeper he loaded the rear of his white Ford Cortina estate with dive tanks, a wetsuit, mask and fins, as well as an inflatable dinghy, and then strapped a kayak onto the roof rack and signed for the equipment. The ensuing drive to North Wales and across the Menai Straits to Anglesey was a five-hour marathon on the then busy, single-carriageway A5 trunk road. As he headed north-west from Shrewsbury to Oswestry, Llangollen and Betws-y-Coed with only the car radio for company, he had ample time to reflect on what he was doing and why. He remembers that it was mostly the practicalities and logistics of the exercise that then concerned him rather than the rights and wrongs. His head reeling with these concerns, he resisted the temptation to stop at the pub opposite the renowned Swallow Falls at Betws-y-Coed, which he knew well from his flight training days in Anglesey. Still deep in thought, he pushed on through the craggy Snowdonia scenery to the university town of Bangor on the Menai Straits. A contact at the university scuba club often acted as a liaison for him when he organized squadron dive outings. The university divers knew the waters off Anglesey better than anyone and Terry relied on them for valuable local information. Correctly, he surmised that it would look suspicious if he had not told them that he was doing a reconnaissance of the *Royal Charter* and sought their advice. As part of his plan he had telephoned ahead to arrange a meeting with his regular contact. After seeing him, Terry headed across Telford's magnificent suspension bridge spanning the narrow straits separating Anglesey from the Welsh mainland and drove to Moelfre, where he arrived in the early afternoon.

He followed a narrow lane out of the village to the seafront. On his right, swards of tufted grass buffeted by the wind clung to a bank that rose steeply to form a round-topped hill. On the summit, a small coastguard hut faced the sea. The building has long since gone but its old concrete foundation marks the spot where for generations men watched for ships in distress as they plied in and out of Merseyside and the great trading port of Liverpool. To his left the uneven, rocky coast swept away in a shallow arc describing Port Eleth, within which lay the rusting remains of *Royal Charter*, in its day the fastest ship between Liverpool and Australia. On the rocks, just below him, in the frothy wake of breaking waves, he could easily make out the much more recent seaweed-covered remnants of the coaster *Hindlea*, driven ashore by a violent storm only seven years earlier.

Terry stood by the car looking out across the grey sea. The sky was heavily overcast and the gusty wind flecked the tops of the waves as they rolled towards the shore. He felt cold in his shirtsleeves and fished a pullover out of his parachute bag to ward off the chill. There were no ships in sight, not even on the horizon towards Liverpool, which was unusual. The coast was equally deserted. No walkers out with their dogs and no sign of any movement from the coastguard hut either. So far as he could tell he was completely alone, exactly what he wanted. Yet the total absence of any signs of life; the bleakness of the surroundings; the whistling of the chill wind and murmuring whisper of the breaking waves combined to unnerve him. Instead of seizing the moment to execute the plan he had by then mentally rehearsed countless times on the long journey, Terry climbed back into the car. He started the engine, reversed up the lane and drove off to find an old friend by the name of Ian Hush. Hush was someone who had been washed out of Terry's original pilot's course and taken up with a girl who owned a pub in Anglesey. Thinking about it now, Terry explains this impulse as a sudden need to talk at the moment when he was confronted by the enormity of what he was about to do. He may well have been searching for a way out. Whether a heart-to-heart with his old friend would have changed anything is impossible to say but it seems a plausible supposition. As it happened though, Hush was not at home. Terry turned the car round and returned straight to Moelfre. The rest as he laconically says 'is history'.

When he parked the car back at the spot below the coastguard hut he wasted no time getting on with what had to be done. So far as he could tell there was still nobody else around. If there was anybody in the coastguard station they exhibited no interest in his presence. He unloaded and inflated the dinghy and then sorted out the scuba gear that he would normally require for a dive. Sitting in the driver's seat with the car door open, he wrote up faked details of an exploratory dive, deliberately noting that he had been forced to cut it short because of a leaking air cylinder. This was followed by another fabricated entry along the lines of, 'it's getting dark now but I'm going to make another dive on the wreck', and then nothing more. Satisfied with the falsified log entries, he heaved the dinghy over his head and carried it down to the water's edge, loaded it with the scuba gear he had selected and shoved it off the rocks into the sea. He smiled as the backwash dragged it away into deeper water, where the offshore breeze would be sure to carry it quickly out of sight.

Returning to the car, he grabbed the parachute bag that he had packed earlier that morning, took the grand total of twenty pounds out of his wallet, nearly all the money that he had, and then left the wallet behind with his service identification card and walked briskly away, leaving the car unlocked with the key in the ignition. He was dressed in a pair of jeans, cotton shirt and knitted, woollen sweater. With the parachute bag over his shoulder, he hurried through the village and headed for the main road. He had not gone very far when a bread van pulled alongside and slowed to a crawl beside him.

'Would you be wanting a lift then mate?' asked the driver in a heavy, Welsh lilt through the open window.

'I don't suppose you're going to Bangor by any chance are you?' responded Terry.

'That's exactly where I'm headed. Come on, hop in,' said the driver leaning across to open the passenger door. Terry jumped in and gratefully accepted a lift all the way to the railway station. The first part of his plan seemed to have gone perfectly.

What he did not know as he left the scene was that his presence had not been entirely unobserved. From behind the twitching net curtains of her cottage, the owner of a small caravan site near the village overlooking the seafront, by the name of Mrs Owen, had seen him launching his dinghy. There was nothing unusual about that since divers frequently used the spot to go off and explore the *Royal Charter* wreck but when Mrs Owen looked out of the window the following morning and saw the white estate car still parked under the coastguard station she called the police. A strong gale had developed during the night and she feared the worst for the car's owner.

Chapter Three
Driving Ambition

At the Woodlarks Workshop School for handicapped children near Farnham in Surrey, Ernie and Annie 'Nance' Peet were relaxing after Sunday lunch when the telephone rang. Ernie, his lungs clogged with coal dust that would eventually cause his early death from pneumoconiosis, heaved himself out of his armchair in their cottage lounge to take the call.

'It's a message about our Terry,' he told his wife cryptically after replacing the receiver, adding 'I'm just going outside for a minute.' Nance, who was the school's principal, went to look for him when he had been gone for some time. Understandably, she was curious to know more about the telephone message concerning their eldest son. She found him in the school office sitting at her desk with his head in his hands. 'He was crying like a baby.'

'What on earth's the matter?' she asked. Then without waiting for an answer: 'It's our Terry, isn't it? Something's happened to him.'

'Yes. They say he's feared drowned,' he replied barely audibly, standing up to take her in his arms. 'He's been missing more than two days now and they reckon there's not much hope of finding him.'

Ernie's disclosure left her reeling in shock. She vomited for three hours afterwards. 'I have three sons and love them all but there was always a special place for Terry. He was our first born.'

Terence John Peet was delivered on 30 June 1935 by Dr Potts, the village general practitioner at Carlton-in-Lindrick, a small mining community five miles north of the Nottinghamshire town of Worksop. His parents rented a modest cottage in an old stable yard adjoining a public house called the *Blue Bell Inn*. Today the cottage has gone, as have the local coal mines. The *Blue Bell* alone remains, with a prosperous new look reflecting the more affluent times. Its stone walls gleam with fresh, white paint; the leaded windows sparkle, and its whole façade is prettily festooned with flower-filled, hanging baskets. The landlord obligingly pulls Terry a free pint of beer as his birthright whenever he calls in. However, back in 1934 when Terry's parents arrived to take up residence in the converted outhouse, the *Blue Bell* was a grimy, colliery local dedicated to quenching the parched, dust-filled throats of thirsty pit men after a gruelling day's work underground.

As a young girl, Terry's mother wanted to be a teacher but she was pushed out into service as a lady's maid as soon as she was old enough to work. Her own mother was a widow struggling to support ten children. Annie Dean was barely seventeen when she met Ernest Peet at Creswell in Derbyshire, where they then both lived. He was eight years her senior; dark haired with a miner's muscular build; with strong, sinewy arms; and smiling brown eyes that concealed his own disappointment in life. A gifted young organist, he abandoned his boyhood hopes of going to music school and ran away to join the cavalry after losing both parents and being entrusted to the care of an aunt when he was thirteen. This adolescent adventure was brought to a summary conclusion when his aunt tracked him down and exposed him for enlisting under age. Unhappily returned to Creswell, the only future he had was underground at the colliery. Shortly after meeting and marrying Annie, however, he found a marginally better-paid job at the then relatively new Firbeck Colliery across the county line and they moved to Carlton-in-Lindrick. Every morning Ernie squeezed into the steel cage filled with sweat-soaked men for the clanking journey to the coalface after walking two miles to the pithead from their new home. Meanwhile, Annie supplemented his wages by taking whatever menial jobs she could find until her pregnancy with Terry stopped her working. After he was born she baked bread and cakes to sell and scrape together extra pennies. They never had any spare money.

Nance Peet lived into her nineties before dying in March 2009. Silver haired and animated, with a beguiling smile and indefatigable spirit, she looked radiantly well almost to the end despite long battles against cancer. Before her death she talked freely and fondly about Terry's childhood. 'He was a beautiful baby: big brown eyes and golden hair. Right from the day he was born he never complained. He was a lovely child to have around; no bother and always willing to help.' When Terry was aged three, his father was in hospital suffering from pleurisy for eight of the nine months of his mother's pregnancy with her second child. There was virtually no money coming in and she was giving Terry most of what little food she could afford. Finally, she was forced to send him away to be cared for by her older sister Ethel, who had no children of her own. 'It was very, very hard. I think that had a big effect on him because he was never quite the same afterwards.'

With the arrival of Terry's brothers, Barry and then some years later Graham, the family moved house, eventually settling in a typical 1930s, terraced three-up-two-down with long, thin garden in Vessey Road, Worksop. This was where Terry spent the remainder of his boyhood. His father's long hours at the mine meant that as a toddler Terry rarely saw him. Later, during the Second World War, his father was often away for long periods at a time working on airfield construction after being seriously injured and only narrowly surviving a roof collapse in the pit that ended his mining days.

> He liked a drink and smoked Woodbines, which I had to go out and buy for him five at a time because that was all he could ever afford. That was really about the extent of my relationship with him. I was much closer to my mother and when I was older she was the one, God bless her, who made sure that I didn't become a miner like him. She always wanted something better for me.

By all accounts, Nance Peet's ambition for her son was matched by his own determination and ability. He could read before the age of five and excelled academically at the Stanley Street Primary School three miles from where they lived. He walked there twice every school day since at the time pupils used to go home for lunch and his parents could not afford the bus fare. After primary school he attended St John's Middle School in Worksop and won a much sought after place at the King Edward VI Grammar School ten miles away in Retford. For a boy from Terry's background this was a huge achievement. A grammar school education would unlock opportunities that a miner's son could normally only dream about. 'Mother was very proud even though she found it a real struggle affording the uniform and all the other things I needed. I can still picture her sitting there smiling, pleased as punch as she sewed on all my name tapes.' Shortly before leaving St John's, Terry was caned for misspelling someone's name. The headmaster warned him severely: 'When you get to King Edward's, you'll soon learn that the head there is called Mr Pilkington-Rogers, boy. If you spell his name wrongly he'll beat you within an inch of your life.'

As events were to prove, it was not canings by the double-barrelled Pilkington-Rogers that Terry needed to fear at King Edward's, but hostility on the part of boys from more well-to-do homes than him, who apparently resented his presence in their midst. They wasted no time in cruelly mocking his dialect and mercilessly belittling his working-class background.

I was dead chuffed at getting to King Edward's. It was like being plunged into the elite at the time. The trouble is that for a boy like me, when you got there you found you didn't fit in very well. The bullying started almost straight away. I went to the head about it but nothing was done.

On one occasion, as Terry waited for his train at Retford railway station, one of his tormentors pulled his new school cap off his head and hurled it onto the tracks in front of a passing locomotive. He lied to his mother saying that he had lost it and was duly scolded since she could ill afford another. Despite facing a daily ordeal at the hands of his middle-class bullies, Terry never breathed a word of complaint at home. 'I must've been a real pain in the arse to the other boys because they never let up.' Then something happened that he could not disguise as a mishap.

A group of older boys grabbed hold of Terry on the platform at Retford and bundled him into a large, wicker postal basket on a train bound for Lincoln. His muffled shouts for help eventually attracted the attention of a railway guard, who called the police after releasing Terry. His father was summoned to the police station to retrieve him and inevitably the prank was reported to Pilkington-Rogers by the police. Although Terry remained stoically silent, the guilty culprits were soon unmasked and punished. 'Them getting into trouble for what they'd done didn't make things any easier for me, I can tell you. Things just went from bad to worse.' Finally, he could take the unremitting persecution no longer. He decided to run away, making his escape by catching a train bound for the west coast after leaving a weekly Boy Scouts meeting, still dressed in his scouting uniform.

I only had enough money to take the train to Sheffield. Then I hitched lifts by lorry and ended up on the seafront in Blackpool. I met another scout, about my own age, who took me home with him. I spun some unlikely yarn to his mother about being lost after getting separated from my troop on an expedition. She called the police and my poor father had to come and fetch me again. After that Pilkington-Rogers washed his hands of me.

Terry had just turned fourteen.

His mother was in hospital giving birth to his youngest brother at the time. When his father brought Terry home he took him straight round to see her. 'He just stood there by my bed looking so sad. I burst into tears. I couldn't be angry with our Terry. The only thing that mattered was having him back again.'

'I'm sorry Mum. It's not you or me dad,' he apologized. 'One day, when I'm grown up, I'll show them who's best of the lot. You'll see.'

His mother accepted that the bullying must have been very difficult for him.

He never told us anything about what was going on; he just bottled everything up. I suppose in the end it was just too much for him and he was getting away from all his troubles. It was just the same when he left Tern Hill. He came to see me on his own sometime beforehand. I could tell he wasn't himself, but all he'd say was that he had a lot on.

Terry refuses to speculate about how differently his life might have evolved if he had not been driven away from the grammar school.

I was bitterly disappointed because I could see the value of a decent education and getting one in those days if you were from a background like mine was very difficult. I ended up going to the Central School in Worksop and enrolling at a night school.

He also joined the Sea Cadets, an act that would determine the future direction of his life.

They became a very big influence on me. I was able to go away on camps, one of which was at a naval air station, where I experienced my first taste of flying. From that moment on, all that I ever wanted to do was be an aviator.

He saw the Royal Navy as the route to this flying career. In 1952, just before his seventeenth birthday he enlisted as a boy sailor. His father was adamantly opposed but eventually signed the papers on his mother's insistence. They both accompanied him to the railway station and waved him off to start life at the stone frigate of HMS *Ganges* on Shotley Peninsula near Harwich on the East Anglian coast of England.

Before being closed in the mid-seventies HMS *Ganges* had a well-deserved reputation as the toughest British armed services' training establishment. Almost a relic of Nelson's navy, it was famous for producing the finest sailors in the world. The accepted saying was that you went in a boy and came out a man. Terry remembers it as 'dog eat dog' where 'you either survived or you didn't, simple as that'. Nozzers, as new entrants were known, spent their first couple of months in an annexe under the watchful eye of instructor boys who, although only a year or two older, were revered like gods. In common with his fellow newcomers, Terry quickly learned how to sew name tapes into every item of clothing in a red-cotton, regulation chain stitch. That was the easy part of a life filled with spit and polish, parade-ground drill, study, compulsory boxing and other sports, and climbing *Ganges*'s 183 feet high mast. On his first ascent, Terry admits to being 'scared shitless', although he quickly discovered that 'it got easier the more times you did it'. He never joined the ranks of the 'stupid nutters who climbed it for fun' or those who nimbly stood on the truck, the small wooden disc surmounting the mast's top, who were rewarded for their vertigo-defying zeal with an extra half-a-crown in pay.

After electing to train in wireless telegraphy, he took the unusual step for a boy of his age of writing to the Admiralty explaining that what he really wanted to do was learn to fly. Shortly afterwards he was confronted by his sub-divisional officer, a man by the name of Gunner McNeil.

'I understand you can bloody write,' McNeil remonstrated. 'Don't you realize that it's not permitted for low life like you to communicate directly with their lordships?'

'No, sir,' Terry responded.

'Well, because you have, I've been given the job of getting you ready to be an aviator,' McNeil protested.

As Terry quickly learned, McNeil's bluster was just that. He conscientiously steered the young recruit to specialize in air telegraphy and then made sure that he understood the full extent of the challenge he faced to fly as anything other than a crewman. In the navy, McNeil pointed out, the only way to be a pilot was by becoming a Fleet Air Arm officer. That would have to be his goal.

Terry has no complaints about his treatment in the navy, where he insists he was given every encouragement and practical help. 'They were impeccable, they really were. If you had an ambition and stated it, they would do everything to help you achieve it.' After successfully passing out from *Ganges* he was assigned to the Home Fleet destroyer HMS *Barossa*, and with the help of a Cambridge University correspondence course passed his 'A' levels while crossing the Bay of Biscay. From *Barossa* he was posted to the naval signal station in Ceylon, now Sri Lanka, where his tour was cut short after incurring the displeasure of an officer by flirting too openly with his pretty, sixteen-year-old daughter. As it happened, on this occasion Terry's pursuit of a girl helped his cause rather than detracting from it. The station commander decided to put an end to the flirtation by having him posted.

He knew that I wanted to go into aviation and he called me in one day and said: 'The *Empire Windrush* leaves next week – you'll be on it and the lieutenant's daughter's staying here.' So I wound up at naval aviation school and then went back to sea as an air telegraphist on aircraft carriers. That's how I first got hooked on helicopters.

His first tour was aboard the commando carrier HMS *Centaur* in the Far East. Another followed aboard HMS *Ark Royal* in the Mediterranean. *Ark Royal* was one of two new *Audacious* -class fleet carriers with an angled flight deck and steam launching catapults. She carried a complement of up to fifty aircraft, comprising Sea Hawks, Sea Venoms, Fairey Gannets, Skyraiders and an assortment of helicopters. Terry could not have asked for a better posting. Remembering McNeil's exhortation that he would have to work hard if he was to have any hope of officer selection to the Fleet Air Arm, Terry spent most of his off-duty hours swatting up on the aircraft and learning mechanical details that need not have concerned him as a wireless operator. This quickly paid off when he was involved in an emergency that might easily have caused the loss of an aircraft and cost Terry and the other crewmen their lives. It happened in April 1958 during a routine night exercise off the island of Malta. He was part of a three-man crew flying in a Fairey Gannet[1] submarine hunter at between three and four thousand feet when the pilot, a man named Adrian Hewlett, announced on the intercom that he had lost control of the aircraft.

Terry, a leading telegraphist at the time, remembers Hewlett saying that 'he couldn't do a bloody thing with the elevators' and instructing the crew to prepare to bale out. He ordered Terry, seated in a rear-facing cockpit towards the plane's tail, to put out a Mayday before doing so. He was about to send the distress signal when he spotted something unusual. 'I noticed that the joint in the elevator control rod that ran through my cockpit had come apart. All the nuts and bolts had fallen out and the rod ends were hanging loose.' Impulsively, he grabbed hold of one of the loose ends and shook it.

'Whoops, that's it,' exclaimed Hewlett, reacting to the violent movement of the rod end.

'I think I've found the problem,' Terry informed him. 'The elevator control rod's come apart. I'll try and fix it.'

Holding the rod ends together with one hand, he stuck a pencil through the retaining holes to secure them temporarily and then scrabbled about looking for the missing bolts on the cockpit floor. 'It didn't take me long to find them and I soon had them back in place and screwed up finger tight.'

'There, try that,' he said.

'That's it. You've done it,' Hewlett confirmed as he regained control of the elevators and the aircraft responded. While all this was happening, the navigator, a man named Hoskins, had ejected his canopy cover ready to bale out as instructed by Hewlett. He was halfway out of the aircraft, literally with a leg over, and had to be ordered back in by Hewlett when Terry managed to fix the control rod.

Shortly afterwards they made an emergency landing at the Royal Naval Air Station at Hal Far on Malta. Once safely on the ground they discovered that Terry could not have sent the distress call even if it had been necessary because the navigator's discarded canopy had carried away half the radio antenna. Only Terry's quick thinking and mechanical knowledge of the Gannet as a result of his study in his spare time had averted a disaster. Terry recalls Hewlett and Hoskins being 'taken off to the wardroom for a stiff drink' while he was put in a storeroom and given an enamel mug of milky tea that left him 'really pissed off'. The next day they returned to *Ark Royal*.

When we got out of the aircraft I was greeted by the chief engineer who came over and hugged me saying: 'You've saved one of my aeroplanes, you beautiful man.' That made up a bit for the tea in the storeroom, but then I went off to the lower deck and another cuppa while the officers went off to the wardroom and another drink! That's when I started thinking to myself that I couldn't wait to be an officer.

Fuller recognition than the chief engineer's grateful, bear-hugging embrace came six weeks later in a written commendation from the Commander-in-Chief Mediterranean, Admiral Charles Lamb, who praised Terry for the 'initiative and resource he displayed in enabling a Gannet aircraft to land safely after a mechanical failure in flight ... action that undoubtedly saved the aircraft.' The Admiral was also gracious enough to concede that Terry's DIY mechanical knowledge played a key part in his cool-headed response to what was a life-threatening emergency. The citation was to be Terry's first but by no means last and it formed part of his eventual Queen's Commendation.

Notes

1 A British carrier-borne, anti submarine and early warning aircraft notable for its two co-axial, contra-rotating propellers. It was introduced in the Royal Navy in 1953 and retired in 1967.

Chapter Four
Balancing on a Stick

A few months after the Fairey Gannet incident, Terry was given the chance he craved. He was sent to the shore-based naval air station HMS *Daedalus* at Lee-on-Solent in southern England to appear before a selection board for the appointment of upper yardmen, a term used to describe officer candidates coming from the ranks. It originates from the days of sail when the men who manned the upper yards of square-rigged ships were the acknowledged aristocrats of the lower deck. He was the only member of his intake to be chosen and was understandably 'over the moon'. At last he had taken that first step towards graduating to the wardroom and fulfilling his bedside promise to his mother to show who was 'best of the lot'. *Daedalus* was next door to HMS *Siskin*,[1] where Terry went to camp and experienced his first taste of flying as a sea cadet. He found it 'rather poetic' when years later that was where he was selected for pilot training.

Qualifying as an upper yardman, of course, was what took him to Lochinvar in Scotland and his fateful romance with Joan McKay. 'That's when all my troubles began. But I can't blame her for failing my course; that was my own stupid fault. I didn't fail by much, but I failed and I was gutted.' One of his instructors, a lieutenant by the name of John Cobb, tried to console him with the suggestion that although he had not made the grade for the Fleet Air Arm he should consider transferring to the RAF since its selection standard was not quite as gruelling. So on his twenty-fifth birthday he joined other hopefuls to face a five-man RAF officer selection board.

I was the last to go in and nervous as hell after sitting outside waiting for several hours. I stood out like a sore thumb; all the other candidates were in civvies but I wore my naval petty officer's uniform because I thought it was the right thing to do. When I sat down in front of them the chairman of the board said: 'Good evening. Now let's see what we can do for your birthday.' I remember thinking, that's encouraging and welcoming. But the next question was: 'So why do you want to leave the navy and join the air force?' I could hardly say because I failed my upper yardman's course, so I said that I found the RN a bit stuffy about taking you as an officer if you didn't come from the right background, which I didn't. That seemed to strike a chord and they all nodded and said: 'Yes, yes, of course.' Anyway, I got in.

Terry still regrets this disingenuous criticism of the navy.

I can't say if my background would've been a problem in the wardroom but it obviously bothered some of the higher-ups in the air force, especially the Australian commanding officer at Butterworth when I arrived there. I didn't know it at the time; in fact I thought he liked me.

His assertion is based on remarks contained in an early confidential assessment disclosed in his service record. Although his first squadron commander was full of praise, writing that he believed Terry could make a very 'sound operational helicopter pilot' and that socially he 'is courteous and takes his full part in squadron and service functions', the air commodore in overall charge at the base felt compelled to note that he 'came from the lower deck and although making very good progress, at times this background breaks through'. Quite what about Terry's behaviour provoked this criticism is difficult to judge. Perhaps the answer lies in what his record discloses as impressions of nonchalance and overconfidence on his part. This behaviour might easily have been a natural enough display of self-assurance engendered by his naval training and service. Or it might have been his way of compensating for his lack of self esteem for failing to qualify for the Fleet Air Arm. It is difficult to underestimate the impact on him of not getting the Royal Navy commission. In recent years he has written an unfinished novel featuring two brothers. The hero is a naval officer, who is clearly Terry's alter ego. He has a happy marriage, achieves high rank and wins recognition in everything he does. The other brother is an RAF officer, who never quite lives up to expectations. Terry is being hard on himself in the story but the truth is that the RAF was always his second choice and a constant reminder of his great disappointment. Given this, a little bravado on his part when he arrived at Butterworth is not really surprising.

There may also have been a simpler explanation for the air commodore's initial reservation. Rather ill advisedly, Terry conducted a brief flirtation with an Australian group captain's daughter, a former New

South Wales beauty queen who caught his eye before his wife and children arrived to join him. As Terry now freely conjectures: 'Australians aren't usually stuffed shirts but I suppose he could've thought that dating this girl was not quite what you'd expect from a married officer and gentleman.' Maybe not, but infidelity is hardly confined to men from the lower deck either.

Terry's introduction to the RAF was not the most auspicious. As he recalls somewhat bitterly:

> They didn't exactly welcome me with open arms. I left the navy as a petty officer and was led to understand that I was transferring to the RAF and would be able to carry over my seniority. But I was designated as an AC1 (air cadet one), the lowest of the low, and had my pay cut by almost half.

His naval petty officer's pay was thirty-one shillings[2] a day. This was reduced to just seventeen shillings and sixpence, a serious setback for a married man with a child and yet another knock to his self respect. Not one to take this kind of thing lying down, Terry complained in writing to the top brass at Headquarters Flying Training Command. His appeal provoked a flurry of correspondence with the Air Ministry, finally resulting in a ruling against him. According to the Ministry's penny-pinching verdict he had not been transferred from one service to the other but resigned voluntarily from the navy on one day and joined the air force as a new recruit on the next. There was therefore no question of maintaining his substantive pay since he was 'starting a new career – at the bottom'.

Although angry and disappointed, Terry put the rebuff behind him and concentrated on securing his wings. He thoroughly enjoyed flight training. In part this was due to being teamed up with two white Africans, one from Kenya and another from Rhodesia, with whom he 'got along very well'. They became thick as proverbial thieves, something not lost on their instructors. At the end of the course all the cadets were told to fall in on the parade ground where the officer in charge announced that he would read out the names of those who had passed. They were instructed to fall out as their names were called. He started going through the list alphabetically and when he passed the 'Ps' and reached the end Terry was still standing there with his two African chums. 'I was thinking, oh fuck I've failed. Then the bastard grinned and said: 'Parker, Pallister and Peet – okay, off you go'.

By then Terry had already come to the attention of the RAF top brass again and not for anything as mundane as his rate of pay. Early during training he saved his aircraft after experiencing a potentially fatal mechanical failure in flight. It happened in April 1960. He was flying back to No. 2 Flight Training School's base at RAF Syerston, five miles north-west of Newark in his home county of Nottinghamshire in a Jet Provost Mark III[3] trainer at the end of his first solo, general handling sortie. While cruising at 9,000 feet the engine flamed out. After a momentary panic he succeeded in relighting it. His relief turned to cold sweat when he opened the throttle and the engine flamed out again. Now showing great nerve, he stayed calm and methodically repeated the relighting procedure. The engine started again but as soon as he increased thrust it died, leaving him powerless.

> By then I was obviously losing height and knew that I was going to have to try and glide back to base. It's something you do all the time in training. The only trouble was that I hadn't reached that stage of my training yet so it was pretty nerve racking.

In fact, the record shows that he was a complete novice and in the circumstances exhibited remarkable cool-headedness. At the time Terry had fewer than four hours of solo flying experience and only twenty-five hours in the air in total. In contrast a newly qualified pilot would normally have a minimum of around 250 hours' flying time, about a third of them solo.

He initiated a glide descent to make an emergency landing, radioing his instructor to report his predicament. Before he could see the airfield he had to break through a heavy layer of cloud cover.

> My instructor on the ground back at Syerston was a man called Squadron Leader Fillingham. He decided to talk me down rather than passing me to regional flight control, which would have been the normal procedure. When I could see the airfield I told him that I didn't think I could make it to the duty runway, which you were always supposed to use. I remember him saying: 'The whole airfield is a patch of concrete. Never mind the duty runway, just land wherever you can!' He saw me coming in low and dip just below the crest of a hill on the approach and he was about to press the button and tell me to eject when I popped over the top and landed. When something like that happens it focuses the mind.

In awarding Terry what is called a 'green endorsement' Air Vice Marshal Charles Scragg, the officer commanding No. 2 Group responsible for training, wrote that his 'judgement, airmanship and control of the aircraft were exemplary throughout the emergency', adding that through 'an exceptional display of competence and calmness in a critical situation he ensured the safe recovery of the aircraft'. This then was the second time Terry had been officially credited with saving an aircraft. What it tells us is that he was not the sort of man who was easily rattled. Only three months later, he would experience another engine failure flying a Jet Provost and again make a successful emergency landing, but by then it could be said that he was something of an old hand at gliding home. As Terry would learn, this is more easily done in a fixed wing aircraft than a helicopter.

After earning his wings he elected to specialize in helicopters, much to the chagrin of his squadron leader flying instructor, who at the time scoffed, 'Helicopters: they're a complete backwater; they'll never come to anything.' Terry felt differently. He had seen helicopters in action on *Centaur* and *Ark Royal* and felt instinctively that they had a big future. At any rate, he knew he was not cut out to be a fighter pilot and the alternatives of flying bombers or transports held little appeal. His request was granted with alacrity since there were so few willing volunteers for helicopters at the time. He was sent to Tern Hill, where the Central Flying School had just established its helicopter basic training unit using Sycamores.

Terry admits that learning to fly a helicopter did not come easily to him. Controlling the collective and cyclic levers simultaneously is not dissimilar to patting your head and rubbing your stomach at the same time. Both hands are doing different tasks at different speeds. Moreover, in early helicopters like the Sycamore, the controls required physical strength. Eley recalled: 'You needed both hands, both feet and both eyes working independently.' A contemporary US helicopter ace compares the control required to fly a helicopter with the difficulty of juggling a rolling marble into a small hole in the middle of a flat board with no sides. The slightest movement or touch makes the difference between success and failure. For Terry it was 'like learning to balance on a stick. Suddenly it comes to you; well that's how it was with me anyway. One day it just clicked.' At this stage Terry, of course, was learning to fly in the right-hand seat. The mind-twisting feats of ambidexterity required of being an instructor were yet to come. Even so, the course was not without its moments of high drama. Twice, Terry experienced mechanical failures, each of which could easily have ended in disaster and the loss of the aircraft and his life.

His basic training instructor was a sergeant pilot named Charlie Spinks, who Terry acknowledged had a sort of Midas touch on the collective and cyclic controls. Yet even Spinks might have felt the hair on the nape of his neck bristle in the face of what Terry experienced early in October 1961 on only his second solo sortie. The all-important collective lever controlling his ability to change altitude jammed in the cruising position. 'It was one of those classic "oh shit" situations. I couldn't go up or down in the normal fashion. Anyway, with Charlie's help on the radio I got the thing down in one piece.' This laconic recollection is typical of Terry. The truth is that landing a Sycamore with a jammed collective would not have been a simple feat for an accomplished pilot, let alone a beginner. As a subsequent citation recognized, Terry had to show 'outstanding coolness and presence of mind' and deftly use the throttle, cyclic and rudder controls to override the collective. All this is much more easily described than practised. To use Terry's own analogy, probably like juggling balls while balancing on a stick.

Potentially fatal mechanical failures of this sort were not commonplace in training. Indeed Terry might have had good reason to feel jinxed when only three weeks after the incident involving the jammed collective lever he faced another equally alarming crisis. He was flying at seven hundred feet over partially forested land to the south-west of the airfield at Tern Hill when his Sycamore's engine cut out. 'It just stopped. There was no warning, nothing.' The only place he could see to land was a small field totally enclosed by tallish trees. To make matters worse, there were 'bloody power cables' going over the top of the field, which was also full of cows grazing on the lush grass. By then Terry had clocked fourteen hours of solo flying under the legendary Spinks. Fortunately, this included practising auto-rotation techniques to exploit the airflow through the rotors in order to control descent in the event of an engine malfunction. In a fixed-wing propeller-powered aircraft, the prop on a dead engine is feathered to eliminate friction. The reverse is true in auto-rotation, when the collective is used to create enough drag by the airflow through the rotors to keep them turning. The trick is to maintain enough airspeed to fly. Too little or too much and all is lost. About a hundred feet above the ground the pilot pulls back on the cyclic to put the nose up and kill forward speed and then at the absolute last moment, when ten to twenty feet above the ground, pulls up on the collective to flatten the rotor blades and cushion the landing. Learning this manoeuvre was essential in the early days of helicopter flight when engine failure was a real hazard. With today's more reliable and mostly twin-engine machines, auto-rotation training holds more dangers than the risk of losing power and is reserved for elite pilots.

Despite his comparative lack of experience at the time of his sudden engine failure in training, Terry mastered the intricacies of auto-rotation to execute a perfect landing on the edge of the field, avoiding not only the power lines crossing it but the cattle grazing in it. An unsuccessful nomination for a Queen's Commendation for Valuable Service in the Air citing the four training incidents, as well as the earlier panic involving the naval Gannet, described this feat as another display of 'exceptional calmness, skill and judgement'. In some ways then, it could be said that Terry was probably better prepared for the new challenges of flying in jungle terrain than most of his contemporaries when he arrived to join 110 Squadron at RAAF Butterworth. In retrospect, he thinks that both the helicopter training incidents may well have been contributory factors in saving his life in Malaya later when he suffered what is normally catastrophic tail rotor failure.

Notes

1 Now HMS *Sultan*.
2 Equivalent to almost £60 at today's values based on average earnings data.
3 A purpose-built trainer manufactured by British Aircraft Corporation and used by the RAF from 1953 until 1993.

Chapter Five
Exciting and Vital

As a young man Terry was naturally athletic. He played rugby and basketball and enjoyed track and field events. High and long jumping were his specialities, although a schoolboy knee injury plagued him. When the damaged cartilage flared up after a hard, high-jump landing in the sand pit at flying school, it very nearly jeopardized the outcome of his flight training exam by making it torture to push the rudder pedal on his Varsity[1] trainer. Nonetheless, he was always looking for sporting challenges and eagerly seized the chance to learn scuba diving during a spell on detachment to Gan. The most southerly island of Addu Atoll in the Maldives, this was then the RAF's strategically vital Indian Ocean staging post for the Far East.[2] Following a brief outbreak of local unrest, 110 Squadron had been ordered to transport a Sycamore to Gan and undertake aerial surveillance of the atoll, maintaining it there on standby as long as necessary. When Terry arrived at the island outpost in November 1963, the disturbance was over. He 'flew the helicopter round the islands every morning and then went diving in the afternoons; there was nothing else to do'. Diving was still a relatively new sport then and Terry found it 'absolutely exhilarating and out of this world'. The atoll enclosed a shallow lagoon of crystal, turquoise water full of exotic corals and reef fish, a far cry from the murky waters of Port Eleth at Moelfre.

The Gan detachment provided him with a welcome interlude from the more gruelling demands and occasional privations of jungle flying operations in Malaya. The island base consisted of a single runway and neat assemblage of corrugated ironroofed, wooden buildings including a large transit mess dubbed *The Blue Lagoon Hotel*, which housed the constant procession of aircrew and military personnel en route between the UK and Singapore. A signpost at the centre of the base highlighted Gan's remoteness, recording distances in miles to other far flung corners of the British Empire: Hong Kong 3,191, Singapore 2,135, Aden 2,142, Nairobi 2,510 and so on. What Terry remembers best, however, was another Gan fixture – a solitary woman in this male bastion with the sobriquet Carlsberg Kate. Her role at Gan was a mystery to Terry but he remembers her cycling around the base during the day and spending every evening alone at a table in a corner of the officers' mess.

'She always arrived at the mess just as the shutters were going up and, of course, as an officer and gentleman, you were obliged to offer her a drink whenever you bought a round. Since she wasn't exactly a beauty this was something you only did out of politeness.' As a newcomer and perfect gentleman, Terry was promptly caught by her well-rehearsed routine. He duly offered to buy her a drink.

'Oh, thank you, I think I'll have a Carlsberg,' she answered demurely. As he discovered, this was her stock reply, hence her nickname. One evening during Terry's stint on Gan, Carlsberg Kate left her customary corner to complain loudly to the station commander at the time, Wing Commander Geoff Moss, as soon as he walked into the mess. A transport returning to the UK with troops going on leave had been delayed and she alleged that some of the soldiers gathered outside her room after a few beers and behaved lewdly.

'Commander Moss, they were extremely rowdy and extremely rude,' she remonstrated. 'Do you know what they said? If we find you, we're going to fuck you!'

'And did they find you Kate?' an unmoved Moss enquired, grinning broadly and evoking cruel laughter from the men who overheard.

'That's despicable, quite despicable,' she spat back, turning red with anger, adding: 'I'll have another Carlsberg,' as she retreated to her corner amid more raucous guffaws.

Terry knew Moss from Butterworth. He had been the squadron leader in charge of 52 Squadron and the most senior British officer at the base, when Terry first arrived there in December 1961. In this capacity he signed off one of the earliest confidential assessments of him shortly after he completed his induction to become operational. Terry's immediate commanding officer at the time, Squadron Leader Cedric Simons, described him as 'spirited, energetic and ambitious'. Endorsing this appraisal, Moss added that the new arrival was 'most likeable and cheerful'. They were promising first impressions and probably not far from the mark. Spirit, energy and ambition were traits from boyhood. Terry had an indefatigable determination to succeed. Underpinning this was his ability to bounce back from real reverses, what they call 'character' in a sportsman or team coming back from behind. His mother confirmed that even as a baby he was always cheerful, a characteristic that he carried into adulthood. He was, without doubt, likeable. Men warmed to his quick humour and unassuming nature. Women wilted under his good looks, unassertive charm and old-fashioned good manners. He may have failed to make the wardroom but his upper yardman's course had thoroughly instilled the basics of being a gentleman.

Terry has quirky recollections of both Moss and Simons.

> Whenever Moss had too much to drink he would blame his drunkenness on his brother, with the result that he was always known as Moss Bros. Simons only sweated on one side of his body. One half of his shirt would be wringing wet and the other half bone dry. Imagine that!

Although he was unaware of both men's favourable comments about him following his debut, Terry sensed that he had made a good start. Within months of arriving at Butterworth he was nominated to take over as 110 Squadron's operations officer from Flight Lieutenant Doug Eldridge, who was returning to the UK.

> This was an amazing opportunity. I was brand new in the squadron but Doug took me under his wing and supported me all the way. He was quite incredible really and I have a lot to thank him for.

Butterworth was on the Straits of Malacca in north-west Malaya opposite the small, heavily wooded island of Penang, famed for its Buddhist temples and known as the Pearl of the Orient. The RAF handed over jurisdiction of its wartime airfield there to the Royal Australian Air Force in the mid-fifties, a status subsequently maintained with fierce Aussie pride since it was the only RAAF base outside Australia. When Terry arrived, Australian Sabre jet fighters and Dakota transports jostled for space on the apron with RAF Canberra fighter-bombers, Beverley and Valletta transports and the Sycamore helicopters of 110 Squadron, all then sharing the base. The sticky, tropical air reeked of high-octane fuel and vibrated almost continually to the discordant scream and chatter of engines as aircraft arrived and left from the two, three-thousand-yard runways. Occasionally, the deafening roar of visiting Vulcan and Valiant bombers amplified the familiar din of the resident aircraft. Butterworth was more than just a vibrant symbol of military virility. Throughout the twelve-year-long Malayan Emergency[3] it was in the front line of one of Cold War's first hot spots. Even when the Emergency officially ended in 1960, the base continued to be the principal staging post for mopping up operations against communist insurgents.

Against a backdrop of the shimmering, tropical sea, the base comprised a large military hospital as well as a cinema, swimming pool, spacious bungalows for the more senior officers, and well-appointed officers' and sergeants' messes. The colonial-style buildings were surrounded by white-washed kerbstones, swaying coconut palms and vibrantly colourful, bougainvillea-filled flower beds. Most of the married pilots lived on Penang, then a fifteen-minute ferry ride away. This was where Terry was allocated a comfortable, three-bedroom villa when Joan arrived to join him with the children. One of Penang's golden, palm-fringed beaches was nearby. He concedes that as a setting for early, married life it could hardly have been more romantic. Inevitably however, in the small, tongue-wagging community of RAF wives, Joan soon learned about Terry's brief but public dalliance with the former Australian beauty queen. Not surprisingly in the circumstances, she also took exception to the amount of attention paid to him by one of the Australian nurses at the military hospital. Terry is still sheepish about both liaisons. He was not a womanizer in the sense of constantly looking for female conquests but he could not resist the temptation to flirt with a pretty woman or return their advances. His confident aura disguised a deep insecurity in constant need of approval. Just as he continually sought to prove himself in the air, so he enjoyed esteem from the opposite sex. For this reason Joan appears to have had good reason for feeling distrustful. Before long their relationship began to founder. She was jealous, he resentful. With the gilt off the marital gingerbread she became an unreasonable scapegoat for his abiding melancholy over failing to make the grade as a naval officer. However, so long as Terry had the jungle for refuge he could handle the growing iciness at home.

No. 110 Squadron's training officer when Terry arrived was a grizzled, former wartime sergeant pilot named Bill Barrel, who was then a pilot officer.

> He took me all over the jungle teaching me the terrain. It was like flying over endless miles of cabbage: dark green and thick, almost impossible to distinguish one part from another. We were in the mountains too, the Cameron Highlands, and you needed to be able to read the weather because it had a nasty habit of playing tricks on you. One minute visibility would be fine and then the next the clouds would come down and you couldn't see your nose in front of your face.

According to Terry, Barrel was a first-rate teacher so long as you flew with him in the morning. By the afternoon he was frequently pickled after a boozy lunch of ice-cold Tiger beers and not much else. So, after two months of early starts with Barrel at his elbow, Terry was ready for a solo into Bongsu, the final test then required of all newcomers before they became operational.

Bongsu was a notorious jungle cul-de-sac, literally a compact clearing at the end of a long, very narrow approach flanked by trees towering two-hundred-feet high. There was only one way in and out. In Terry's words:

> … it was like flying into a pocket and when you reached the end you just had room to turn the helicopter round in its own length and fly out again. It was a legend in itself, like a bogey man being held over your head throughout familiarization training.

Bongsu tested a lot of basic helicopter flying skills. The first was a pilot's judgement about whether to go in at all. If you miscalculated the wind conditions, you risked reaching the clearing only to find it impossible to turn round and escape. Once committed, you had to be able to manoeuvre in a confined space. A moment of lost concentration could have you clipping the trees down the approach or knocking the tail rotor off trying to pirouette in the clearing. Either could be disastrous. Then there was the added challenge of landing the Sycamore on the uneven terrain in the clearing without experiencing ground resonance, an interaction between the wheels, the ground, the hydraulics, the shock absorbers and the rotors, which could literally shake the aircraft to pieces. Newcomers used to go into Bongsu with Barrel a few times before then attempting it alone.

> When my turn came I remember Bill coming in to the crew room after lunch one day and whispering something to one of the flight commanders. I knew that he was full of Tiger and everyone stopped playing their usual game of crib when he looked at me and said, 'Come along, let's go to Bongsu.' That cul-de-sac was bad enough at any time and with Bill after lunch it was an even hairier prospect but I was young and felt immortal and so off we went. As it happened it was a good day with practically no wind and I nailed it pretty well, maybe clipping a few bushes with my rotor blades. Bill either didn't notice or didn't care and he signed me off. I was ready to go.

Terry admits to feeling euphoric relief when the clearing was behind him and he headed out. Later he used Bongsu as a personal test on numerous occasions. 'I did, in fact, manage a forward exit out of the clearing once but I'd have been scalped by the CO for even trying if he'd ever heard about it.' As Eley testifies, he was always trying to prove himself.

The Sycamore, named after the way the sycamore tree's seeds rotate as they flutter earthward, was a small, first-generation helicopter. Its glued, wooden rotor blades were powered by a 550 horsepower Alvis piston engine, which quickly lost power in vertical ascent. The throttle required two complete twists to open fully and operating both the collective and cyclic levers required some strength if not brute force. Getting airborne in confined jungle spaces surrounded by towering trees with a full payload required total concentration, as well as a fair amount of physical exertion. Even in perfect conditions it was an extremely hazardous business, certainly by comparison with later aircraft. Even once safely in flight, the aircraft shook the whole time. 'When you got your beer in the bar after a long day flying it was difficult not to spill it because you were still shaking so much,' recalls Eley. The Australian air commodore in overall command at Butterworth was scathingly dismissive of Sycamores. 'Those things couldn't lift the skin off a custard tart,' he was fond of saying. However, in Eley's opinion, although the Sycamore had its drawbacks he believes that it proved a worthy aircraft nonetheless. 'It wasn't impossible to fly but it wasn't easy. When you think that it could do so little we had to really push it to accomplish what the army wanted.'

Throughout flight, pilots had manually to update details of payload, fuel consumption and distance to go on a kneepad log, easier said than done with both hands needed for the controls and the whole machine vibrating like a drum skin. There were no fancy, computerized avionics to do the sums or help with navigation. Weight was so crucial that the 110 Squadron aircraft had bathroom scales fitted to them. During troop lifts, soldiers were weighed with their gear so that pilots could calculate exactly how much fuel they could afford to carry without exceeding the aircraft's restrictive payload. Often they would have to plan several stops along the way to refuel from dumps using hand-operated, toggle pumps. Sometimes a crewman would be left behind or the aircraft's doors taken off. As Eley recalls:

> ... it was so near the bone the whole time. I mean, you'd put on maximum revs, you'd pull the collective but you'd quickly run out of steam and have to get into forward flight and then you'd be dragging your undercarriage through the tops of the trees. It was exciting because it was so vital.

At the height of the Emergency, Sycamores were known to return to Butterworth with the macabre cargo of a jute sack filled with severed rebel heads for identification because whole corpses were too heavy for the helicopters to transport.

Flying helicopters demands considerable skill, as anyone who has used a flight simulator will quickly testify. For most who try simulators, learning to land a jumbo jet in a storm comes a lot more easily than learning to manoeuvre a helicopter through a series of gates over hilly terrain in perfect weather. Even today with all the advances in technology, flying helicopters in extreme conditions carries risks not associated with fixed wing aircraft. Flying the primitive machines of Terry's day over jungle terrain without instruments was insanely hazardous. As a latter day veteran of helicopter flight with over 10,000 hours of rotary flying – many of them over jungle in countries like Guatemala and Colombia – confirms: 'Even now there's no flying in the world more dangerous than flying helicopters in jungles without instruments, let alone those old machines in the early days of helicopter flight.'

Terry revelled in the challenges and the danger. Apart from the difficulty of getting the Sycamore airborne from a tight spot fully loaded, worrying about its mechanical reliability and navigating it in unpredictable weather, flying the aircraft posed another test. It was particularly susceptible to the phenomenon of ground resonance owing to its three-wheel undercarriage. If a pilot tried to land too gently, putting one wheel down first and not following quickly with the others so that the weight was evenly balanced between the wheels and the rotor head, resonance developed dramatically fast. Within four seconds the aircraft could literally disintegrate. As Eley recalls, this unenviable fate befell an Army Air Corps pilot who was left sitting strapped in his seat looking dumbfounded and lost, surrounded by wreckage and nuts and bolts.

> He had been tasked to pick up a general and attempted to make a very gentle landing close to him. Suddenly ground resonance took over and reduced his helicopter to scrap. After recovering his composure, he jumped out, smartly saluted the general and explained that there would be a short delay while he ordered up another machine. 'I don't think so,' replied the general. 'I'll take my car.'

In his role as operations officer, Terry was responsible for the daily tasking of pilots and aircraft in their vital function supporting ground operations against communist infiltration along the border.[4]

> We were supporting the Malay police field force, who held strategic forts across the country, as well as putting Gurkhas and New

Zealand SAS troops into areas where insurgents were suspected. Apart from being a fantastic opportunity so early in my posting, it also meant I could task myself to go out on ops a lot, which I did. I was young and exuberant and wanted to be where the action was, not sitting on the beach.

He also wanted to be away from the growing marital tensions at home. What Eley recalls as Terry's volunteering spirit was not just enthusiasm for the job but a form of escapism too. During June and July of 1962, 110 Squadron's eleven Sycamores worked round-the-clock ferrying troops and supplies and carrying out life-saving casualty evacuations after remote jungle fire fights. The squadron's Operational Record Book chronicles well over three hundred operational flying hours each month and the movement of nearly six hundred troops and more than nine thousand pounds of supplies and equipment in July alone. These were significant achievements for a squadron equipped with such small, primitive helicopters. Men and machines were being pushed to the limit. In his quest to prove himself, Terry was always in the thick of it, accumulating operational flying hours faster than most of his comrades. Something had to give. It did, when Terry was ferrying Gurkhas to a remote, jungle landing zone.

The squadron despatched four Sycamores in response to an urgent need to airlift troops to the Thai border and cut off a reported guerrilla incursion. Terry was flying one of them. 'We could only carry two or three Gurkhas at a time with all their gear, so we each had to make several trips, going into the LZ [landing zone] one at a time.' By then, the routine checks before take-off were second nature to him. Dressed in a lightweight, Australian air force flying suit of olive-green, cotton overalls – preferred by most pilots to their heavier RAF suits – with a revolver holstered at his waist, he approached the Sycamore carrying his helmet, a survival haversack stuffed with sufficient rations for two weeks, and a machete. After placing these behind his seat he walked round the aircraft, climbed to the rotor hub to verify the oil and fuel levels, releasing a little fuel to check for water, and then inspected the hydraulics before jumping down and walking to the tail. 'You always gave the tail rotor a good yank because you were never sure when the damned thing was going to come off.' Satisfied with the tail rotor, he gave each of the main rotor blades a pull downwards to check for play and then climbed the single fixed step and settled into the leather, right-hand cockpit seat and ran through the other pre-flight checks. Everything was fine. He signalled for his passengers to join him, one seated beside him and another squeezed behind, their haversacks and weapons tucked into the remaining space. Terry reached behind the seat for his helmet and strapped it on and then pulled the seat harness over his shoulders and secured it.

Starting up was a bit like cranking a Bentley. The engine would whirr and growl and groan a bit and then burst into flame and smoke, mostly smoke, and then the rotors would start turning. I loved the smell – it was like old racing cars.

After dropping off the first two men, Terry returned for three more.

It was a really tight squeeze with three of them and the aircraft was at the limit of its payload. I had to pull like mad on the collective and give it full power to get off the ground.

Cruising comfortably about halfway back to the landing zone, the engine suddenly caught fire.

I got the warning light and then it just burst into flames. The last place you want to be when that happens is a thousand feet above the ground. We were over thick jungle and the only place I could see to get down was a dry river bed flanked by tall trees.

Using the auto-rotation technique that saved him during training at Tern Hill, Terry started a controlled descent, praying that the fuel tank would not explode before they could reach the ground and scuttle to safety. With the heavily laden machine he had to fight the controls. 'It was looking good until one of the rotors caught the treetops. That did for us.' The little Sycamore dropped like a stone, hitting the ground with explosive force before rolling over onto its right side. In the pilot's seat Terry was at the bottom of the pile of men and equipment. The three Gurkhas managed to lever open the twisted door and clamber out of the burning wreckage. One of them lingered long enough to haul Terry up with some of their gear. They dived for cover into a shallow dip in the river bed as the stricken Sycamore exploded. Terry had just lost an aircraft.

He lay in the sun-baked sand, shaken but unhurt, as tins in their ration packs popped in the flames, sounding like bursts of small arms fire. The ensuing silence was broken shortly afterwards by the unmistakable chattering of a helicopter's rotor blades. Knowing that it had to be one of the other Sycamores returning from the LZ, Terry pulled himself to his feet and rummaged in his haversack for his Very gun. Seconds after the flare arced skywards the Sycamore turned towards him. Its pilot dropped down for a closer look, giving Terry and his companions a reassuring wave before flying away. Rescue could only come once the stranded men hacked enough of a clearing for one of the helicopters to land safely.

'I thought you were a goner when I saw that lot,' remarked Flight Lieutenant Dave Tennyson when he finally dropped down on the make-shift landing zone later the same day. Tennyson was a former lawyer and wartime glider pilot, about ten years' Terry's senior. They were destined to share many operations together and become the closest of friends. Yet, ultimately, when Terry needed him most, Tennyson would disappoint him.

Notes

1 A twin-engine crew training aircraft introduced into service with the RAF in 1951.

2 Following the disbandment of the RAF's Far East Air Force, Gan was formally closed as an RAF base in 1975 and handed over to the Maldivian civil authorities. RAF aircraft gained access to the US air base 200 miles to the south on Diego Garcia, the largest island in the Chagos Archipelago, a British dependent territory.

3 The conflict began in June 1948 when the Malayan Communist Party, dominated by ethnic Chinese, resisted British post-war policy for an independent federated state of Malaya, leading to the murder of three British planters and the declaration of an 'emergency' by the colonial administration. The proscribed MCP formed an armed wing known as the Malayan Races Liberation Army (MRLA) and a full-scale guerilla war followed. Some 40,000 British and Commonwealth troops and up to 60,000 Malayan police were involved against an estimated guerrilla force of around 12,000 fighters and 30–40,000 supporters.

4 Although the last serious resistance by MRLA forces ended in 1958 and the newly independent Malayan Government declared the emergency over in July 1960, remnants of the MRLA fled to the Thai border from where they continued their struggle.

Chapter Six
Defying Death Again

Terry's popularity with most of his fellow pilots soon ensured that he added the all-important responsibility of bar officer to his role as operations officer. He was happy to accept the honour. 'Being bar officer in an Australian mess is not such a bad thing I can tell you. It's not like being bar officer in the RAF and having to account for every pint and penny.'

'Here you are mate; here are the keys to the bar and good luck,' said the Australian he was taking over from. 'Just make sure the fucking beer's cold and don't forget the Pommy bastards like those thick glasses on the shelf over there. But don't worry mate, the waiters know what to do.'

That was the extent of the handover. Terry was left standing in the bar surveying his new realm. The mess was a three-storey building overlooking the ocean, cooled by the sea breeze and giant ceiling fans whirring lazily overhead. Sundowners were frequently accompanied by spectacular sunsets that turned the sky over the Straits of Malacca myriad hues of pink and orange. However, as Terry emphasizes, this was an Australian mess and the view was much less of an attraction than the beer.

One of Terry's closest friends at this time was Flying Officer John Martin, a young bachelor from Newark, not far from Terry's home town of Worksop. They had first met during Terry's initial flying training course. Then, when Terry arrived to join 110 Squadron, Martin immediately made him welcome. They occupied adjoining rooms before Terry moved to married quarters and often spent off-duty hours in the mess together. They became mates. 'He'd been sent out to Butterworth shortly before me and his was the first friendly face to greet me when I arrived. I got to know him very well.' Terry describes Martin as a meticulous man. His white, Cape-leather flying gloves that Terry rarely wore because he found them 'a bit prissy' and prone to getting filthy dirty, were always spotless, like the white lanyard to his revolver. He was always immaculately turned out. Martin had a reputation for being just as fastidious in the air, a man who normally took absolutely no chances.

This made his accidental death during a private display of flying for rubber-planter friends all the more shocking.

As Terry recalls it, 'he was showing off to a girl who was sunbathing semi-naked on the roof of the plantation house by flying backwards at full speed.' The absolute first rule of flying backwards is that great care is required when converting back to forward flight. Make a mistake and the aircraft is liable to tuck its nose under and flip over onto its back, leading to a certain crash. That is what happened to Martin. He was killed outright. As his closest friend, it fell to Terry to collect his personal effects so that they could be returned to his family. Meanwhile, the Sycamores were grounded until the cause of the accident was determined. However, even without accidents at any one time at least half the squadron's aircraft were frequently unserviceable because of persistent problems with their tail rotors and a desperate shortage of spares. Nearly fifty years on, British servicemen struggling with similar equipment defects and shortages in Iraq and Afghanistan may reflect ruefully that nothing much has changed. The Sycamore ground crews worked miracles of improvisation to keep the helicopters airborne but it was often necessary to restrict operations to urgent casualty and medical evacuations, known by the shorthand 'casevac' and 'medevac'. The squadron was still contending with pressing tail rotor shortcomings at the end of 1962, when a cable from headquarters in Singapore signalled the start of a new crisis, this time in Borneo.

Britain had proposed the creation of a federation[1] comprising Malaya, Singapore, Sarawak, north Borneo and the Sultanate of Brunei, sparking violent opposition from left-wing nationalist groups, supported and encouraged by President Sukarno of neighbouring Indonesia. What was to become another prolonged Cold War guerrilla conflict, commonly known as the Indonesian–Malaysian Confrontation,[2] began when nationalist rebels staged a revolt in Brunei in early December 1962. Although this was swiftly and decisively crushed by British forces, Indonesian-backed guerrillas began infiltrating across the thousand-mile long Kalimantan border into Sarawak, provoking a conflict that would last four years and at times involve attempted incursions by Indonesian regular forces. Perversely, the US Government was openly providing military aid to Sukarno in order to keep him out of the Soviet camp, while at the same time both the CIA and MI6 covertly backed anti-communist generals in his army with the aim of provoking a military coup, as well as arming Indonesian anti-government rebels in Sumatra and Sulawesi.[3]

Two days after Christmas in 1962, 110 Squadron was ordered to provide helicopter support for security operations in Borneo in the aftermath of the Brunei revolt. Terry, along with his friend Dave Tennyson, two other pilots and twelve ground crewmen, formed the first detachment. The partially dismantled Sycamores were flown to Labuan, on the northern coast of Borneo, in Beverley transports and then reassembled to start operations within forty-eight hours. Day after day the four Sycamores made repeated trips to jungle LZs carrying SAS troops and their equipment. Once dropped, the troops lived rough for weeks at a time looking for insurgents. Terry will never forget the wild sight of the men when he returned to collect them – they were often pale, emaciated, bearded and stinking.

The army commander in charge of military operations was the neatly moustached General Sir Walter Walker,[4] who had already made a name for himself in the Malayan Emergency. He was about to do the same in Borneo, making that conflict another text-book example of how to deal with an insurgency. Terry was his pilot on a number of occasions.

> He was an astonishing man. Once I flew him out to this jungle fort and after landing he called me over and said: 'Pilot, come with me.' We climbed into a dug-out canoe with some of his men and paddled for miles up this river. Eventually, we arrived at a spot where we slid alongside the bank and after clambering ashore the men disappeared into the undergrowth leaving me standing there with the General.

'We'll walk back from here, pilot,' Walker announced, turning to Terry and striding off, with him obediently following. Every few hundred yards, Walker would stop and turn round.

'Are you all right?' he enquired each time, to which Terry would answer: 'Yes, fine thank you sir.'

Terry wouldn't have minded only the General was twice his age. In the end they arrived back at the fortified jungle camp where they had flown in earlier and General Walker walked up to the sergeant major in charge.

'Have you got any beer?' he asked. 'I'll have one for myself and one for my pilot, please.' Two warm beers were duly produced. 'God, these people can't even keep the bloody beer cold,' Walker complained playfully.

The flight back to Labuan involved crossing a high plateau and then diving down to the coast but the approach was shrouded in thick cloud and Terry grimaced, turning to Walker: 'I'm not about to fly into that lot, sir,' he announced. 'It'll get us killed.'

'Now come on pilot; I've got to get back,' Walker insisted.

Suddenly there was a little hole in the cloud and Terry could see the whole valley spread out below, so he dived down through it and they landed without any problem.

'Well done. Not bad, not bad,' said Walker, hurrying away.

Just before the start of the Borneo crisis, Squadron Leader Derek Eley arrived to take command of 110 Squadron. Terry remembers him as a balding, thin-faced dynamo of a man with piercing eyes. He would later play an influential role in helicopter warfare developments and become Britain's military attaché in Saigon for much of the Vietnam War. Making his first assessment of Terry, the new squadron commander wrote that he possessed 'a great deal of initiative', while noting that 'his enthusiasm has to be curbed at times'. Although he acknowledged that Terry took 'unnecessary risks', Eley assessed him as 'above average' with the 'interest and ingenuity to make the most of a difficult situation'. By contrast, the Australian base commander, Air Commodore Phil Ford, a short man with a giant personality, drew attention to what he described as the 'nonchalance with which Peet approaches almost everything he does', adding that any pilot who took unnecessary risks should never be assessed as anything but 'below average'. He was the man who ridiculed Sycamores and in an earlier report referred scathingly to Terry's 'lower deck background'.

Before they were replaced by much-easier-to-fly larger, more powerful jet-engine Wessex Whirlwind Mk 10s with power-assisted controls, the Sycamores of 110 Squadron played a vital role in supporting ground operations in the initial phase of the Borneo conflict, where the long border in dense, primary jungle could not be effectively occupied or patrolled. This made life for helicopter pilots like Terry completely different from that of their fixed wing counterparts. On fixed wing aircraft you flew out of the airfield, did your sortie and then came back and spent the evening in the officer's mess. In their role supporting the army, helicopter pilots might have to spend the night out in the jungle and sleep in a hammock slung between the trees. This sort of experience was critical in encouraging Terry's later belief that he could make a contribution in the Congo. Just like the jungle terrain, he would find that the equatorial climate there bore striking similarities to the monsoon conditions of Malaya and Borneo. The weather in mountainous Borneo in particular could be treacherous. There were no meteorological forecasts and pilots had to rely on being able to read the tell-tale signs in the clouds for themselves. The early mornings were always thick with mist and fog that shrouded the jungle and lifted from the forest canopy like steam as the sun rose. Most of the day would then be clear until late afternoon, except during the wet monsoon period, when towering clouds started to build quickly, obliterating the landscape. Terry relished these sorts of challenges with their inherent risks and he soon learned to read the sky and stay out of trouble.

By the end of his second year in the Far East, he had completed a couple of three-month detachments in Borneo, interspersed with operations ferrying troops and freight as well as carrying out scores of casualty and medical evacuations back at Butterworth; several weeks supporting intensive border security patrols working out of Kroh in the Cameron Highlands; and the interlude on surveillance duty in Gan. Normally he would have been assigned to a new posting. With Eley's support though, he succeeded in extending his tour with the aim of logging over a thousand hours of operational helicopter flying. Terry had by now discovered enough about himself to know that he enjoyed the isolation of being a helicopter pilot. Apart from being alone in the cockpit, many missions were flown without the company of other aircraft. Airborne in a Sycamore he was in complete control. Everything was down to him. This gave him an enormous buzz. Being alone and in charge made him fearless.

The other discovery was that his most satisfying missions were casevacs and medevacs. Being able to evacuate military casualties or seriously ill civilians quickly from even the most remote and inaccessible locations was often the difference between life and death. This is taken for granted today but it was still pioneering stuff in the early 1960s. The Sycamores could be fitted with stretchers attached to the undercarriage or hastily laid athwart the cockpit to pluck the wounded to safety. This was a significant morale booster for troops combating insurgents on the ground. It made Terry feel good about what he was doing too. He experienced an intoxicating thrill in saving lives. Risks were worth taking to accomplish rescues.

> Knowing that you were probably going to save someone's life by getting them out gave you an incredibly good feeling; well at least it did me. It wasn't just the soldiers we were evacuating either. Often it was a case of going in to some village in the middle of nowhere with a doctor to treat serious cases of illness, or bringing sick villagers out for treatment in hospital. I found all that very rewarding.

He is proud to have played a cameo role as the life-saving Sycamore pilot in a short, black and white Pathé newsreel film called *Doctor on Call* about the RAF's 'hearts and minds' flying doctor service in Malaya.

Both these discoveries about himself – his need to be in control and his sense of reward in performing humanitarian missions – informed his later life-changing decision at Tern Hill.

Towards the end of January 1964, shortly after participating in making the Pathé film, Terry was flying alone carrying freight to a remote outpost at Tapong, near the Thai border with Malaya. After taking off from a jungle clearing, where he had stopped to refuel, the tail rotor on his aircraft failed.

> There was an almighty crack and the aircraft lurched violently. I thought at first that I'd been hit by something but when I realized that the fuselage was starting to spin I knew that I'd lost my tail rotor.

This was every Sycamore pilot's worst nightmare. That was why they religiously gave the rotor a swing during every pre-flight check and Terry always paid particular attention to it.

> Losing the tail rotor's usually a killer. It's Black Hawk Down and all that. More often than not it's curtains, simple as that. The aircraft swings violently because it's lost its anti-torque device and wants to go round the rotor, instead of the rotor round it.

Terry knew instantly that he faced certain death unless he kept completely calm and put everything he had learnt in training into immediate effect. But there was no training for tail rotor failure and so he had to improvise. The first step was to kill the engine and eliminate the source of torque rotating the fuselage. He reacted instinctively and urgently.

> With the power off I pushed down on the collective to go into auto-rotation. This changed the centrifugal forces creating an anti-torque, which slowed the violent rotation of the fuselage and then started turning it the other way at the same rate. So I pulled the power in again saying 'no, no, not that way, this way' so that I started to fish tail.

Terry knew that he had to time his use of the throttle and collective with absolute precision to keep control and stay alive. 'You have to get it just right. If you can't or you panic and don't, well then you're a goner.' Very few pilots are good enough to do this in a genuine emergency. The skill and sheer nerve required are difficult to exaggerate. Any hesitation, any loss of concentration, any false move and there is no second chance.

Terry could see a small clearing in the jungle canopy, the site of a disused helicopter pad used during the Emergency. He managed to stop the violent motion of the fuselage and rhythmically fish-tailed towards the pad, putting down squarely in its centre. Extraordinarily, the only damage to the helicopter was a broken windshield caused by the impact of his flying helmet hitting it on landing. He slumped forward, conscious that he was soaked in sweat and shaking feverishly. 'It took me a few minutes to pull myself together and radio for help. Then it was a question of waiting patiently for rescue.' That did not come until the following day when a Sycamore flown by one of his colleagues hovered overhead and lowered a rope for Terry to climb. 'Sitting out there alone for the night gave me plenty of time to think about how ugly it could have been.'

Another day later, Flight Lieutenant Ted Blackwood, who had by then taken over from Barrel as the squadron training officer, flew out to the site of Terry's downed Sycamore, accompanied by an engineer. Their task was to assess the cause of the tail rotor failure and determine how best to recover the stricken aircraft. Blackwood was in his mid-thirties, a rotund man who liked to sing madrigals in the mess. 'He loved madrigals. He was one of those guys who used to go bright red like a lobster in the Malayan sun; an ordinary sort of bloke who should really have been a banker.' Ordinary or not, he was an experienced enough pilot and Terry was aghast when he heard that what should have been a routine mission became a disaster.

The old landing pad was on a piece of ground leading to a stream with heavily tree-clad hills rising behind.

> For some reason Blackie approached the clearing downwind rather than dropping in upwind over the treetops. The outcome was inevitable. When he reached the clearing, the tailwind was too much and he couldn't stop. By the time he realized he wasn't going to make it he didn't have the power to pull out. His rotors caught the trees, sending the aircraft straight into the river bed, where it exploded in a huge ball of flame on impact. The engineer was thrown out behind a large boulder, which saved him from the worst of the blast. Blackie was not so lucky. He took the full force and was dreadfully burned.

The two men were rescued by another Sycamore and Blackwood eventually invalided back to the UK, where he became a life insurance salesman. 'I bought a policy from him at Tern Hill; one of the ones I had to cancel before I left.'

Saving his aircraft despite losing the tail rotor earned Terry yet another 'green endorsement'. Air Commodore Ford was obliged to sign it, much to Terry's subsequent amusement. 'That must have hacked him off a bit considering he thought I was so lower deck and below average.' The citation commended Terry for 'an extremely high degree of skill and competence' in landing safely in 'such acutely difficult circumstances'. Eley is still incredulous.

It's unbelievable really. Terry experimented with the collective and cyclic controls on the way down and found he could control the aircraft. As I said before, anyone else would have crashed and been killed and that's why I put him up for his gong.

In the latter half of 1964 Terry was non operational for a lengthy period after needing surgery on the old parrot-beak fracture of his knee cartilage. The day before he went in for the operation, he had flown out into the jungle to pull out a New Zealand army captain who had been badly burned by phosphorous. Throughout the flight back he juggled with the controls so that he could drip feed water from his canteen onto the man's raw wounds. 'The phosphorous was still burning and the water seemed to help him a bit.' The following day, by sheer coincidence, Terry found himself in a hospital bed alongside the New Zealander.

'Good on yer mate,' said the Kiwi. 'What happened to you then?'

'I don't know. It's something to do with having to go into the jungle and pull buggers like you out all the time,' Terry joked. 'How are you?'

'Well mate, it's not really as bad as it looks. They thought the Charlie Tangos[5] got me but they didn't. I was using grenades to clear rats out of a hole and one of them bloody blew back on me.'

That evening a pretty, young Australian nurse came into the ward pushing a drinks trolley. She explained that since the ward's occupants were all officers they were allowed an alcoholic beverage. The New Zealander asked for a beer, which she poured for him. Then she looked across at Terry.

'What'll you have?' she asked.

'A Scotch, please,' he answered.

'Oh, this is my first day doing this. How much should I pour?' she wanted to know.

'Well, you've just poured my friend here a beer; it's the same thing really,' he teased.

'She poured me a beer glass full that night and for several nights afterwards. Matron was livid when she discovered why the Scotch was disappearing so fast.' The anecdote typifies Terry's wicked humour and charm.

When he came out of hospital most of 110 Squadron's Sycamores had been replaced with Whirlwinds and the whole squadron relocated to RAF Seletar, near Singapore. Terry was assigned light duties flying communications flights in one of the surviving Sycamores. By then, any misgivings about him at the most senior level appear to have been forgotten. In another glowing report, Eley wrote that he was 'keen as mustard and has a considerable amount of drive, initiative and sheer guts', adding that he was a 'sterling asset to the squadron'. Even Air Commodore Ford was gracious enough to temper his scepticism, admitting that although he had on occasions thought Terry to be accident prone 'he has survived and in fact proved extremely able in extricating himself from very difficult predicaments'. A little later a new base commander would go even further and commend him as 'an extremely keen pilot, who would do anything and go anywhere in a Sycamore'.

For the most part, communications flying meant ferrying VIPs around, particularly Air Chief Marshal, the Earl of Bandon, the former Commander-in-Chief Far East Air Force, who was then involved in sensitive, top-level talks on the future of the Federation of Malaysia.[6] Terry had complete control of the air space over Singapore for ten minutes every morning and every evening as he ferried Bandon to and from the talks.

> I wore white overalls and had a white helicopter and used to fly across the golf course and land on the helipad near the C-in-C's house at precisely eight o'clock every morning. He'd be walking towards the helicopter from his limousine having been driven all of a hundred yards as I landed; and that happened every day for several weeks.

Finally, Terry was told he would be returning to the UK to join the Central Flying School at Tern Hill. 'The Air Chief Marshal didn't know me from Adam really, but one morning he tapped me on the shoulder and leaned forward.'

'I believe you're leaving us next week,' he said.

'Yes, that's correct, sir,' Terry answered.

'Well, good luck in your future career and thank you very much for everything you've done for me here.' Terry thought that was 'very unusual, almost what you'd expect from a naval officer', betraying his abiding affection for the Senior Service.[7]

Notes

1   The Federation of Malaysia came into being in 1963. The Sultanate of Brunei refused to join and Singapore had to secede in 1965.
2   Although of much shorter duration than the Malayan Emergency, the Indonesian Confrontation required the deployment of more than 30,000 British and Commonwealth servicemen before it ended in June 1966.
3   Sukarno was eventually deposed by General Suharto, leading to mass killings that left the Indonesian communist party annihilated and over 100,000 of its sympathizers dead.
4   Walker was director of operations in Borneo from 1962–65. A distinguished soldier, he later earned widespread scorn as a right-wing political activist. He died in 2001 aged eighty-eight.
5   A term used to describe Communist Terrorists, also called Terrs or CTs.
6   Singapore was expelled from the Federation because of intractable ideological differences between the city's government and the federal government in Kuala Lumpur, becoming an independent city state in 1965.
7   Air Chief Marshal The Earl of Bandon – an Irish peer often known by the nicknames 'Paddy' or the 'Abandoned Earl' – was noted for his distaste for officialdom and his common touch.

Chapter Seven

Absent Without Leave

Back in Anglesey in 1965, the police launched an extensive search shortly after caravan site owner Mrs Owen raised the alarm on the morning of Thursday 30 September. They knew they were looking for Terry after finding his identity card in the white estate car, still parked where it had been the previous evening below the coastguard hut. A helicopter from the search and rescue unit at nearby RAF Valley – where at the time of writing Prince William, the future heir to the throne, is serving as a helicopter pilot – joined the Moelfre inshore lifeboat scouring the coastline and off-lying sea area, while policemen helped by local residents combed the rocky foreshore for any sign of him. Concern mounted rapidly when they found nothing. There was no trace of the dinghy or diving gear. The urgent quest continued the following day and into the weekend, by which time an RAF air-sea rescue launch arrived to reinforce the effort. There are no details of the search in the relevant operational record books for RAF Valley or Tern Hill, and the North Wales police files covering it have been destroyed, leaving a few sketchy newspaper reports as the only remaining source of information. However, it is clear that any hope of finding Terry alive was abandoned by the weekend, prompting Squadron Leader Garwood to telephone his parents on Sunday afternoon. This was the call taken by Terry's father informing him that Terry was missing and presumed drowned.

According to the newspaper reports, RAF and police divers started an underwater search of the dangerous sea bed at Port Eleth in a bid to recover his body on the Monday morning following his disappearance. His parents were informed of this grisly development. As frogmen continued their painstaking task in the cold, murky water the following day, Terry's father and youngest brother, Graham, arrived on the scene after driving up from Surrey overnight. His mother recalled that 'by then they were dragging the bottom to try and find him'. The only indications about what had happened to him were his car and the clues he had deliberately left in it. Based on these, it was a clear-cut case of tragic, accidental drowning. Yet, according to his mother, Terry's father was not convinced.

> My Ernie stood on the cliff at the spot where he was supposed to have disappeared and when he came home he said, 'He's not drowned.' He couldn't explain it to me but he said he felt there was something sinister about the whole thing.

Local fishermen speculated that the absence of any trace of Terry or his dinghy could be attributed to a strong gale that blew up the night after Mrs Owen triggered the search. The Moelfre lifeboat coxswain at the time, the famous Dic Evans, now memorialized in the bronze on the village seafront, was more circumspect. 'It seems a complete mystery,' he was reported as saying.

In the absence of the police files on the case, it is difficult to be precise about when official suspicion that Terry's disappearance was not a straightforward case of accidental drowning first arose, or what in particular prompted the doubts. Nonetheless, it is fairly clear that although Terry had achieved his objective of disappearing 'without trace' he had certainly not succeeded in doing it convincingly enough to fool the RAF for long. His younger brother, Barry, who was a corporal in the RAF military police serving in the NATO Provosts Office in Germany at the time, was immediately summoned to Tern Hill to help with the investigation. He admits to being suspicious about Terry's disappearance as soon as he arrived at the Shropshire base. After trying to console Joan, who he found in a distraught state, he was allowed to look at what little evidence investigators had turned up. Based on this he concluded quickly that 'there were too many things that didn't add up'. In fact, he was so confident that Terry was not dead that he did not even go up to Anglesey. 'I didn't need to. I knew that it was a put up job.'

Barry, who is four years Terry's junior, admits that their boyhood relationship was never a close one.

> As an older brother he was like most older brothers, I suppose. When you have to look after your younger siblings there's a lot of hide and seek, well there was with us. In our case I did the hiding and Terry did the seeking and mostly not finding.

As teenagers they rarely saw each other. Terry was usually away in the Navy, which Barry confirms was 'always his first love', adding that he 'never really got over not getting his commission'. He acknowledges that

Terry was academically gifted and found learning easy but believes this put him under a lot of pressure.

He knew that Mum and Dad expected a lot of him and he didn't ever want to let them down. I think that's why he bottled stuff up so much. It would never come out at the time; you'd get to know years later. That's how it was at Tern Hill: he didn't like the instructing job, he wanted more action. When they didn't give it to him he took matters into his own hands.

Ironically, Terry's disappearance for once turned the tables on Barry. Now it was his turn to do the seeking and not finding. What aroused his immediate suspicion about the drowning theory was Terry's falsified dive log.

They showed me the notes they'd found in the car about the leaking cylinder and stuff like, 'it's getting dark now and I'm going for my last dive'. I knew there's no way Terry would have dived with a leaking tank or at nightfall without a buddy; that's just not his style. He was prepared to take calculated risks but he was never a reckless sort and wouldn't have gambled with his life like that. That's probably why he's still alive today given all the things he's done.

Barry's doubts were reinforced after a search of Terry's locker and home led by Squadron Leader F R Cox from the RAF Special Investigations Branch (SIB) at RAF Dishforth. This revealed that his flying equipment and passport were missing. The thorough search of his house also turned up the brochures for the Irish ferry that Terry had deliberately planted. Taken together, these discoveries were enough to quash the previous assumption that Terry had accidentally drowned. As Barry puts it, 'I think that's what finally convinced everyone that the drowning was a hoax.'

Former Flight Lieutenant 'Lofty' Marshall, whose gangling height earned him his nickname the day he joined a fighter squadron in 1952, was a helicopter instructor at Tern Hill at the time of Terry's disappearance. He eventually retired with the distinction of being the oldest flight lieutenant in the RAF. In 1965 he and his wife lived in married quarters almost opposite Terry and Joan. 'We never got to know them very well. She was a bit of a loner. In fact, to be honest they both kept themselves to themselves.' Nevertheless, he recalled that at first the news that Terry was missing off Anglesey came 'as a real shock and caused quite a stir around the place'. Initially, most personnel on the base were convinced by the drowning ruse, although there was some open speculation about the improbability of a diver of Terry's standing undertaking a solo underwater exploration. The speculation gained momentum when Squadron Leader Cox appeared on the scene. Marshall recalls Cox 'asking to see Terry's locker and searching it'. When news then leaked that the subsequent search of his quarters had failed to locate Terry's passport or flight log, 'the rumours really started flying'.

Another of Terry's co-instructors at Tern Hill, former Flight Lieutenant Mike Bailey, a Second World War Typhoon pilot who transferred to helicopters towards the end of his career, confirms:

> ... there was a lot of speculation on the base at the time he went missing because we all knew that there was a basic rule if you were a professional scuba diver or amateur professional as he was, that you never dived solo. Every book and every article you read says that you always dive with a buddy. Some people said that he'd gone and committed suicide because of domestic problems but that didn't really stack up because what the hell was he doing taking all his flying gear, his helmet, his suit, his overalls and his log book if he was going to kill himself? He was such a pleasant, unassuming, quiet guy; I simply can't believe he went off to join the CIA.

The RAF Tern Hill records show that an official board of inquiry was convened there to consider Terry's disappearance on the Monday after he was reported missing, while frogmen started the search for his body. This was what triggered the arrival of Squadron Leader Cox the following day. Cox eventually correctly concluded that Terry had not drowned at all but faked his death and was illegally absent. On 26 October a separate board of inquiry, unusually made up of very junior officers considering the seriousness of the case – two pilot officers under a flight lieutenant – rubber stamped Cox's finding and posted Terry officially 'absent without leave'. Astonishingly, this finding was never formally communicated to Terry's wife or parents, who were allowed to go on believing that he was presumed to have drowned. As his mother confirmed, 'It's hard to believe, I know, but we were never told anything else officially or unofficially by the RAF until he was arrested.' She had no idea why she and her husband were not told the truth then or later when the RAF had categorical evidence that he was alive.

One explanation, although on balance totally unsatisfactory, is that the RAF may have assumed that Terry would let his parents know. But as he rightly points out, 'There wouldn't have been much point in going to all the trouble of making it look like I'd drowned, then picking up the phone.' Anyway, he argues that WIGMO had made it clear that his family, and he took that to include his parents, should not know the truth until the dust settled. Importantly, he also knew that if he had told them and they did not then report what they knew to the authorities, it may well have landed them in serious trouble. 'It was just much better all round for nobody else to be involved.'

A couple of years after Terry's disappearance, air force SIB officers visited his wife with a photograph of a man who they believed was Terry, standing beside an aircraft in Africa. She was asked to confirm his identity. Shortly afterwards, one of the children told Nance Peet about the men's visit and the mystery picture. By then her own relationship with Joan had become difficult and the girls' mother flatly refused to discuss the visit or the existence of the photograph. However, some months later Nance received a letter from a nun at a convent in Somerset, which seemed to confirm that Terry was alive and flying in the Congo. The letter recounted the nun's rescue and that of other nuns by an English helicopter pilot working alone out of Stanleyville. Apparently, a former kitchen worker from Woodlarks School, who knew from Nance of Terry's disappearance and the possibility that he was in Africa, was then working at the convent, where she had heard the nun's story. Nance concluded that 'she must have put two and two together and given the nun my address.' Unfortunately, she destroyed the letter, along with other reminders of Terry, during a weak moment when she thought she would never see him again. But she remembered the nun writing that 'this man had saved a lot of lives and she was deeply thankful for what he'd done'. She can only have been referring to Terry because he was the only British helicopter pilot in the Congo at the time.

Chapter Eight
Escape to Brussels

AFTER hitching the lift to Bangor aboard the bread van on the day of his disappearance, Terry took the night train to London. He was feeling physically and mentally exhausted after the day's exertions and found a corner in a sparsely occupied second-class compartment where he closed his eyes and tried to sleep. The last thing he wanted was to be drawn into conversation with a stranger.

> I don't remember much about the journey except that it seemed to take for ever. There were a few stops at places like Crewe where I half expected the compartment door to fly open and reveal a pair of MPs waiting to drag me away. But I needn't have worried. Nobody paid me the slightest attention and I managed to get some kip by the time we arrived in London at some god-awful hour in the morning.

Terry sat around killing time in the only cafeteria he could find open at that early hour at Euston Station, the capital's principal terminus for trains to and from the North West, drinking revolting British Rail coffee that looked and tasted like dishwater. He retrieved a lightweight coat from his parachute bag and pulled it on to stave off the October morning chill and watched the hands on the terminus clock laboriously tick off minutes as if they were hours.

> I remember buying a newspaper and reading it a dozen times, but don't ask me what the stories of the day were; all I could really think about was what was going to happen when I turned up at the WIGMO office.

Conscious that he should not arrive there at an unrespectable hour of the morning, he killed more time with a greasy breakfast as Euston slowly came to life. Then, after asking a cab driver for directions, he set off on foot for Wigmore Mews, a useful way to dispose of another half-hour and conserve his limited reserve of cash.

He arrived at WIGMO's address in the heart of London's West End just north of Oxford Street, shortly before eight o'clock and pressed the doorbell. A bleary-eyed female wearing a dressing gown and slippers opened the door.

'Good morning. I'm Flight Lieutenant Peet,' he announced.

'Oh, yes. We've been expecting you,' the woman answered, inviting him in and offering him coffee, an infinitely superior brew to the foul-flavoured strain at Euston.

> There was a man present in the background but he didn't say anything. I exchanged a few pleasantries with the woman, who then went off to make a phone call while I drank my coffee. When she returned a few minutes later she told me that I had to go to the Belgian Embassy, where they'd make arrangements for me to go straight on to Brussels.

The woman sketched a rough map with directions to the embassy, then located off Eaton Square[1] in fashionable Belgravia, and ushered Terry out. He enjoyed the walk across Hyde Park as the rush-hour traffic crawled along Park Lane and had no trouble finding the embassy building adorned with the black, yellow and red tri-colour of Belgium. After a short wait a Congolese officer in military uniform introduced himself and escorted Terry into a lift. 'He took me to a room downstairs where we talked for a while, mostly idle chit chat about my flying background.'

'We're going to process you through Brussels,' the officer explained, finally getting down to business and handing Terry a wallet containing train and ferry tickets, as well as a map pinpointing the location of the Congolese Embassy in Brussels. 'Go there as soon as you arrive. They'll be expecting you and will make all the arrangements for sending you on to Leopoldville,' he instructed.

After the short walk to Victoria Station it was still only mid-morning. The boat train for Brussels was not due to leave until early afternoon, so Terry had more time on his hands. 'I cleaned up as best I could in the men's at Victoria and then went to a bureau de change to change my money, keeping a few bob for a coffee and sandwich.' He asked for francs, by which the cashier wrongly presumed he meant French francs without checking. When Terry realized the mistake he went back and changed them for Belgian ones. 'I was angry with myself because I only had about thirteen quid left and I lost out twice on the exchange rates and commission.' He found a dark corner in a cafeteria where he could sit unobtrusively and wait for the platform indicator to inform him when to board his train.

> I think it was about two o'clock when it finally pulled out for Dover. I was a bit nervous going through immigration for the ferry because I was travelling on my passport in my real name, but nobody looked at me twice and I repaired to the bar as soon as I was on board.

If immigration officers had been advised to keep a lookout for Terry, the brochures found in his quarters may well have proved the red herring he intended and confined the alert to the Irish Sea ports. It is worth emphasizing here that in spite of staging his death in order to disappear without trace as required by WIGMO, Terry never subsequently used a false identity. He was given a CIA alias, actually an agent cryptonym – W I Mossie – after arriving in the Congo. However, he never publicly used this and he never travelled under any name other than his own, using his British passport. 'After a while I stopped worrying because I was convinced that I'd been cleared all the way by the CIA, just like they'd promised.'

The popular three-and-a-half-hour ferry crossing of the English Channel from Dover to Ostend was a Belgian Government monopoly at the time, operated by Belgian Marine Administration with a ten-strong fleet of freight and passenger ships working almost round the clock. After boarding the *Roi Leopold III*, Terry quickly fell in with a group of young Australian men occupying a central table in the saloon bar and amused them with reminiscences about his experience as bar officer in the Australian mess at Butterworth. By the time they set sail the bar's limited seating was filled with passengers and their baggage. Terry recalls 'every seat at every table being full' except one beside him. 'I was blathering on with these Aussies when this hippy girl came up and asked whether the empty seat was taken.'

She was Joan Milner, a twenty-four-year-old Canadian medical graduate nearing the end of a short summer sabbatical visiting family in England. Terry gallantly jumped to his feet and pulled out the vacant chair, making an immediate impression on Joan. She smiled her thanks, reached into her bag for the book she was reading and sat down. Terry was captivated by what he describes as her 'uncanny resemblance to Audrey Hepburn in *Roman Holiday* before the famous hair-cut scene'. She was slim, with a gazelle-like, long neck; dark liquid, almost black eyes, thin lips and long, black hair to the middle of her back. To make conversation he started asking her about her book. 'She spoke very softly with the hint of a lisp that made you want to listen hard in case you misheard what she was saying.' Afterwards Joan noted in her diary: 'We talked and talked, all about Vietnam, the East, Malaya etc. He'd been a pilot there and led a jolly interesting life.'

After disembarking in Ostend they agreed to make the onward train journey to Brussels together. Joan had booked accommodation at a youth hostel in the city and since Terry had nothing arranged and they were not due to reach the Belgian capital until late that night, he willingly agreed to accompany her. They took a bus to the hostel's address, arriving there around midnight only to find it firmly closed for the night. Joan spoke fluent French, learned at school in Quebec. She explained their predicament to a patrolling gendarme who took them to a small bistro-cum-hotel where the female proprietor was starting to close the bar. She had one room vacant and they gladly took it. So began a relationship that would eventually lead to marriage, although that was still several years and long periods of separation away when they spent that first night together. Joan had no idea what she was getting herself into. Terry told her nothing about being married and having children, or of how he had left the RAF. What he did volunteer, was that he was a miner's son who had been in the Royal Navy and that struck an immediate chord, giving them something in common.

Joan told Terry that she was a Geordie by birth. She originated from a mining village in Durham, in the North East of England. Her grandfather on her mother's side had been the manager of the village colliery. Her own father, like Terry, had been a Royal Navy petty officer. He was from Yorkshire, where she went to live as a young girl. When he came home at the end of the Second World War, after surviving repeated Atlantic convoys, he joined a Sheffield-based, tool-making company that eight years later appointed him as manager of its Quebec-based operation in Canada, where the family then migrated. They crossed the Atlantic aboard the P&O liner *Franconia*, an experience that kindled a lasting love of travel in the young Joan. In future years she would take off several weeks every summer to return to the UK to visit family and then explore different parts of Europe. This was what she was doing when she boarded the ferry for Ostend. She had a month left of her break when the chance meeting with the runaway helicopter pilot launched their romance. Over the next few days they shared an adventure neither has ever forgotten, although Joan admits 'the events and the order in which they happened are rather hazy, not only because so much happened that I find it really hard to believe in retrospect, but also because it was such a wonderful experience in living'.

At the end of it she confided in her diary of Terry, that he was 'dynamic, action-packed, exciting, lover of good things – fast cars, big dogs etc – and quite out of my league'.

The observation that he was out of her league is interesting because the reverse was probably true. What it underlines was Terry's easy-going self assurance and his natural ability to convey the impression of sophistication and experience. He achieved this more through brevity than exaggeration; more by what he did not reveal than what he said. Terry finds it difficult to express his thoughts and inner feelings but he is an avid listener. When they parted after knowing each other for barely a week, Joan knew precious little about him. By contrast, he knew her intimately. He heard about her 'quite wonderful childhood in Yorkshire' where her father was much loved in the small community in which he had lived all his life surrounded by extended family before going to Canada. He was a scout leader, who loved to walk, play the ukulele, sing, and entertain family and friends. Joan would go on long walks with him as soon as she was old enough to spend the whole day out on the moors or valleys or commons around the village. Her mother died prematurely in her early fifties of a heart condition that took the family by surprise but 'she was a very positive, game lady; a wonderful cook who could throw things together to make inspired meals', qualities that Joan inherited. She and her younger brother were exposed to a huge variety of personalities both in Yorkshire and in Quebec and she developed an outgoing, trusting personality that enabled her to socialize easily and make long-lasting friendships. After leaving school in 1957 she was accepted by McGill University in Montreal to study occupational therapy and five years later joined the physical medicine department at the city's Royal Victoria Hospital. As a student and young therapist she led a flamboyant life filled with visits to the theatre and concerts. She skied with friends every weekend in the Laurentian Mountains in winter and drove to New York to see a matinee or evening play every Sunday during spring and summer. By comparison, Terry's upbringing had been nothing like as rounded or colourful. She was a graduate, a lover of the arts, a girl-about-town who could mix freely in any strata of society. Yet she was in complete awe of him.

The morning after their arrival in Brussels, Terry informed Joan that he had to call at the Congolese Embassy. He told her that he was on a job-hunting mission and hoped to find work as a helicopter pilot in the Congo. He gave her no inkling of his agreement with WIGMO and the promise of a role in search and rescue operations. She accompanied him to the embassy, wishing him luck before settling down to wait patiently at a nearby café while he went off to present himself as instructed by the officer at the Belgian Embassy in London. All went as he hoped.

Just as I'd been told, they were expecting me. I didn't have to wait long before a Belgian officer appeared and led me upstairs and along a corridor. We passed a group of white men, who I took to be mercenary recruits, sitting on a bench and then I was shown into an office and introduced to another Belgian officer and his aide.

'Now, you're the RAF pilot, aren't you?' the officer said, gesturing for Terry to sit down. 'Do you have your flight log with you?'

'Yes,' responded Terry, handing over his log. A moment's silence followed while the officer flicked through the pages.

'Good,' he said closing the log and handing it back. 'When did you last have a medical?'

'Less than a couple of months ago,' answered Terry.

'Well in that case you don't need another. You're wanted in Leopoldville as soon as possible so you'll be leaving on a Sabena flight as quickly as we can arrange it next week. We'll have your ticket and papers ready after the weekend. Everything else you need to know will be explained to you when you get there.'

The officer volunteered no information about the terms of Terry's employment. 'No questions were invited and I didn't ask any.' He gained the distinct impression that even if he had, he was unlikely to have been given answers. 'It was as though I was expected to know everything and he didn't need to tell me.' One cannot help feeling that Terry must have been apprehensive about going off to a war-ravaged African country without having the slightest idea of his conditions of service. In the same situation most men would have insisted on knowing what they were going to be paid and by whom at the very least. Terry took all this on trust. This may seem stunningly naïve and out of character for a calculating man. After all, Terry took risks but he was never stupid. However, he had already gone much further than most men would have done on the basis of an anonymous telephone call. He was simply continuing along the same course, having decided that the WIGMO venture was his salvation. In his fertile imagination the cloak and dagger stuff was part of the fantasy of being on a special operation. At any rate, if he is to be believed, the lure of mercenary money was not his motive. He had abandoned his children and family and forsaken the RAF to go and do great deeds saving lives, not fill his bank account. To him this was the honourable way out of the dissatisfying mess he felt his life had become. He was not about to jeopardize it by getting pernickety over conditions of employment. However risky, he felt the gamble was better than facing the alternative. Anyway, he was comforted by how smoothly everything seemed to be going. Further reassurance, if it was needed, came in an envelope embossed with the Congolese Government's insignia containing one thousand francs.

'Here, take this. On Monday go and open an account with the *Banque Belgo-Congolaise*,' the officer told him. 'We've also arranged somewhere for you to stay until your departure. It's the *Hôtel la Ruche* near the *Gare Central*; they'll be expecting you and the bill will be taken care of. Bon weekend.'

Terry felt exuberant as he left the embassy to find Joan. He gave her a jubilant thumbs-up as he approached the café and then beamingly announced: 'The job's mine. Let's go and celebrate.' They went off to check-in and leave their bags at *La Ruche*. This turned out to be a small, rather run-down establishment with a shabby, smoke-filled bar harbouring an equally scruffy-looking clientele. At first sight Terry took them to be a mixture of hoods and hookers. If the middle-aged *Madame* at the desk was surprised by Joan's presence with Terry when he signed the register, she gave no hint of it and casually acknowledged: 'Yes, yes, *Monsieur*; we know about you. We have a lot of people staying here sent by the embassy.' Although their first impression was off-putting, they soon discovered that *La Ruche* was a charming, family-run hotel where they were made to feel completely at home and enjoyed delicious meals. They celebrated Terry's success in securing the Congo assignment with a walk to the magnificent *Grand-Place*, acknowledged as one of Europe's most beautiful city squares, where they sipped wine in one of the terrace cafés and talked late into the night. Joan remembers Terry telling her 'about the Rhodesian crisis and the British Government's attitude to it', although she did not understand the connection between Rhodesia and the Congo, except that they were neighbours in Africa. 'He was determined to go to Africa and save lives. I had absolutely no idea about what was going on there.' Nor in truth did Terry, apart from what he had read in a few newspaper reports. From these he knew that people were being needlessly butchered when they could be saved. That was all that mattered.

On Sunday morning they took a bus to explore other parts of the city but returned to the hotel early when it started raining and went to the bar for a pre-lunch beer. A shrivel-faced man with skin the texture and colour of dried parchment was sitting at the next table, a single crutch propped against his chair. After a few minutes he leant across to Terry and in halting English offered to buy them another drink. Terry declined politely, explaining that he could not accept since he was short of money and unable to return the compliment. 'With that the stranger pulled a huge roll of one-thousand franc notes out of his trouser pocket, peeled one off and put it on the table in front of me.'

'There, that's for you,' he proffered.

'No, no. I can't possibly accept,' Terry responded while Joan looked on in complete astonishment.

'Yes, my friend. You can take that and pay me back another day when you have money,' the man insisted, stuffing the roll back into his trousers and spilling several raw diamonds and revolver bullets as he withdrew his hand. Terry and Joan looked startled as the rough stones and cartridges rattled to the floor. The man smiled and nonchalantly swept them together with his foot before reaching down to scoop them up.

'Oh, just some rubbish I carry around,' he beamed. With that he stood and stuck a gnarled, mahogany-coloured hand out to introduce himself. He was short and wiry, and in his mid-to-late thirties. 'My name's Oscar. Oscar Koksa,' he announced. 'I've just come back from the Congo.' Then pointing to his left foot, he added: 'I had this blown off in Bukavu; that's why I have that thing,' nodding in the direction of the crutch. Later Joan recorded the meeting in her diary in her usual staccato style.

> He was a commando, gangster, smuggler, alien, no passport and a wallet full of one-thousand franc notes, gun and pocket full of uncut diamonds! Fantastic! He'd lived and fought in the Congo and got on well with Terry.

Early on Monday, Terry returned to the embassy to pick up his ticket and documents and then opened his new bank account as instructed. He discovered that he was booked to leave for Leopoldville with Sabena in three days and was determined to enjoy to the full his remaining time with Joan. After more sightseeing they went to a risqué show entitled *Embrasse-Moi Vite* and then returned to the hotel for dinner in the long, narrow and poorly lit restaurant, where the excellent food comprehensively outclassed the dingy surroundings.

Oscar was at his usual table in the bar and greeted them enthusiastically. He insisted on taking them for a drive into the country with his girlfriend, Fabiola, the next day. As Terry explains, 'That wasn't her real name. Oscar called her Fabiola because that was the name of a

Belgian princess and he wanted her to think that he thought she was one too.' Fabiola was the hotel owner's daughter and Oscar spent most of his time hanging around *La Ruche* in pursuit of her. She looked nothing like a princess. In fact, she was rather plain with mousy hair but she must have had something of the adventuress about her to go with Oscar. From what Terry gathered: 'He was one of the original *affreurs* [2] and very bitter about having his foot blown off by a rebel mine, although he'd collected a handsome insurance payout and was living off that and the diamonds he'd looted.'

Oscar owned a bright red Thunderbird convertible and the following morning he arrived in the hotel car park, revving the engine impatiently. Terry held the door open while the two women clambered into the back and squeezed onto the narrow bench of a back seat. As he pulled the door shut and sank into the leather luxury of the passenger seat, Oscar accelerated away. 'He had the top down and off we raced, the girls with their hair blowing round their ears.'

'It's automatic so I can drive with one foot,' shouted Oscar above the screaming engine as they sped off in the direction of Charleroi.

Terry recalls:

We'd only gone a mile or so when the police stopped him for speeding. He pointed to his missing foot saying, '*blessé de guerre*' and they let him go without another word and we roared off again.

Both the subsequent days were spent in Oscar and Fabiola's carefree, live-and-let-live company. Going on Terry and Joan's memories of them, they had an unquenchable zest for life and Oscar seemed genuinely delighted to share this with his new-found friends, asking nothing in return. On one day he drove them to Ostend to see a performance of *My Fair Lady* and then treated them to a slap-up dinner in a smart restaurant where he was clearly something of an *éminence grise*. The next day, he drove them 250 kilometres to Malmédy in the Ardennes, on the border with Germany, infamous for a massacre of American POWs during the Battle of the Bulge in 1944. Here he introduced them to an idyllic, lake-side hotel and booked rooms for the night. 'Gorgeous ride – quite exhilarating,' and 'lovely spot', Joan recorded.

Terry was due to fly out to Leopoldville the next day and so they had an early start. Joan at the time noted: 'Up at 5.30 am for Terry to be at the embassy by ten. Very quiet us both [sic].' Terry recalls hurriedly packing when they arrived back at *La Ruche* then heading off to the Congolese Embassy with a very subdued Joan at his side. She cheered up when they discovered that his flight was not scheduled to leave until 7.30 that evening and they could spend the rest of the day together, although she slept most of the afternoon, leaving Oscar to occupy Terry with his Congo memories. Terry recalls that he:

… went on quite a lot about the war generally and how the rebels were really bad news and how dangerous it was out there: that sort of thing. He didn't know much about the flying side of things but did tell me that there were aircraft involved in strafing and rocketing rebel positions. To be honest he was more concerned with his own injury and his contempt for Africans; he would have fitted in well in South Africa's old apartheid regime because to him a kaffir was a kaffir was a kaffir and they should all be killed anyway.

Writing in her diary, Joan expressed her dismay at their eventual parting with characteristic style. 'Time for one last of *Madame*'s super suppers then off to the *Gare Central* for a fast goodbye. Pow!' Terry was understandably wary of an effusive promise by Oscar to console her.

Shortly after take-off on the Sabena 707, Terry was invited to leave his economy seat and go up to first class by the chief stewardess. She was a statuesque blonde with an hour-glass figure who immediately made an impression. Her name was Maria Dvardswaard and he flirted with her enthusiastically as she filled and refilled his champagne glass. 'She didn't have much to do on the flight because the first-class cabin was almost empty, so she spent a lot of time talking to me and telling me how difficult life was in Leopoldville.' She promised to bring him fresh milk every time she flew the route. Terry willingly accepted. It seemed as good a way as any of making sure he would see her again. As he was to discover, Sabena air hostesses like Maria, who lived with an American boyfriend in Brussels, would provide more than a few small sought-after luxuries once he reached the Congolese capital. 'We used to say that the only thing that hadn't been over them was a Brussels tram.'

Notes
1   The embassy has since moved to Grosvenor Crescent
2   The first white mercenaries to fight in the Congo.

Chapter Nine
Operation *WITHRUSH*

Had Terry done his homework on the Congo's wretched history, he would have known that the savage murder of European settlers, missionaries and nuns that captured worldwide headlines merited little more than a paragraph in a bloody chronicle of violence stretching back to pre-colonial times. He would have known, too, that between 1880 and 1908 Belgium's King Leopold and his henchmen indelibly wrote by far the most brutal chapter of that history in African blood. Their barbaric behaviour outraged civilized opinion when finally exposed. Joseph Conrad's classic novella, *Heart of Darkness*, featuring the notorious head collector Mr Kurtz, is a portrayal of what he described as 'the vilest scramble for loot that ever disfigured the human conscience' after witnessing events in Leopold's cynically dubbed Congo Free State. It is essential reading for any student of the Congo. If Terry had taken the time to study it he could not have failed to understand that the participation of white, mercenary adventurers in post-independence bloodletting would inevitably resurrect distasteful spectres. He may justifiably have taken comfort in the knowledge that his motive in going was humanitarian. Even so, he could not escape the fact that while meeting Oscar Koska in Brussels may have been an entertaining diversion, encountering men with his attitudes in the Congo would be blood chilling. In the end their behaviour overshadowed the achievements of the more well-intentioned, attracting international condemnation and making mercenary a dirty word. Notably, the CIA always described its hired hands as 'contractors'. As one of their employees, Terry would be a 'contract pilot'.

The brutal civil war that embroiled the country when he arrived had its roots in the chaos that immediately followed independence from Belgium in 1960. Political and tribal differences provoked a power struggle fuelled by a new 'Scramble for Africa'. The protagonists in this were not European powers extending their empires but the principal adversaries in the Cold War. As Africa's single largest country with massive reserves of mineral wealth, including all-important cobalt and uranium as well as zinc, copper, diamonds and gold, the fledgling Democratic Republic of Congo became an immediate proxy battleground. The USA and its NATO allies, including Belgium, were determined to thwart any influence from the Soviet-bloc and China. Direct intervention by either side was politically impossible; in the post-colonial world, Africans had to appear to be conducting their own affairs. Behind the scenes the truth was very different. From the outset the CIA was deeply involved in influencing events in the Congo as its station chief in Leopoldville, the late Larry Devlin, candidly admitted in a memoir.

> The Cold War, like it or not, had come to a hot country and the battle lines were rapidly being drawn in the streets of Leopoldville and across this enormous, fragile country. It was my job to do something about it, and the first task was to create a network of agents and then mount clandestine operations against the Soviet Union and its allies, which were clearly setting their sights on influencing, if not controlling, Lumumba's fledgling government.

Patrice Lumumba was the charismatic, left-wing prime minister of the Congo and Devlin was instructed to assassinate him using poisons – one of them a lethal polio virus concealed in toothpaste – on orders approved by President Eisenhower. In his memoir he refreshingly owned up to all this, while categorically absolving himself and the CIA of any responsibility for Lumumba's eventual murder.[1] Significantly, he also confirmed that one of his last major efforts as station chief, before being reassigned to CIA headquarters at Langley, Virginia, to oversee the East Africa station, was 'trying to obtain an air force for the Republic of the Congo [sic][2] because up until then it didn't exist'. Initially, neither Devlin's bosses nor the State Department believed that there was any justification for escalating US involvement to this extent. However, Devlin pressed the case assiduously. His conviction was that a few planes would provide the insecure government with a valuable psychological weapon, particularly in the event of a rebellion or civil war. As he pointedly recalled in his book: 'God knows, their army was a weak reed to lean upon.' Devlin knew that the Congolese 'looked on planes much as if they were a sort of talisman', really believing that once they had them they would be safe. He felt that an air force would be 'symbolically important for the government and deter its opponents'.

Washington finally relented, agreeing to send six unarmed Second World War-vintage T-6s[3] to Leopoldville. The CIA was entrusted with locating pilots and maintenance personnel who would ostensibly work for the government of the Congo. This was the opening move in what would later become Operation *WITHRUSH*, still privately hailed by the CIA as one of its classic paramilitary successes. The T-6s, single-engine fighter trainers, otherwise known as Harvards, were new aircraft purchased in Canada and they arrived in the Congo in mid-1963 with a group of Cuban-exiles hired to fly them. The pilots had all been on the CIA's payroll for the Bay of Pigs fiasco and needed a morale booster. What better than a show of strength against a then imaginary enemy? Given the key psychological value of the aircraft, no secret was made of their arrival and they were publicly proclaimed as the new *Force Aérienne Congolaise* (FAC).

Just over six months later, in early 1964, a former Congo government minister led a revolt of the kind Devlin had feared, making his commitment to an air force prescient indeed. The FAC's six T-6s were hastily equipped with gun pods and rocket launchers. However, it was soon apparent that they were nothing like adequate given the size of the country and the widespread nature of the rebellion. This was the signal for the CIA's subsequent under-cover, paramilitary intervention. While the FAC would remain the public face of the air force, the CIA was charged with covertly providing the real firepower.

At the time all CIA clandestine operations and agents were given cryptonyms. As a rule these consisted of a digraph identifying the country and a single word denoting the specific activity or individual. The digraph for the Congo was WI, correctly pronounced as the single sound 'Y'. The word 'thrush' was chosen to denote Air Support Programme, hence *WITHRUSH*. The digraph followed by the names of birds became the crypto-langue of the operation. This explains Terry's CIA alias of W I Mossie, a 'mossie' being a Cape sparrow. Cryptonyms were mostly used for coded cable traffic and they were often whimsical. The avian theme was obvious enough but Terry was not thrilled by his *nom de guerre*. 'I can't think of any bird more boring than a sparrow, although I suppose it was better than being a tit.'

At the time Devlin, a Californian who joined the CIA in 1949 after leaving the army with the rank of captain, was heavily committed with events then unfolding in East Africa, a revolution in Zanzibar and army mutinies in Kenya and Uganda. 'I had a lot on my plate and was travelling a great deal and so I wasn't involved in the founding of the operation.' According to Leighton Mishou, one of the air operations officers who would work closely with Terry, this responsibility fell to Dick Johnson.

Johnson was a former Marine Corps officer gifted with a photographic memory and sharply analytical mind who was then regarded as one of the agency's[4] most valuable case officers and counter insurgency experts. However, although Johnson undeniably later headed-up the paramilitary operations under Devlin, he insists that he did not play any part in the founding of *WITHRUSH* and this was also Devlin's recollection. That said, Johnson certainly had the right credentials for such an assignment. During the Second World War, he worked behind the lines with Chinese nationalists involved in the dual objectives of ousting the Japanese and stemming the spread of communism, later becoming a specialist in guerrilla warfare. Then, in the run up to the Bay of Pigs invasion in 1961, he worked alongside Richard Bissell, then the CIA's Deputy Director of Plans (DDP)[5] – the covert 'black ops' arm of the agency. In the acrimonious aftermath of its failure he was quietly moved to a teaching post at the Army War College in Pennsylvania, until his services were needed again. He became a key player in *WITHRUSH* when Devlin returned to the Congo and chose him as his paramilitary supremo.

Devlin claimed not to know who masterminded putting the clandestine air support operation together but believed 'it was probably someone in the CIA's Air Wing.'[6] Whoever it was, he would most likely have been allocated desk-space on the third-floor of CIA headquarters with its off-white walls and green, vinyl-tiled floors where DDP's Africa Division hung out. Routinely, CIA operations start with a thorough background briefing. In this case the priority would have been to get up to speed with events then rapidly unfolding. At the time, the agency's recommended reading list for the Congo was headed by *Heart of Darkness* but the country book, an internal bible chronicling every notable development since independence, would have been a better starting point.

Upstairs on the sixth floor of CIA headquarters, in the wing occupied by the Deputy Directorate of Intelligence (DDI) – the overt intelligence gathering arm – a new analyst by the name of Sam Adams[7] had been charged with running the Congo desk. The rebellion shrewdly foreseen by Devlin and the catalyst for *WITHRUSH* had started a week after Adams arrived for work in a row of sunlit cubicles in January 1964. His report on the revolt in Kwilu province made the lead story in the next day's *Bulletin*, a daily newsletter circulated at CIA headquarters. The reaction from seasoned Congo watchers was muted, almost dismissive, a kind of collective sigh of 'here we go again' boredom that bemused Adams. Then he discovered why: the Congo country book, a blue-bound, loose-leaf folder containing all the pieces written by agency analysts, was already thicker than all of Africa Division's other country books combined and one of the weightiest tomes in DDI. The country had staggered from crisis to crisis since independence and the Kwilu uprising was seen by most as simply the latest episode in a long-running saga.

The country book's opening pages described Congo's independence but fresh entries then followed on an almost daily basis documenting the rapid slide to chaos. Firstly, the army mutinied and went on the rampage, leading to the wholesale flight of panicked Belgian nationals whose departure left the country dysfunctional. Shortly afterwards the mineral-rich Katanga Province under the Belgian stooge, Moise Tshombe, broke away to form an independent state. Then growing rivalry between the West-leaning president Joseph Kasavubu, and the leftist Prime Minister Lumumba, ended with Lumumba's arrest and subsequent assassination, effectively scotching any hopes of unity. Shock over Lumumba's death was still reverberating internationally when a rebel regime acting in his name formed another breakaway government in Stanleyville with Soviet backing. It collapsed within a year and the focus shifted back to ending the Katangan secession. To maintain control Tshombe resorted to hiring white mercenaries, who quickly earned the epithet *les affreurs* owing to their looting and violence. In December 1962 a heavily armed, United Nations force, with US financial support, invaded Katanga and succeeded in restoring Leopoldville's authority. Tshombe fled to exile in Spain and his Belgian, South African and Rhodesian mercenaries were rounded up and deported.

For six months the country enjoyed a period of comparative calm. Then came the Kwilu revolt. Leopoldville despatched an Israeli-trained parachute battalion – supposedly the most elite unit of the *Armée Nationale Congolaise* (ANC) – to end the uprising. Instead of rounding up the rebellion's ringleaders, the troops characteristically chose the easier option of terrorizing, raping and robbing the local population, provoking the rebels to respond with brutal revenge killings of European priests, nuns and missionaries, as well as Congolese civilians. Over successive weeks and months the situation rapidly worsened, as the graphic and often gruesome reports in the new pages of the country book added by Adams made painfully clear. Fuelled by the central government's incompetence and corruption and the ill-disciplined brutality of its soldiers, the rebellion steadily gained momentum, spreading to Kivu Province in the east of the country under the leadership of a left-wing firebrand from the former French Congo.

Initially, the rebels were poorly armed and organized, relying on machetes, spears and *dawa* or 'magic water' dispensed by witch doctors, which they believed transformed them into *Simba*s – the Swahili word for lions – rendering them immune to government bullets. However, the CIA soon received reports that in neighbouring African countries, notably Tanganyika, Uganda, Burundi and Sudan, Russian and Chinese diplomats – actually agents of the KGB and Peking's Ministry of Public Security, the CIA's chief rivals – were establishing smuggling nets to run guns and munitions to the *Simbas*. Emboldened, the rebels terrorized and massacred white settlers and missionaries and thousands of Congolese suspected of sympathizing with the central government. Alarm bells started ringing in Washington when Devlin's successor predicted the likelihood of an open revolt toppling Kasavubu's struggling administration.

By June, as UN peacekeepers started withdrawing from the country, a full-scale civil war with the super powers ranged on opposing sides seemed inevitable. In desperation Kasavubu recalled Tshombe from exile and installed him as prime minister in a belated attempt to restore some semblance of unity. Although Tshombe was anathema to the US State Department and CIA, the Americans welcomed his resolve to crush the communist-backed *Simba* rebellion. They and the Belgians supported initiatives to re-hire white mercenaries to stiffen the ill-disciplined and often cowardly ANC and to fly the original American-supplied T-6s of the FAC. Meanwhile, the Cubans were to provide the nucleus of pilots for a larger, more powerful behind-the-scenes CIA air force.

The final pages in the country book summarising the *Simbas'* capture of Stanleyville, taking some 1,600 hostages, over 900 of them whites, including the entire American consular staff, of whom at least one was a CIA agent,[8] left no doubt about the urgency of Operation *WITHRUSH*. So far as the CIA was concerned, it had to deliver the kind of firepower that would give the shaky Leopoldville government a lot more than another psychological boost. Nothing less than a killer punch would do.

The *WITHRUSH* team urgently set about assembling a lethal squadron of better-armed T-28s and B-26s that would quickly terrorize *Simba* rebels. Given the ANC's poor marksmanship and tendency to turn tail and run at the first sign of a fight, it was little wonder that the *Simbas* believed in being immune to bullets after swallowing their witch doctors' *dawa*. They would soon discover that the witch doctors' mumbo jumbo provided no protection from a hail of fifty-calibre machine-gun fire and rockets raining from the sky. As Devlin affirmed:

T-28s and B-26s were hardly what you could call up-to-date, but we really didn't need super jets for the kind of operation we were involved in there. The rebels had never been under attack from the air and happily for us they didn't have any anti-aircraft weaponry either.

Thirteen beefed-up, US Navy versions of the T-28,[9] known as the T-28B, equipped with two fifty-calibre machine guns and two rocket pods, each capable of holding seven folding-fin rockets, were soon on their way to Leopoldville. These aircraft, fitted with a mighty 1,425-horsepower engine and three-bladed propeller, made the standard USAF model with an 800-horsepower engine and two-blade propeller look like a kindergarten version. Sourcing the Douglas Invader B-26,[10] twin-engine bombers proved more problematic. Most had been grounded due to fatigue problems. However, four old B-26Bs were found languishing in the US Air Force bone-yard at Clark Field in the Philippines after service in Vietnam and they were resurrected for WITHRUSH. One never made it any further than Okinawa in Japan and another crashed in Aden en route. Meanwhile, three refurbished versions, known as B-26Ks, were diverted to WITHRUSH from a factory in Florida, where their wing struts were being strengthened, to complete the combat line-up. They were flown out via Ascension Island with British Government approval. Although the use of bombs was ruled out, the B-26 was a formidable enough aircraft without them, having eight, fifty-calibre machine guns in the nose and sixteen, five-inch rocket launchers under each of the wings. All the aircraft were 'sterilized', wiped clean of any identifying marks or part labels, and were officially part of the newly formed Congolese air force, although the B-26Ks remained on USAF charge and their record cards listed them as being in storage in America throughout their Congo service. In addition to the T-28s and B-26s, there were three C-47 transports and two small, twin-engine liaison aircraft in the initial allocation. Helicopters were to follow later.

Procuring the aircraft was one thing, finding men to direct their operations and fly and maintain them, something entirely different. The CIA knew that it could have American air operations officers and technicians on the ground masquerading as civilian advisors and contractors but there were serious problems over using Americans in the air, especially on combat operations. The air force pilots who delivered the aircraft flew a handful of early missions but any ideas of using them on a long-term basis were dismissed after one was killed in an accident and the news media exposed their presence. There were still no trained Congolese pilots available despite the best efforts of Italian and Belgian training programmes. A mixed bag of European and South African mercenary pilots had been hired by Tshombe to fly the FAC's T-6s while the original batch of Cuban-exiles stood by for the first T-28s. For the CIA the obvious answer was to recruit more of the Cubans' old Bay of Pigs chums to fly the other aircraft when they were delivered. It had no trouble finding willing volunteers. One of the recruits later reportedly confessed: 'It was a lot more exciting and better paid than parking cars in Miami.'

Maintaining the clandestine nature of the programme and ensuring that the US was publicly distanced from it was a key policy requirement. Devlin admitted:

> ... we certainly did our best not to advertise their presence. This wasn't always easy with T-28s and B-26s but they were scattered around the country. Journalists saw some, not others.

The FAC provided a public face for air operations but any claim that the *WITHRUSH* pilots or maintenance personnel worked for the Congolese Government was a complete smokescreen. This was how it was meant to look; the reality was quite different. They were there with Congolese approval but the funds and direction came from Washington.

The inspiration for the maintenance operation that metamorphosed into Anstalt WIGMO was a Panamanian-registered company named Aerovias Panama already operating in the Congo, where it had been contracted to the UN. The founders of this business were Winston Guest and George Monteiro, whose initials supplied WIGMO's name, the first two letters of which by pure coincidence also happened to be the same as the CIA's digraph for the Congo. The beauty of the Aerovias Panama solution was that, apart from already being present on the ground, the change to CIA ownership as WIGMO could be made easily and quickly without attracting any untoward attention.

By the middle of August 1964, *WITHRUSH* was a fully fledged air force comprising seventeen combat aircraft, as well as a fleet of transport and liaison planes, thirty Cuban pilots, four field-based air operations officers reporting to a senior central controller, and well over a hundred mechanics and armourers. It was designated as 22 Squadron or 22 Wing to differentiate it from FAC's 21 Squadron, although to most of those involved it was never known as anything other than WIGMO. Devlin was well satisfied with the development of his brainchild when he returned to head the Congo station again at the beginning of July 1965, although he instigated some immediate personnel changes, one of the first being Johnson's selection to oversee the air force and other paramilitary operations based in Leopoldville. In this role he would be Terry's overall boss. There is even some circumstantial evidence that he may have had a hand in his recruitment.

Notes

1 The poisons were specially produced by Sidney Gottlieb, who headed the CIA's Office of Technical Services, and designed to imitate African diseases but Devlin decided against carrying out the order and threw them into the Congo River. The assassination plot was originally investigated by a Senate Select Committee in 1975 that found no evidence of CIA involvement in Lumumba's death. However, in June 2007 the plot was publicly acknowledged when the CIA finally released classified documents known as the 'family jewels'.

2 He meant the Democratic Republic of Congo. The Republic of Congo is the neighbouring, former French colony.

3 Originally designed and built by Northern Aviation in the US, the T-6 Texan (or Harvard) prototype first flew in 1935 and later variants were used to train fighter pilots during the Second World War. The six aircraft sent to the Congo were the ultimate Harvard 4 Canadian-built models.

4 The CIA never refers to itself as 'the agency'. It uses 'the company' instead and fronts like WIGMO are 'customers'.

5 Shortly afterwards the DDP was renamed the Deputy Directorate of Operations (DDO).

6 The CIA was already operating Air America and a number of other small aviation operations.

7 Sam Adams, a direct descendant of President Adams and a member of one of America's oldest families, was a graduate of Harvard who spent ten years as a CIA analyst from 1963 to 1973. He resigned to expose CIA involvement in a deliberate government policy of misleading the American public over the true strength of Viet Cong forces during the Vietnam War.

8 The vice consul, David K Grinwis

9 The T-28 Trojan was Northern Aviation's replacement for the T-6 and there were several variants.

10 Not to be confused with the earlier B-26 Marauder.

Chapter Ten
Bienvenue Capitaine

Just over a year after the start of *WITHRUSH* and shortly after Devlin's return, Terry arrived in Leopoldville on the Sabena 707 from Brussels. A blast of hot, clammy air with the pungent smell of melting tar and rotting vegetation greeted him, standing second in the queue to disembark, as the chief stewardess unlocked the aircraft's forward door and swung it open. Even in the early morning the sultry, equatorial climate steamed, reminding him of Malaya and Borneo.

'*Au revoir et à bientôt,*' Maria smiled, as he headed for the boarding steps, adding in English, 'don't forget, the *Hôtel Memling.*' This was a coy reference to an arrangement to make contact again through messages left with the concierge at Leopoldville's swankiest hotel, where the Sabena crews normally stayed on stopovers.

Sweat started to trickle down Terry's face and dampen the back of his shirt as he made the short walk across the tarmac to enter Ndjili's domed, terminal building.

There were armed Congolese soldiers everywhere. They were at the bottom of the steps, all over the tarmac and inside the terminal, where they herded us towards the immigration and customs people.

Getting through Ndjili had already become a nerve-racking lottery of humouring and bribing officials determined to milk passengers in return for a trouble-free experience. Fortunately, Terry was spared this ordeal. Just inside the doorway a portly, middle-aged and balding man dressed in Belgian air force uniform stepped forward to block his path.

'*Bienvenue Capitaine,*' he said, holding out his hand. 'Please come with me. I'm Captain Leon Van den Bon.' After shaking his hand, Terry followed Van den Bon out of the building.

He recognized me immediately and shepherded me away from the other passengers to a waiting Volkswagen minibus. My bag appeared within minutes and we surged off through the gates without any sort of challenge.

Van den Bon's English was fluent. He quickly filled Terry in on where he was taking him as the minibus bounced along the potholed road towards the capital some eighteen kilometres to the west of the airport. The journey was slow, uncomfortable, hot and dusty.

'We're going to the *Force Aérienne Congolaise* base at Ndolo,' announced Van den Bon. 'It's a military airport just this side of Leo. Commandant Noël is expecting you. He's in charge and will tell you everything you need to know.' Terry nodded in reply, intent on taking in the squalid roadside scenes that were his introduction to the Congo. 'Welcome to Africa,' Van den Bon gestured with undisguised contempt, as if he could read Terry's thoughts. 'You should have seen this place before independence. Now it's every man for himself and to hell with the country.'

The traffic slowed to a crawl as they entered the outskirts of Leopoldville and turned off to the right to pass the intimidating, barbed-wire topped walls of the city's notorious Camp Kokolo prison and head towards Ndolo, a short distance further on. The airstrip occupied a flat expanse on the edge of Stanley Pool: a crescent-shaped, lake-like widening in the lower reaches of the Congo River, below which navigation is prevented by a series of white-water cataracts descending hundreds of metres through deep gorges before the river continues westward to complete its 2,900-mile journey to the ocean at the small fishing town of Muanda. The Congo may be second to the Nile in length, but it is easily Africa's largest river measured by flow, being second only to the Amazon in the volume of water it drains from a vast basin on both sides of the equator, meaning that parts of the river are always subject to a rainy season. Leopoldville as it was known then – or Kinshasa as it became later – sprawls along the southern bank at the western end of Stanley Pool, faced on the opposite shore of the swirling, brown water filled with floating clumps of hyacinths and debris, by the equally sprawling city of Brazzaville, the capital of the Republic of the Congo, the former French colony.

'Here we are,' said Van den Bon as the minibus turned towards the entrance gate for Ndolo, where a group of ANC soldiers slouched indolently over their automatic rifles. 'They're completely useless,' he muttered derisively as he flashed his pass and they nodded him through without a second look. 'The only thing you can trust them to do is run away or beat up women and kids. Without the mercenaries, half the country would still be in rebel hands.' Terry immediately understood that Van den Bon was an old colonial stager embittered by Congo's independence and subsequent chaos. 'He didn't have a good word to say for any Congolese and I couldn't fathom why he bothered to stay. But after a while I would learn; Africa gets into your blood.'

At the outset of *WITHRUSH*, helicopters were not a CIA priority because the Belgian *Force Aérienne Technique Assistance au Congolaise* (FATAC), a unit primarily responsible for training, had three H-21[1] helicopters available for search and rescue. The Congolese wanted more and although General Joseph Mobutu, then the military commander-in-chief, pressured the Americans either to acquire the UN's or supply others, none materialized. This changed about a year later when the last of the Belgian H-21s became unserviceable, the other two having crashed. The Americans then offered to add helicopters to the WIGMO force at no expense to the Congolese Government. However, a disgruntled Tshombe chose instead to order fifteen French Alouette IIIs, no doubt encouraged by the promise of a lucrative personal 10 per cent kickback. The order was later reduced to five. None had been delivered owing to disagreements over payment but the knowledge that the helicopters were coming, despite the absence of anybody trained to fly them, galvanized both the Belgians and Americans to look for pilots. The search took on a particular urgency in early 1965 when the CIA finally acquired three Bell-47 helicopters to replace the H-21s and illusory Alouettes. A few months later Terry had his chance meeting with the RAF officer who put him in touch with WIGMO, by then a well-established recruitment channel.

To this day Terry has no idea if the encounter at Tern Hill with the American helicopter pilot named Leach had anything to do with his subsequent recruitment by WIGMO.

> I don't know if I said anything to him that may have suggested I was worth targeting and that's why my RAF 'friend' then showed up or whether they were totally unrelated coincidences. What I am sure of is that the Americans had obviously got to one of our people and he'd done a bloody good job for them.

Previously classified US State Department telegrams between the embassy in Leopoldville and Washington reveal an urgent need for the recruitment of non-American pilots for a range of aircraft, including helicopters, in case of a worsening military situation. One, in February 1965, urged 'that sources of contract pilots be investigated soonest' so that a lack of pilots 'will not prove a stumbling block'. There can be no doubt then, that at the time of Terry's disappearance, the CIA was actively looking for recruits and would have put feelers out wherever possible, including presumably through any relationships with serving RAF officers. A man like Terry with jungle flying experience would have been a prize catch. The fact that he was also a qualified instructor and could train or convert other pilots would have been a valuable added bonus.

Significantly, in addition to making close studies of the French campaigns in Indo-China and Algeria as part of his counter-insurgency expertise, Johnson had also been an observer with British forces in Malaya. This would have given him the opportunity to have working contact with RAF and army personnel there and possibly even to develop a more influential relationship. Whether this played any role in Terry's subsequent recruitment to the *WITHRUSH* adventure is purely conjecture. Terry can only speculate.

> He was always very familiar and took a lot of interest in me but he was also very professional. I mean, he would never have said anything to me even if he'd had a hand in my recruitment.

Johnson's Malayan experience may be nothing more than an intriguing coincidence but Terry's former CO, Eley, has no doubt about the CIA's ability and willingness to recruit a serving RAF officer if it suited the agency's purpose.

> I'm absolutely sure of it. As military attaché in Saigon I had a lot of dealings with CIA agents. I often wondered about them and the way they went about things. I don't think there's anything they'd have stopped at.

From Ndolo airport's entrance gate the road followed the perimeter fence running parallel with the long, tarmac runway on its right before arriving at two cavernous, corrugated-iron hangars. The first hangar was occupied by an Italian air force contingent responsible for training Congolese pilots, a hang-over from Italian involvement in the UN mission, using a handful of ancient T-6s and Piaggio P148 jet trainers.

'You won't believe this but they've got one Congolese who's done three hundred hours dual and still can't go solo; the fools are still trying with him,' scoffed Van den Bon. 'They're a joke,' he added dismissively, providing Terry with his first insight into seething Belgian resentment over the presence of the Italians, whose unit supplemented the larger Belgian FATAC training facility based at Kamina in the Katangese south of the country, where the Belgians had their major air station during the colonial era. Significantly, FATAC had been no more successful in producing competent Congolese pilots.[2]

On arriving outside the second hangar, the minibus slewed to a halt. Van den Bon threw back the door and climbed out, gesturing Terry to follow him inside.

There were a few mechanics about working on some T-6s and a de Havilland Dove with tools that looked remarkably like those flimsy spanners you find in bicycle repair kits. It was really hairy scary to see – like something out of a comedy.

Van den Bon must have recognized the utter disbelief in Terry's face because he immediately started making excuses.

'We have to do the best we can. By the time everyone from the army chiefs down have helped themselves to our orders for equipment and spares, there's not much left,' he explained. 'Those crooks steal just about everything we requisition.'

In a building added to the rear of the hangar, Van den Bon led Terry to Commandant Pierre Noël's office and introduced him to the short, thin officer who commanded the FAC squadron but never flew combat missions. He wore an immaculate, Royal Belgian Air Force khaki uniform with sharply creased trousers that belied the ramshackle appearance of the maintenance operation in the hangar. Terry immediately recognized him as a by-the-book, staff-officer type, well suited to his job flying a mahogany desk rather than one of the squadron's armed T-6s.

'Welcome to 21 Squadron, *Force Aérienne Congolaise*,' Noël announced formally in perfect English. 'You're the new helicopter pilot from England, aren't you? We've been waiting for you but I'm afraid we don't have any helicopters here at the moment. Not to worry, you're here now and you'll have the rank of captain. I presume you can fly other types of aircraft?'

Terry bristled at Noël's offhand assumption that the absence of helicopters did not really matter. For the first time since leaving Tern Hill he felt uneasy and had to suppress a visceral urge to ask why he had been recruited under false pretences.

'Of course I can fly other aircraft,' he answered abruptly. 'But where are the Americans? I thought I was going to be working for them.'

'Ah yes, the Americans – they have some helicopters,' Noël admitted lamely. 'They're based at Ndjili where you arrived this morning but I'm informed that they've got all the pilots they need at the moment. We had to lend them one of our men and they've also trained a couple of their

Cubanos, so you've been assigned to us for the time being on the orders of Colonel Bouzin. He's in charge.'

As Terry would soon learn, Emile Bouzin was the most senior Belgian Air Force officer in the Congo and the official air advisor to the Congolese Government. He was a short, dapper, Douglas Fairbanks look-alike who worked closely with the CIA air operations officers and although he was technically in overall command of the FAC, the truth was that it, too, fell under CIA control on an operational basis. This had come about a year earlier during the Stanleyville hostage crisis. According to the CIA, uncoordinated FAC attacks on rebel positions during the 111-day stand-off had endangered the hostages' lives. Understandably, this so infuriated the Americans that they temporarily suspended their air support operation and threatened to withdraw it altogether, forcing Tshombe to accept the change.

'We work closely with the Americans,' Noël added. 'I can also tell you that we've been waiting for a delivery of new Alouettes from France. They should've been here months ago and Colonel Bouzin has been trying to find out where they are but as usual nobody in the government will give him a straight answer. They're coming, they're coming – that's all he ever gets.'

Reassured by Noël's explanation, Terry's anger subsided. 'Well, I suppose there's no point crying over spilled milk,' he grinned to Noël, who frowned, clearly bemused by the English expression. 'Look I'll fly whatever you've got for the time being. Just remember though, helicopters are my speciality and I came here to do search and rescue work and that's what I expect to be doing before long.'

'Yes, yes, of course. I'm sure our American friends will send for you when they need you,' answered the Commandant. 'But they've given us an important assignment for you based here with us until the Alouettes arrive and then you'll take charge of our new helicopter wing. Now, please go with Captain Van den Bon. He'll deal with the formalities and take you to your quarters in the city where I hope you'll be comfortable.'

Terry sensed that Noël was making excuses. All the same, he decided not to press him then on the so-called important assignment.

I got the impression that I was a bit of a special case and they really didn't know what to do with me. Later I learned that I had to be allocated to the FAC initially because WIGMO was still waiting for the official nod from the British on using me. Noël probably didn't know that and he'd been told to keep me busy. He knew he was in the dark but didn't want to admit it.

In Terry's view Nöel was puffed up and full of self importance but about as useless as his diminutive presence suggested. He soon discovered that the Commandant had the very dubious distinction of having crashed at least one of every type of aircraft he had ever flown.

> That apparently was his forte: there was absolutely no doubt about it, it was on the record. Now that's some claim to fame. Happily I never had to fly with the little jerk.

Van den Bon took Terry to his own small office where he gave him a cap and set of captain's insignia for his uniform, apologizing as he did for the fact that he had not been allocated a higher rank.

> I told him not to worry about that; what I really wanted to know now that I was finally signing-on, so to speak, were the terms of my contract. Van den Bon looked embarrassed and told me that there was no contract. I wasn't required to sign anything; my lodgings and meals would be paid for and I was to be given an expenses allowance until further notice, all on the orders of Bouzin.

First no helicopters, then no contract; not surprisingly Terry began to wonder what was going on. With the so-called formalities complete, he followed Van den Bon down the corridor to a sparsely furnished room with paint peeling off the walls, which served as the crew rest area. Two other pilots were sharing a joke about one of their comrades who had succeeded in convincing his gullible wife that he had contracted a vicious dose of gonorrhoea from a lavatory seat. Van den Bon introduced them as Bob Brannon and Glen Cohen. Brannon was a big, husky South African who had learned to fly in the Royal Canadian Air Force and been one of the earliest recruits to 21 Squadron when it was formed on Tshombe's return. He and Terry were to have an enduring relationship. Cohen was a lanky Canadian who Terry rarely saw again.

On this occasion the two men took Terry off to be measured for his uniform and then dropped him outside the *Hôtel Regina* just off the *Boulevard Albert* in the heart of Leopoldville, where FAC pilots were often temporarily housed. Until a year earlier the hotel had been the UN mission's headquarters. On the first floor Terry was shown into a large room that looked pleasant enough except for an unmade bed, an untidy pile of children's toys and a wardrobe jammed with male and female clothes. When he complained he was told that an FAC pilot named Jock 'Mac' MacDonald had been living in the room with his wife and child. They had vacated it earlier in the day to go on leave. The hotel manager was reluctant to tidy the room or allocate Terry another because the government was more than a year in arrears with payments for the pilots' lodgings. 'I eventually persuaded them to clean the room up for me and then spent the evening in the bar fortifying myself with Chivas Regal.' No doubt, with more than a little help from the Scotch, he convinced himself that 'WIGMO wouldn't have gone to all the trouble and expense of recruiting me and getting me to Leopoldville if they had no use for me'.

Terry was waiting in the *Regina* lobby when the minibus arrived to collect him for the ride out to Ndolo at eight o'clock the following morning. At the airport he made his way to the crew room. Two or three pilots were present including an older Belgian by the name of Vic Verloo, who was dark-haired and on the short side. He was an old Congo hand, a Katanga veteran then working with Air Brousse, a small, independent air charter and maintenance outfit that also operated out of Ndolo. He immediately approached Terry.

'You must be the new helicopter pilot,' he said, sticking out his hand. 'Noël's asked me to check you out in the Dove. But first let me show you the only helicopter they have here.'

'Noël said they didn't have any helicopters,' Terry answered, as he shook Verloo's hand.

'Well that's not entirely true. Come with me, I'll show you,' said Verloo.

With some of the other pilots tagging along close behind, they went outside to the rear of the hangar. Verloo stopped and pointed across the grass to an aircraft graveyard filled with pieces of wrecked UN aircraft. Near the centre Terry could make out a twisted mound of metal, barely recognizable as the rusting remains of a Sikorsky 55 lying on its side with buckled rotor blades pointing crazily at different angles.

'There – that's the only helicopter,' laughed Verloo.

'Oh, very bloody funny,' grinned Terry, looking round at the others, who having quite obviously conspired in the jape, were enjoying every minute of it. 'Now let's go fly the Dove.'

No. 21 Squadron's sole Dove – an eleven-seat, British-built, light-transport aircraft – had an interesting history. It was originally part of Tshombe's break-away Katangese air force where MacDonald, whose room at the *Hôtel Regina* was then being occupied by Terry, had been one of the mercenary pilots. When the UN finally crushed the Katangese secession, MacDonald, a tall, laconic New Zealander who smoked heavily and rolled his cigarettes from corner to corner of his mouth, made a daring escape in the Dove and flew it to Leopoldville. On Tshombe's return as prime minister of the Congo, MacDonald was another of the first recruits to 21 Squadron.

Terry had not flown a fixed wing aircraft for over three years but Verloo knew immediately that the check-out was a mere formality. As they accelerated down the runway for take-off he pointed out the wreckage of more UN aircraft: a couple of DC-4s and a DC-6 that had been stripped of their engines so that their tails rested on the ground, their noses pointing skyward in a futile attempt to become airborne. Opposite, on the other side of the runway, was the control tower and the building occupied by Air Brousse. They climbed away over Stanley Pool and then banked sharply to the right, giving Terry in the co-pilot's seat his first aerial view of the surrounding country. 'More bloody cabbage,' he thought to himself as he looked down on the forest stretching away to the east as far as he could see with the wide, brown trail of the Congo River the only identifiable feature. Verloo gave him the controls and they completed two or three circuits. On his first approach Terry had to remind himself to land the aircraft and not try to hover it. After only half an hour they were back on the ground with Verloo heading off to confirm enthusiastically to Noël that the new man would have no trouble flying any of the squadron's aircraft.

Notes

1   Transport helicopters having a curved fuselage with main rotors at each end of the kind used in Korea and the early years of the Vietnam War and nicknamed the 'flying banana'.
2   Many Congolese suffered from sickle-cell anaemia, which affected them at altitude, although this was little understood at the time.

Chapter Eleven
Special Assignment

Terry's arrival at Ndolo provoked idle speculation among the other pilots who regarded the stranger in their midst with a certain amount of suspicion. They saw him as reticent and aloof. For his part, Terry was being naturally guarded. He could hardly come clean about his dramatic exit from the RAF and he was feeling understandably cagey about his role after Nöel's less than satisfactory explanation. Unbeknown to him, one fantastic rumour that started gaining currency was that he was one of the Great Train Robbers on the run. News of the escape from prison of some members of the gang responsible for what was then Britain's largest-ever heist – the £2.6 million[1] hold-up of a London-to-Glasgow express in August 1963 – was still a major talking point in the crew room.

Most of the pilots had been with the squadron since its outset or shortly afterwards. In addition to Brannon and Cohen, there were three South Africans named Ares Klootwyk, Kevin 'Dinger' Bell and Charlie Vivier; an Englishman named Tom Sadler; a Portuguese man named Eddie Ip; a Belgian named Degaugier, and the New Zealander MacDonald, who was away on leave. With the exception of Sadler, who was quite a bit older, the men were all around the same age as Terry or a little younger. They had spent most of the previous year and a half flying aggressive combat missions in support of the English-speaking, 5th Commando, a mercenary unit then led by Colonel 'Mad' Mike Hoare.[2] While Nöel and Van den Bon directed operations from the relative safety and comfort of Ndolo, the pilots operated from crude airstrips in remote parts of the country. Their T-6s were not fitted with radios and there were no navigation aids apart from occasional radio beacons that rarely functioned, making the missions hazardous without the added danger of retaliatory ground fire from rebel positions. Two aircraft had been lost. In one attack Brannon was badly wounded in the arm by gunfire and nearly bled to death flying back to base. Vivier, too, was lucky to be alive, as Terry would shortly hear.

Terry decided to try and win their respect by demonstrating his flying ability. In the days immediately after his introductory flight in the Dove with Verloo, he simply took whatever aircraft was available and put it through its paces over the Ndolo airfield. Everyone agreed he could fly; yet the frosty atmosphere prevailed. Even Brannon, who would become his flying partner and a close friend, avoided him at first.

> Terry would sometimes come up, obviously looking for a friend, but I usually ignored him. I never believed any of the nonsense about him being one of the Great Train Robbers because I couldn't see how a Royal Air Force officer of his capability and standing could possibly have been involved. All the same, something made me wary.

The men's misgivings turned to outright resentment when word spread that the newcomer had been selected to fly a brand new C-45 Beechcraft[3] on which Air Brousse had just completed a costly nose-wheel conversion. The aircraft had been a gift from President Kennedy to General Mobutu in his capacity as commander-in-chief and was known to be under CIA control. Terry's 'special assignment' in the absence of any helicopters, was to pilot the Beechcraft for Colonel Leonard Mulamba, then the ANC's second-in-command and the most popular and respected Congolese army officer. He asked the standoffish Brannon to be his co-pilot in this prestigious undertaking.

Early one morning before operations started, Terry and Brannon went out to Ndolo to start familiarization on the Beechcraft. Terry was checking Brannon out on engine-out circuits and landings and they were doing a single-engine overshoot, turning into the dead engine, when Tom Sadler arrived for work. As the squadron's regular transport pilot, Sadler was particularly peeved about Terry's preferential treatment in being chosen for the Mulamba assignment in the spanking new aircraft. According to Brannon, all the men were 'cheesed off because none of them had been allowed near the plane. They were all really beside themselves with jealousy, particularly Tom who was also angry about losing me as his co-pilot.' When Terry and Brannon landed after a few more 'touch-and-goes', Sadler stormed up to them and waded into Terry with a torrent of abuse in front of everybody else in the crew room. Terry smiled back condescendingly but said nothing. Sadler continued his tirade. Finally, Terry retaliated.

'Oh, why don't you get stuffed, you old fart,' he shouted in exasperation.

This merely encouraged Sadler to scream even more abuse. The other men were now doubled up with laughter. Incandescent with rage, Sadler yelled for Noël, who scuttled round from his office to determine the cause of the uproar. Sadler ranted about Terry flying dangerously, claiming that turning into a feathered engine was against all the rules and reckless. Terry calmly refuted this.

Of course he was old school and didn't know what the hell he was talking about. There was an old myth that you never turn into a dead engine but aerodynamically that's complete bullshit, which is what I tried to explain to that buffoon Noël. Of course, he didn't have a clue what I was talking about.

Sadler refused to have it either, insisting to Noël that he should have Terry arrested to face a court martial.

'Would you prefer close arrest or open arrest?' a blustering Noël asked Terry.

'Open,' replied Terry, grinning.

'Good. Then you're under open arrest,' Noël told him. 'Now go to Ndjili. You need to collect Mulamba and take him back to Stanleyville.'

That ended the incident. Nothing more was ever heard about it, although Sadler would never speak to either Terry or Brannon again. Terry appeared completely unperturbed by the whole affair. As his new comrades were to learn, he rarely lost his cool. All the same, the truth was that he rarely showed his true feelings at all. What he seemed to shrug off as inconsequential nagged at him inside and he disliked anything that belittled his ability. He never forgave Sadler.

After getting to know Mulamba, Terry held him in high regard.

He was the hero of Bukavu. Stanleyville would never have fallen and there would never have been a hostage crisis if Mulamba hadn't been called away to save Bukavu at the time. He was brave, intelligent and, by the standards of the ANC, in a league on his own. Working with him was a real pleasure.

In their role as his pilots, Terry and Brannon shared a room in Stanleyville's former *Hôtel Victoria*. This was where most of the white hostages had been held by the *Simbas* less than a year earlier before an audacious, joint US–Belgian operation to free them. In many respects, Stanleyville typified the Congo more than any of its other towns. Standing on the Congo River in the heart of the country a thousand miles to the east of Leopoldville and just north of the equator, it was a colonial gem of wide, paved boulevards, green lawns and tropical gardens with huge trees whose canopies provided cooling shade. The residential areas boasted elegant, stucco-walled houses with high ceilings and spacious verandas. However, the *Simbas* had trashed much of the city after occupying it when the ANC garrison fled without a fight, abandoning most of its guns and equipment along with the 300,000 beleaguered citizens. Among those remaining were 1,600 foreigners who were then held hostage. Negotiations for their release continued for over three months. Finally, the US and Belgian Governments decided to act. At first light on the morning of 24 November 1964, four USAF Hercules C-130 transports laden with a crack force of 600 Belgian paratroops appeared over Stanleyville's airport preceded by CIA T-28s and B-26s. Operation *Dragon Rouge* was underway. At the same time the mercenary 5th Commando approached by road to recapture the city once the hostages were freed.

The sight of aircraft overhead, paratroops falling from the sky and gunfire from the airport panicked the *Simbas*, many of whom were intoxicated with a cocktail of alcohol and hemp. Dressed in manes of monkey fur and feathers, they herded around three hundred of the white hostages from the *Hôtel Victoria* into the street and started marching them towards the city park and the Patrice Lumumba monument, where they habitually executed government sympathizers. Before they reached the park, a rebel radio station blared orders to 'kill, kill, kill' and the deranged *Simbas* opened fire on the captives, gunning down men, women and children with automatic weapons and brutally hacking others to death with machetes. Almost thirty died. The survivors included the American consulate staff and CIA operative, who escaped by fleeing in different directions just as the paratroops appeared on the scene. They and the other surviving hostages were flown to safety in the Hercules transports but the bloody images of the slaughtered filled the world's front pages. The rebels were also holding smaller groups of hostages in other towns, notably Paulis. A similar attempt was made to save them in Operation *Dragon Noire*, but again many of the captives were slaughtered before the paratroops could secure their release. Two other rescue missions were cancelled but more hostages were butchered in brutal revenge killings. Newspaper reports of these killings accompanied by gruesome images of the slain, outraged people throughout the world. They were a key factor in persuading Terry that he could play a valuable role in the Congo.

When the mercenary relief column arrived in Stanleyville, captured *Simbas* were shown no mercy. With the city back in government hands, Congolese retribution was just as pitiless as the *Simba* butchery. Leighton Mishou, one of the CIA air operations officers who later worked closely with Terry, arrived in Stanleyville two days after *Dragon Rouge*. Bloated, decomposing *Simba* corpses still littered the streets. He took over the *Hôtel Victoria* to house the WIGMO pilots and ground crews, and in subsequent weeks witnessed examples of the ANC's summary justice. In a private memoir, Mishou described how one group of *Simba* suspects was rounded up, trucked out to the airport and gunned down in front of the WIGMO crews, the heap of writhing bodies then soaked in kerosene and set alight. Later, executions were carried out more efficiently in the city park with a single bullet to the back of the head after trials that resembled Roman arena justice. 'A suspect was paraded on a reviewing stand. If he was booed or jeered by the crowd he was sentenced to immediate execution. If he was cheered he was set free.' Hundreds more suspects were reportedly thrown off a bridge over the Tshopo River and fed to crocodiles. Some 10,000 are said to have died by these means.

Memories of the *Simba* occupation were still raw in Stanleyville and surrounding areas when Terry arrived there on his special assignment to fly Mulamba. One of the Colonel's key roles was to go around making hearts-and-minds speeches assuring people that the rebels had been defeated. From their base in Stanleyville, Terry and Brannon flew him to government-controlled towns to preach his message as well as making leaflet drops spreading the word. In fact, the *Simbas* still occupied large tracts of the countryside and the uprising was by no means over. All the same, even the conscientious Mulamba liked to return to Leopoldville at the weekend. This meant that Terry and Brannon could also enjoy haunts there like the bars at the *Memling* and *Regina* or the popular *Blue Note* nightclub. 'At that time Leopoldville was not the squalid dump it soon became. You could have a lot of fun and we did.'

Although Terry was disappointed not to be flying one of WIGMO's Bell-47s on search and rescue, he was content to bide his time being Mulamba's pilot with the pristine Beechcraft more or less at his disposal. He made a point of getting to know the CIA air operations officer in Stanleyville, a hulking Polish American named Ksary Wyrizimski, whose name was such an unpronounceable mouthful that he was only ever known as Big Bill. He had been a squadron leader in the Polish air force when Hitler invaded and after a vain struggle against overwhelming odds escaped to Russia with his aircraft, although Hitler's pact with Stalin ensured his immediate imprisonment in barbaric conditions. Later, when Hitler invaded Russia, Wyrizimski was freed and went to Britain to join the RAF's free Polish squadron as a Spitfire pilot. When the war ended he migrated to the US, where his hatred of the Russians made him a willing recruit to the CIA. He had been part of *WITHRUSH* from the outset. With a little persuasion from Terry, he readily agreed to allow the Beechcraft's use to rescue refugees whenever Mulamba did not require the aircraft.

Within a few days of arriving at Ndolo, Terry had accompanied Verloo to Stanleyville in an old tail-wheel Beechcraft to make several refugee evacuations from primitive, dirt airfields out in the bush. These were usually narrow, deeply rutted, strips of red, laterite clay with no windsocks or any other kind of aids.

> Reports of besieged missionaries or nuns came through the church grapevine or by tom-tom messages drummed from village to village and picked up in Stanleyville by the CIA air operations officer and then passed to us.

The short strips were in jungle reminiscent of Malaya. Verloo was familiar with most of them. Terry would later copy his landing procedure.

> We'd come in low, no more than five hundred feet above the forest canopy, and then fly over the strip to clear off any animals or people. After a quick keyhole turn we'd make the landing approach, almost clipping the treetops. Then it was flaps down hard to hit the strip and just as we touched flaps up to make the aircraft stick to the ground and stop.

Once on the ground they crammed the aircraft as full as they dared with Congolese nuns and mission workers fleeing from rebel-held enclaves. Terry had never seen people in such a desperate condition.

> They were in a pitiful state: hungry and traumatized by fear. Some of them had been raped repeatedly. I can't remember how many we got out altogether but it must have been ten or twelve each time; little Congolese nuns didn't take up too much space or weigh very much either and we could squeeze a lot of them in. We didn't bother with seat belts or anything like that.

With the aircraft so full, getting off the ground required nerves of steel.

Together with Brannon, Terry made a number of similar evacuations using Mulamba's Beechcraft, as well as going out to collect casualties. One of these was an ANC soldier with severe machete wounds who had been brought to the airstrip at Buta, about 175 miles north of Stanleyville. On the way up, flying over dense jungle, Brannon recounted the story of Charlie Vivier's crash and lucky escape in the area, not long before Terry's arrival. He spared none of the grisly details about the fate of Cuban pilots who had fallen into rebel hands.

'Be warned, if the bastards ever catch you, they'll eat you,' he told Terry. 'Charlie was bloody lucky to get out in one piece.'

Vivier was below average height. However, whatever he lacked in stature was overshadowed by a demonstrative character and attention-grabbing, piercing blue eyes. Like Barrel in Malaya, he was prone to bouts of heavy drinking but a first-rate pilot nonetheless. Terry listened enthralled to Brannon's gravely-voiced narration above the hum of the Beechcraft's engines. Vivier had been on a mission from Buta to re-supply ground forces right up in the north of the country near the Sudanese border. He was flying with Klootwyk and two Belgians in a flight of four T-6s when the weather closed in on them and heavy cloud cover prevented them landing at the forward position. Klootwyk had been another of 21 Squadron's earliest recruits. He was Vivier's regular wing man and they were close friends, having served together in the South African Air Force, where Vivier had been an instructor when Klootwyk was learning to fly. Stocky and dimple-chinned with boyish good looks and blond hair, Terry recognized Klootwyk as a classic female, locker-room pin-up. 'All the girls loved him. He was a bloody good pilot too.'

The base at Buta had no direction-finding equipment. So to get back, Vivier and his comrades had to try and find a river to help them navigate over the uniform jungle canopy. The cloud cover progressively worsened until they could see nothing to help pinpoint their way. Vivier flew up close to Klootwyk, indicating by means of hand signals that he was low on fuel. Waving back, Klootwyk signalled that Vivier should follow him but soon afterwards he saw him pumping furiously with his left hand and realized immediately that his friend was either completely out of fuel or very low indeed. Ironically, by this time the cloud had lifted slightly and although they were still over dense jungle Klootwyk spotted a clearing of sorts ahead. He urgently gestured to Vivier that he should try to crash-land in the clearing and then watched as Vivier expertly belly-flopped into the space in a cloud of dust, narrowly missing the surrounding trees before his aircraft slewed to a halt. Vivier clambered out of the wreckage as Klootwyk circled overhead to drop an Uzi sub-machine gun and pistol to him. He knew only too well that Vivier's chances of surviving were poor if there were rebels anywhere in the vicinity.

Klootwyk eventually found the river leading him back to Buta, where he refuelled, collected a ration pack and, accompanied by one of the Belgian pilots in another T-6, flew back to where Vivier had come down.

They dropped the food and then circled protectively over him for three hours until darkness started falling before making the forty-five-minute dash back to Buta. The next day they did the same thing and then arranged for a third pilot to relieve them on the following one. Eventually, a FATAC DC-3 Dakota from Kamina dropped a small contingent of well-armed, Belgian paratroops at the crash site and they escorted Vivier out of the forest to safety. Back at base a Congolese mechanic admitted that when he was refuelling Vivier's aircraft, the drum emptied before the tanks were full but he failed to warn Vivier. Klootwyk also discovered that the sub-machine gun he dropped would have been useless had Vivier needed it because the barrel bent when it hit the ground.

Vivier later admitted that his worst moment had been on the first night. He decided to sleep in the aircraft with the canopy open and he was woken by a scratching sound on the fuselage. When he looked out he saw at least two lions pulling at the wreckage. He had forgotten that they were carrying meat supplies and the lions had obviously picked up the scent. Two rounds from his pistol were enough to frighten them off and he spent the other nights up a tree. However, for Klootwyk and his comrades the worst aspect of the drama was the refusal by the CIA to send the Bell-47 based at Stanleyville to rescue Vivier. Stanleyville was only about two hours away but the CIA claimed the helicopter was busy on other operations. Much later Terry heard that the CIA disapproved of the FAC mission on that occasion because it involved crossing the Sudanese border. Refusing to send the helicopter was meant as a rebuke.

Through stories from Brannon, Terry gradually learned more about the FAC and the unusual mix of characters in its ranks. Although he had not met the Kiwi MacDonald, he knew all about his escape from Katanga in the Dove. He sensed that Vivier and Klootwyk were the squadron's acknowledged aces while Bell was the new kid on the block. He had set out to be a Roman Catholic priest but stayed on in the South African Air Force after national service. A slight man with youthful features, he was the youngest of the group. Degaugier and Ip kept to themselves and nobody seemed to know much about them. The ranting Sadler was a former RAF transport pilot who struck Terry as a complete misfit in the small, hands-on operation where the pilots pretty much ran their own show. Commandant Noël's role was obviously little more than a formality and he was generally regarded as a reject anyway. The small back-up team of Air Congo engineers included a few genuinely good mechanics and a high proportion of complete duds, like the man whose casual incompetence over refuelling nearly cost Vivier his life. Fortunately, the T-6s were new aircraft and required minimal maintenance.

What then of Brannon, the man he had chosen to be his partner on the special assignment with Mulamba? As usual Terry was learning a great deal more about other men than they were about him. His relationship with Brannon was no exception. During hours spent together in the cockpit of the Beechcraft and bars in Stanleyville and Leopoldville, Brannon opened up. He was softly spoken with only a trace of a South African accent. Terry thought he had recognized something of a loner in him and he identified with that. What he learned was that the big former RCAF man could trace his roots back to the owners of the *County Press* in the Isle of Wight off the south coast of England. His father had been sent to South Africa by the Rhodes Trust and, after growing up there, the young Brannon migrated to Canada where he joined the air force. He was married with a young child when his father died unexpectedly in 1959 and the RCAF released him on compassionate grounds to return to South Africa and run the family business. A few years later he founded a small air charter company near Cape Town. This was what led to his presence in the Congo. Unlike the others, most of whom had responded to recruitment advertisements in the *Johannesburg Star* and other South African newspapers, Brannon had been hoodwinked and pretty much conscripted.

In the middle of 1964 two Polish men who claimed to have been with Tshombe's air force during the Katanga secession approached him. They told him that he could do very well for himself selling aeroplanes to the Congolese Government and promised to pay him a retainer if he flew them to Leopoldville, where they claimed they had all the right contacts. On the face of it this seemed quite an attractive proposition. Brannon flew the men up in one of his air charter Cessnas. Once in Leopoldville he was taken by them to a flat in the centre of the city and told that if he went outside he would be arrested by the ANC and probably killed. After five days as a virtual prisoner without food, he threatened to walk out and expose the two Poles as frauds unless they took him back to Ndjili, where his aircraft was parked. As soon as they approached the plane, they were all arrested and roughly pushed and prodded with gun barrels to explain themselves to a Congolese officer. The Poles were told they could stay if they joined one of the mercenary commando units but Brannon was threatened with being jailed. He immediately volunteered to try and join the Congolese air force and the officer allowed him to go to the *Hôtel Memling* to see Colonel Bouzin. The dapper, moustached Belgian sent him to a room on the hotel's next floor where Jerry Puren,[4] the South African who ran Tshombe's original Katangese air force, had been rehired by the prime minister and was busy putting together the fledgling FAC. He looked at Brannon's credentials and hired him on the spot. The next day Klootwyk came to collect him.

After hearing all this, Terry felt he owed it to Brannon to tell him something about himself. They were sharing a room in the officers' mess at Kamina after flying down there on a liaison errand for Mulamba. Kamina had once been the Royal Belgian Air Force headquarters in the Congo and probably the best air station in all of Africa, although it had been ransacked during the post-independence Katangese secession. The Belgian FATAC unit had since done its best to make the base habitable again. Terry and Brannon were changing for dinner in the mess after the long flight down from Stanleyville when Terry surprised Brannon.

'I expect you're wondering why I'm here?' he started. 'Well, my wife and two daughters were killed in a plane crash. I needed to get away from everything that reminded me of them.'

'Christ, I'm sorry to hear that. I don't know how you can face the days,' sympathized Brannon, who was genuinely moved.

'Life goes on; there's nothing you can do about that,' shrugged Terry.

By his own admission, Brannon 'swallowed the whole story and felt very sorry' for Terry. It would be years before he learned the truth.

Notes

1 Around £37m at today's prices.
2 Hoare, born in India of Irish descent and a former British army major, was regarded as a serious and capable soldier who had been with Tshombe in Katanga.
3 A twin-engine aircraft capable of carrying six passengers.
4 Jeremiah Puren was one of the key architects and chief recruiters for Tshombe's entire Katanga mercenary operation.

Chapter Twelve
Cleared All the Way

After a little more than a month, Terry's special assignment to Mulamba abruptly ended. He and Brannon had been away from Stanleyville making leaflet drops over known rebel strongholds before flying to Leopoldville to participate in a flypast marking Kasavubu's birthday. When they returned to Stanleyville on 23 November 1965, Terry saw a Telex message for Mulamba. This advised that an American DC-3 was scheduled to pick the Colonel up later that day and take him to the capital for a top-level conference with other senior ANC officers who were being collected from their regional headquarters. Terry immediately sensed that something big was happening.

> My instincts told me that putting all your top generals in an aeroplane together, even one provided and flown by the Americans, was asking for trouble. So I went to see Mulamba to express my concern.

'Look, I'm worried about you and the other army commanders being in the same aircraft,' he told him. 'What if somebody wants you all out of the way?'

'I'm flattered by your interest in our well-being but I assure you there's absolutely nothing to worry about,' replied the unflappable Colonel.

'Why don't you let us take you to Leo in the Beechcraft?' Terry suggested.

'That won't be necessary. I can't go against an order from my chief,' answered Mulamba. 'He was very calm, very considerate and thanked me again for worrying about his safety. Nothing I said would change his mind and off he went that afternoon.'

In Leopoldville the following evening, the large American community was celebrating Thanksgiving with traditional turkey dinners when the first news of a military coup broke. As diplomats and CIA operatives raced back to their offices it emerged that General Mobutu, with the full support of his army commanders, had taken over the government and proclaimed himself president. Unusually for the Congo, the change was made without any bloodshed. Mulamba was installed as the new prime minister.[1] As Terry recalls it, 'the Americans were really caught with their pants down. They had no idea the coup was coming, which is extraordinary given that the generals were all collected in one of their DC-3s.' For years afterwards Devlin was accused of engineering the plot. Mobutu was certainly his protégé. However, he resolutely denied any prior knowledge and claimed the first he heard was when his deputy alerted him at six o'clock on the morning of the coup. If he was telling the truth, then it was a spectacular intelligence failure on his part.

With his special assignment over, Terry started to get impatient about the absence of any news from WIGMO or new information on the delivery of the Alouettes. The only consolation was that he and Brannon were free to do pretty much what they liked with the Beechcraft. They volunteered to carry out refugee evacuations and casevacs, as well as undertaking surveillance flights for Big Bill. These missions took them all over the country, from Watsa in the far north near the Sudanese border, to Elizabethville, the Katangese capital, in the distant south near neighbouring Zambia. For Terry it was an invaluable opportunity to get to know the Congo and its hazardous flying conditions. Doing more of the kind of work that had brought him there also helped to keep his spirits up. So did the intrigue of working with Big Bill. 'I learned more than I should about the CIA from the stuff he used to leave lying around on his desk'.

At the time Big Bill was fretting over reports that gold from the massive open-cast mine at Watsa was being looted by mercenaries who were supposed to be guarding it. Watsa had been recaptured for the government by Hoare's 5th Commando only months earlier. The stash of gold bars in the mine's huge vault had been valued at over $60 million[2] before the *Simba* revolt. Over half was missing when the mine was retaken. A contingent of mercenaries was left to protect the remaining twenty-eight tonnes until it could be removed. However, rumours soon abounded of intrigue, murder and secret flights to smuggle out stolen fortunes. Big Bill wanted Terry and Brannon to see what they could find out. He despised looting by mercenaries, whom he collectively dismissed as a worthless bunch of unruly drunks, drug users and thieves. Such scorn earned him plenty of enemies among them, particularly when he openly accused some of looting a local branch of the Banque Nationale du Congo. Whenever he came across conspiratorial groups of mercenaries together,

Big Bill would go up to them, put an intimidating arm round a shoulder and whisper: 'Okay den, who blew de bank at Bumba?'

All that Terry and Brannon could establish at Watsa was that a small 'inner sanctum' of mercenaries guarded the gold jealously. They allowed nobody else near to it, not even other colleagues, some of whom had been threatened with being shot. There was nothing to stop these men from helping themselves. Big Bill was convinced they were doing just that and he made no secret of his suspicion. In August 1967 he was killed near Albertville. The official story was that his jeep overturned after being accidentally driven off the road by an ANC truck. Terry dismisses that version. He believes that in truth a renegade bunch of mercenaries decided to settle old scores. 'He was literally wiped out; that was the way things were done in the Congo.'

The mixture of savannah and thick jungle separating Watsa and Stanleyville still harboured rebel enclaves when Terry and Brannnon took the Beechcraft to the mining settlement. By then Terry knew that the CIA had lost two T-28s in the area earlier in the year. As he looked down at the endless canopy of trees below on the return flight, he grimaced at the thought of the horrific fate endured by one of the two Cuban pilots. 'Wasn't it round here that those T-28s disappeared?' he asked Brannon.

'Yeah. They were on ops out of Bunia,' nodded Brannon. 'I buried what was left of the poor sod the *Simbas* got hold of.'

The two men, Juan Peron and Tomas Trujillo, ran out of fuel after losing their way back to base when heavy cloud cover and rain unexpectedly blanketed any landmarks. An ugly, towering wall of dark-grey storm clouds and squall lines obliterated even the sparkling, blue expanse of Lake Albert, normally easy to find by climbing a few thousand feet. Unlike the T-6s, the T-28s were equipped with radios. Their air operations officer monitored the Cubans' plight while they circled blindly, their panicky conversation bordering on hysteria as their fuel diminished, making their situation increasingly perilous. Eventually, they were both forced to crash-land, triggering an immediate search.

The effort to find the downed men intensified dramatically on news that a CIA case officer named Dick Holm[3] – who had been masquerading with WIGMO as a Canadian technician under the alias Jerry Fraser – had gone with Peron to undertake air reconnaissance. The CIA scrambled two B-26s and asked FATAC to send its H-21 helicopters, two of which were then still flying. At the same time a C-130 transport was sent to Stanleyville from Leopoldville to evacuate the men if they were found while a Special Air Missions 707 raced across the Atlantic to collect Holm. Nothing like as much urgency or effort had been made to recover two T-28 pilots lost a couple of months earlier, although in their case both were fortunate enough to survive.

Nine days after the aircraft went missing Peron was found being escorted along a road by a group of Azande warriors: tall, proud, nomadic tribesmen who roamed freely between the Sudan and Congo. Peron confirmed that Trujillo and Holm were in the Azande village, although Holm's condition was critical. He had been severely burned in the crash-landing. One of the ancient H-21s – nicknamed the flying banana on account of its ungainly, curved fuselage with a main rotor at each end – set off to collect the two missing men. Less than halfway to the village the helicopter was brought down by mechanical failure. After recovering the three-man crew and six mercenaries on board, all of whom escaped the crash unharmed, the second helicopter successfully reached the village and evacuated Holm. He was unconscious and black with gangrene. There was no sign of Trujillo.

Amazingly, Holm survived. However, the H-21 that brought him out never flew again. Its whirling forward rotor blades collapsed, hacking into the fuselage and destroying it as he was borne away on a stretcher at Stanleyville. A little later, news of Trujillo's gruesome fate emerged. Stricken with fever – probably malaria – he left the Azande village and attempted to walk to the nearest town. Knowing that he was in rebel territory he travelled at night, hiding by day until he stumbled on a small mission. There, nuns struggled without the benefit of quinine or any substitute, to reduce his fever. One morning a roving group of *Simbas* raided the mission. After raping and killing the nuns they found the bedridden pilot. He killed several with his pistol and Israeli-made Uzi sub-machine gun before they hacked him to death and then feasted on his brains, heart and hands.

Only a few weeks earlier another T-28 pilot by the name of Fausto Gomez had met a similar fate after his aircraft belly-flopped into the ground when trying to pull out of a steep, strafing dive on *Simbas*. Gomez left it too late to initiate the climb and the T-28's momentum carried it down. The aircraft was notorious for this handling deficiency. He survived the crash and his wingman, by then out of ammunition and low on fuel, circled briefly overhead and watched in muted horror as rebels broke open the aircraft's canopy, chopped off Gomez's harness and dragged him out of the cockpit. Two days later a mercenary unit found the wrecked aircraft. Nearby they found Gomez's mutilated body. He had been hacked to death with machetes and his head, hands and feet were missing.

Thirteen Italian pilots had been butchered and eaten a few years earlier. Terry had heard unabridged accounts of that atrocity. He also knew:

> ... another guy who used to tell a story about watching his friend's ears and nose being boiled in a pot and then being made to eat them. You can't imagine the things that happened. A lot of the refugees I pulled out had watched their families being massacred or mutilated. One of the *Simbas'* favourite meals was a young girl's buttocks cut into steaks and barbecued while she watched. Believe me, they were complete savages.

Both he and Brannon wore pistols and carried an M-15 rifle in the Beechcraft in case of coming down in hostile terrain. Uzi sub-machine guns were standard issue for 22 Wing pilots and most of the FAC pilots carried them as well. 'Being armed was a straightforward matter of survival but it was much better not to end up in the sort of situation where you might need your gun.'

In early December Terry was approached in Stanleyville by the new British defence attaché to the Congo, who was probably also MI6's man on the spot, Colonel Robert 'Barney' Brook-Fox. Slim and of medium height, he walked with a pronounced limp, the result of losing a kneecap when a bomb exploded near his vehicle in North Africa during the Second World War. He wanted Terry to take a despatch back to the embassy in Leopoldville.

'I'll be glad to,' Terry smiled, 'always pleased to be at Her Majesty's service.'

'Thank you very much,' acknowledged Brook-Fox. 'I'm sure we'll be seeing more of each other. I understand you're to be seconded to the Americans. You can expect to hear from a Colonel Weber shortly.'

Terry sensed immediately that Brook-Fox knew exactly who he was talking to. He took the attaché's news as confirmation that he would soon have word from WIGMO and that he had nothing to worry about from the British. 'As I read the situation, I'd been cleared all the way.' He and Brook-Fox were to meet on several occasions subsequently, although Terry never suspected the attaché's heroic past.

Commissioned into the Royal Artillery before the war, Brook-Fox was captured in the British retreat at Dunkirk. After a daring escape from a POW camp, he made it home by crossing into Switzerland and then through France and over the Pyrenees into Spain and Portugal. For this he was awarded the Military Cross. After being seriously wounded by the bomb blast in North Africa, he resisted all attempts to invalid him out of the army and went on to serve in the Sudan, and then India against the Japanese, where he was twice mentioned in despatches. His physical courage was matched by moral bravery. This landed him in the centre of a diplomatic row towards the end of his career when he was refused re-entry to Zambia on a trumped-up spying charge for objecting to the payment of bribes to President Kenneth Kaunda. His despatches from the Congo reveal his abhorrence of the corruption there.

The day after delivering the pouch to the embassy for Brook-Fox, Terry was asked to test fly a new Learjet that Mobutu was planning to buy for himself.

> This was less than a fortnight after seizing the presidency. To be honest everyone should have realized then what was coming. I mean, the country was on its knees, Mobutu was making speeches promising to stay on his army pay and end corruption and yet here he was about to splash out on a Learjet.

Terry took the aircraft through its paces over the next couple of days. He had no inkling then that he was destined to become the president's personal helicopter pilot. However, coming so soon after what he had heard from Brook-Fox, he felt sure that being tasked to test the Learjet was further confirmation of his special status, like his assignment to Mulamba. 'Everything was beginning to fall into place. I decided that I had nothing to worry about. Getting the call from WIGMO was just a matter of time.'

No sooner had Terry completed a second day of circuits in the Learjet, than he and Brannon set off to ferry a couple of senior Belgian army officers round the country in the Beechcraft. The officers were from the army academy in Belgium and they were looking for young Congolese prospects to take back for training. The search started by flying westwards from Leopoldville to Matadi, the Congo's only sea port. As was usual by then, Terry and Brannon were taking turns as pilot and co-pilot. When they landed at Matadi with Terry at the controls, Brannon noticed that the nose-wheel indicator warning light on the instrument panel was flashing on and off. It bothered him because it was his turn to be in the left-hand seat the next day. He was discussing his concern with Terry when a senior pilot with Sabena, who also flew with Air Congo and who they socialized with frequently in Leopoldville, joined them. Brannon said that he did not think they should continue to fly the Beechcraft until a mechanic came down from Ndolo to check out the nose wheel. Terry and the Sabena pilot laughed at him and called him chicken.

So the following morning they took off for Moande, about half an hour's flying time away, where they were going to spend a couple of days in a luxurious beachside hotel while the two Belgians interviewed potential recruits in Matadi. Brannon noticed the nose-wheel warning light flickering. He went to open the throttle to take off again but Terry stopped him.

'No, it'll be all right,' he said confidently. The next instant the nose wheel collapsed. The Beechcraft ploughed into the runway, chewing up its propellers and badly damaging the aircraft. Terry and Brannon clambered out without a scratch but Brannon was furious, both with himself and Terry, who appeared completely unabashed. Again, he was stifling his own feeling of guilt by pretending to Brannon that it was really nothing to worry about.

Shortly afterwards Van den Bon and Kevin Bell arrived in the Dove to collect their two stranded colleagues. As they made the landing approach back at Ndolo with Van den Bon at the controls, they ran into heavy air turbulence. The aircraft started lurching violently, the wings dropping and nose swaying. Knowing that Van den Bon was an inexperienced pilot, Bell decided to help by operating the rudder control and with some difficulty they landed safely. Afterwards, Terry made himself extremely unpopular by criticizing Bell's intervention although it had undoubtedly saved them from a ducking in Stanley Pool.

'The pilot calls the shots. You had no business doing what you did without Van den Bon's say so,' he told Bell. In the immediate aftermath of the nose-wheel collapse on the Beechcraft, this inflamed Brannon. He knew that being in the pilot's seat on that occasion he should have ignored Terry's reassurance. Moreover, by his own admission in rebuking Bell, Terry was wrong to countermand Brannon's decision and he knew it. He really should have kept quiet, not least because he would certainly have done the same thing as Bell in the same situation. The only difference might have been that he would probably have waited until crashing was a near certainty before taking over.

In Leopoldville Terry and Brannon had rooms at *Le Residence*, a small, courtyard hotel on the outskirts of the city reserved for whites-only. Effectively grounded by the loss of the Beechcraft, Terry focused on other aspects of his life. He arranged to start learning French, which he knew he would need to speak in order to survive in the Congo. 'I found it a bloody sight easier than Mandarin Chinese, which I'd had a crack at in

Malaya. People still tell me I speak it like a *petit nègre* and I suppose it's true.' He also bought himself a gramophone player and a few long-playing records of classical music, including his favourite, Debussy's piano solo, *Clair de Lune*.

> I first fell in love with that back in 1957 when I had a crush on a girl in Portsmouth called Mary Diamond. Her father had a beautiful grand piano that he played it on all the time. In fact, that was when I first became interested in classical music and I still play *Clair de Lune* whenever the mood takes me.'

Terry also made the most of Leopoldville's nightspots. At the *Hôtel Memling* he made contact with Maria, the Sabena air stewardess, and they dined across the square at *Chez Felix*, a small, crowded French restaurant run by an affable Greek, as a prelude to many similar evenings. These were often spent with Brannon, who had a delightful French girl friend until his wife found out and made a fuss through the Canadian Embassy. As the men's relationship grew, Terry also began quizzing Brannon on what he knew about WIGMO.

'It's a really slick outfit. The pay's better than ours too,' he confirmed. 'I've been trying to get myself transferred for ages but the nearest I've got to them so far is burying their stiffs.' Dead 22 Wing pilots were automatically an FAC headache. In life they worked for WIGMO but if they were unlucky enough to die, their disposal became an FAC problem. This was part of the masquerade distancing America from the air support programme. As FAC's administration and liaison officer, it fell to Van den Bon to obtain death certificates and burial plots. When Brannon went to him about getting a transfer, the portly Belgian immediately roped him in to help. He persuaded Brannon that it would smooth his passage to WIGMO. Afterwards, burials somehow became Brannon's job, although nothing else changed. Following each fatality he routinely drove out to Ndjili to meet the aircraft returning the corpse, often horribly bloated after days out in the jungle in the fetid heat. He would take the body to the city mortuary and bribe the Congolese assistant there to help him with the nauseating task of transferring the remains to a makeshift coffin ready for burial. While kicking his heels waiting to hear from WIGMO, Terry volunteered to help Brannon with his sixth burial, a Cuban who drowned after flipping his T-28 into Lake Tanganyika at the end of the airstrip at Albertville. So far, that was the closest he too had been to the secretive WIGMO base.

Notes

1 Tshombe had by then already been replaced by a man named Kemba and returned to exile in Spain. Kemba was ousted in the coup.

2 Around $360 million at 2007 values.

3 Holm achieved legendary status in the CIA and on his last assignment was expelled from Paris by the French Government along with other CIA operatives posing as diplomats after an abortive honey trap operation involving alleged economic espionage. At the time he was the CIA station chief.

Chapter Thirteen
You Belong to Us

In the closing week of January 1966, Terry finally received the news that he had been waiting to hear. A WIGMO limousine arrived at *Le Residence* with instructions to collect both him and Brannon. WIGMO's extensive hangar and office complex lay about a mile to the east of the civilian terminal at Ndjili. From the outside it looked little different to a hangar about the same distance to the west of the airport terminal utilized by Sabena and Air Congo. However, the inside told a completely different story. Terry knew from Brannon that the WIGMO operation was in a different league to the makeshift FAC outfit at Ndolo. Now he could see the marked contrast for himself.

> It was just like walking into a USAF base. They had proper tools; a huge store filled with every imaginable kind of spare part; an overflowing armoury, and fully equipped engine bays. There were mechanics everywhere and not a Congolese face in sight. Here, I was back in an air force proper, no doubt about it.

In the vast, door-less hangar a couple of T-28s were being routinely serviced while piped, popular music played in the background. At the rear of the building another T-28 was having sections of aluminium-alloy skin grafted with surgical skill to the underside of the fuselage, which was stripped of its engine, wings and tail.

> Apparently one of the Cubans had crashed the plane landing at Ndjili and done a pretty good job of wrecking it, so WIGMO was rebuilding it more or less from scratch. That was pretty impressive.

Outside in the shimmering heat on the concrete apron a twin-engine, C-46 Curtiss Commando transport[1] was in the final stages of being loaded with supplies for one of 22 Wing's operational bases in the field. Parked nearby, their twin-bladed rotors neatly anchored and the fierce sun glinting dazzlingly off their Plexiglas full-bubble cockpits, were two Bell-47s – the ubiquitous, multi-purpose, light helicopters immortalized in the

M*A*S*H film and TV series – both serviceable and ready to fly. Terry looked across at them longingly. These were what he had come to fly. His pulse raced as Brannon was taken aside and he was escorted upstairs to meet Colonel Ken Weber.

'Hi. You belong to us,' smiled the well-built, middle-aged former USAF fighter pilot who was then running the air support operation under Dick Johnson, the overall head of paramilitary activity reporting to CIA station chief Devlin. 'Sorry about the delay. We had to clear you with London. That's all done now.' Weber – a Korean War hero – was a big, striking man with a classic, square-set jaw and close-cropped hair. 'I thought he looked like the archetypal Marine Corps drill sergeant but he had a big welcoming smile and what he was saying was music to my ears.' Weber stepped round his desk and shook Terry's hand firmly, gesturing for him to sit down.

'Here, you'll need to sign this contract,' he said, handing Terry a few sheets of paper. 'Once we've got the paperwork out of the way I'll take you down to meet Bob Houke. He'll check you out on the Bell and then we can put you to work.'

Terry quickly read through the contract, completed the blank sections and signed the final page. His pay was to be $2,000[2] a month on top of full board and lodging, credited tax-free to a bank of his choice anywhere in the world. There would also be attractive, lump-sum benefits for him or his family if he was unlucky enough to be maimed or killed on operations. Terry maintains to this day that money was never his motivation for volunteering to join WIGMO in the Congo. Sceptics might question this assertion but before arriving there he had no idea of what contract pilots were being paid. Subsequently, he found out from Brannon that the FAC men were earning around $1,500 a month. Nonetheless, he willingly remained on the informal arrangement covering his accommodation and living expenses amounting to much less until receiving the summons from Weber. His RAF pay when he arranged his disappearance had been the equivalent of about $266 a month. With WIGMO he would be earning nearly eight times as much – almost three times the salary of an air commodore at the time – all tax free on top of being housed and fed. He could not help being elated by the realization that at last he would be doing what he most wanted and being paid a comparative fortune for it too.

Back in the hangar, Weber introduced Terry to Ray Tluszez, the fiery head of ground operations, a foul-mouthed, irascible Polish-American from Florida. Tluszez drove his hundred-plus mechanics and armourers with the unforgiving firmness of a musket ramrod, every barked instruction punctuated by the kind of profanity that could even make an old hand from the lower deck like Terry blush. His sidekick was George Barnes, a more mild-mannered American from Oregon. In appearance and character they were as different as men can get. What they had in common was an intimate knowledge of aircraft engineering and with a flood of money from their CIA backers they ran a first-rate ground maintenance operation. It was immediately clear to Terry that the WIGMO mechanics were head and shoulders above the motley Air Congo crew at Ndolo. 'Most of them were Brits from the Midlands; I could tell that from their accents. There was a smattering of Scandinavians among them as well.'

'Good to meet you. Just don't wreck any of those goddam, mechanized palm trees of mine,' growled Tluszez. Terry could not mistake the threatening tone. 'Everybody was shit-scared of him. His deputy also enjoyed a lot of power but he didn't wield it like Tluszez and he got just as much done.'

While in Stanleyville, Terry had come across a number of the Cuban pilots and seen some of the T-28s. As a result he was already familiar with 22 Wing's striking emblem – a stylized caricature of an angry-looking Cape buffalo. This had been unashamedly borrowed from the local brewery, which used it as the trademark for its popular Makasi brand of beer. Painted in black and yellow, the buffalo was depicted with its snorting head down, horns threatening, forelegs braced for the charge and oversized testicles prominent in the background. The Cuban pilots loved its aggressive machismo. They adopted it enthusiastically and made it their own. It adorned the noses of the B-26s, the sides of the T-28s, the doors of the transport aircraft and the fuel saddle tanks of the open, tubular-steel framed helicopters. The pilots had it emblazoned on their flying jackets and stamped on everything from coffee mugs and glasses to Zippo cigarette lighters.

Based on what he had seen of them in Stanleyville, Terry had a low opinion of the Cubans.

They looked like a bunch of cowboys out of a bad B movie set. They walked around wearing shoulder holsters or guns slung round their hips and some even wore cowboy boots and hats. When they were in Leopoldville on leave they lived in this big house on a hill overlooking Stanley Pool in the military compound where Mobutu also lived. If you went up there you couldn't move without tripping over pistols, rifles or Uzi sub-machine guns.

Known as River House owing to its startling view of the rapids below Stanley Pool, the property also served as 22 Wing's operational headquarters with radio links to the American Embassy and the air operations officers in the field. The principal out-stations in early 1965 were in Stanleyville, Albertville and Kamina, then controlled by a handful of air operations officers, including veterans from the start of *WITHRUSH* like Big Bill.

Despite their gun-toting, cowboy-like appearance, most of the Cubans were competent airmen, although as one of the air operations officers later admitted to Terry, 'some of them couldn't fly for beans'. Managing them proved a constant challenge. In some respects they were a law unto themselves; for example they never referred to themselves as belonging to WIGMO or 22 Wing, preferring instead the self-styled moniker of *El Grupo Voluntario Cubano* – The Cuban Volunteer Group. Some also used any excuse to question missions or complain about the serviceability of aircraft until the threat of being returned to Miami to park cars changed their minds. This truculent, confrontational tone began at the outset of operations shortly after the arrival of the ancient B-26Bs. The pilots quickly noticed that the aircraft lacked the wing-strut reinforcements of the later B-26Ks and flatly refused to fly them, claiming that they were unsafe. On this occasion at least, the Cubans had a genuine grievance. Civilian pilots had been engaged to fly the aircraft out to the Congo from their graveyard in the Philippines because they were deemed unfit for US Air Force pilots. By contrast, Cuban exiles were clearly expendable. WIGMO hastily installed reinforcing wing struts in one of the aircraft and afterwards it was used mainly for reconnaissance work rather than combat and jokingly dubbed the 'U-3'.[3] The other was cannibalized for spares.

Most of the time 22 Wing's attack aircraft were based well away from any public scrutiny at Ndjili. At the out-stations they were closer to on-going military operations and less likely to attract unwelcome media attention. When Terry finally received his summons to meet Weber, the principal air action was in support of operations on the shores of Lake Tanganyika, then being used as a conduit for rebel arms supplies out of Tanzania. The B-26s usually operated out of Kamina with the T-28s evenly divided between Albertville and Stanleyville. They only ever returned to Leopoldville for major service checks and repairs. As a result, journalists reporting on the civil war rarely saw the aircraft. The out-station airfields were heavily guarded and off-limits to prying cameramen and reporters, and the air operations officers went to considerable lengths to ensure that the planes were not photographed. Maintaining the clandestine nature of *WITHRUSH* was a top priority. Although the media reported mercenary ground operations and the personalities involved extensively, precious little ever appeared about the air support programme. In Devlin's words, 'the mercenaries loved publicity and sought it out whenever they could. We on the other hand abhorred it and did everything we could to avoid it.' This included sending Johnson on holiday to South Africa with the specific task of dissuading Hoare from including anything more than a passing mention of air operations in his memoir after he left the Congo. No doubt with an eye to the possibility of future operations with the CIA, he willingly agreed.

The distinction between hired white soldiers, who were 'mercenaries', and pilots, who were 'contract employees', was an essential propaganda feature. In a 'Secret – UK Eyes Only' dossier, the British defence attaché Brook-Fox, was less particular.

> The exact functions and means of support of WIGMO are deliberately kept obscure to avoid too much prominence being given to American participation. The aircraft and the equipment are the property of the US, who also pay the personnel. ... Apart from the fact that the Congolese do not pay the bill, WIGMO is an efficient mercenary force.

The three Bell-47s acquired by 22 Wing after the last of the old Belgian H-21s finally self destructed at Stanleyville were 'G' models of the kind first introduced in 1953 and used to great effect during the Korean War. Smaller than the RAF's Sycamores, they were designed to carry up to three people – a pilot and two passengers or a pilot and two litters – and they had a maximum range of 245 miles at their cruising speed of around 85 miles per hour. In this sense they were ideal for short-range, casevac operations. With no trained pilots available when the helicopters were delivered in the early part 1965, the CIA called on one of the 'Company's' old helicopter specialists to help out. He was a man by the name of Tom Baldwin, a portly grandfather, who was ruddy faced and white haired with a white, walrus moustache that made him resemble Captain Kangaroo, a popular American TV character of the day. Inevitably, this became his nickname. He arrived with a young Cuban trainee pilot to form the nucleus of the new helicopter group. In addition, one of the

Cuban T-28 pilots was trained to fly the Bell-47s by Baldwin. However, when Terry was called to join 22 Wing the only active helicopter pilot was the Frenchman Bob Houke, who had been seconded from the FAC. 'Flying unarmed helicopters on rescue work wasn't macho enough for the Cubans. They only wanted to fly the B-26s and T-28s with their rockets and machine guns.'

Houke, a former French air force officer, was average height, thin faced with a long, lean jaw and ready smile. He spoke impeccable English and Terry liked him immediately.

'Bob will take you through familiarization and then you'll be relocating with him to Albertville. Five Commando's in a bit of a scrap up there and needs constant casevac back up,' Weber told Terry when he introduced him to the Frenchman. 'Bob's been doing a great job and you'll be relieving him.' Terry was impatient to get back into a helicopter. He had never flown the Bell-47, also known as the Sioux, but knew of its unrivalled reputation for manoeuvrability. Although smaller and less powerful than a Sycamore, the skeleton-framed Bell-47G was much less cumbersome and awkward to fly and WIGMO's models had the added advantage of turbo-charged engines, making them superior on a straight power-to-weight ratio.

> It was a very game little aircraft and could carry a lot more than appeared at first sight. The design specification was for a pilot and two passengers in the cockpit or in litters but I flew on many occasions with two passengers inside and both litters full. It was a case of necessity.

Rather like Verloo's perfunctory check-out in the Dove when he first arrived, Houke wasted no time in clearing Terry on the Bell-47. He had lost none of his deft skill in handling the collective and cyclic levers and was pleased to see that the Bell-47 sported dual controls so that swapping seats required none of the mind-twisting antics of the Sycamore. After just over an hour of familiarization routines they landed and Terry returned to *Le Residence* to pack a bag for his detachment to Albertville. Brannon rode back with him and explained that he was being sent to Stanleyville to convert to the T-28s before going to Albertville.

'Looks like we'll be up there together,' he said grinning.

'Yes. You can't get rid of me that easily, mate,' Terry laughed.

Albertville at the time was a one-street town on the shore of Lake Tanganyika in the extreme east of the country. For the past several months it had been the operational base for a campaign to clear rebels from a

Terry as a boy (right) with his younger brother Barry. (*Terry Peet*)

Terry during his service as an air telegraphist with the Royal Navy at about the time of his commendation for saving a Fairey Gannet during an exercise from HMS *Ark Royal*. (*Terry Peet*)

Officers on the helicopter instructors' course at RAF Tern Hill. Terry is seated in the front row second from right. Derek Eley, his former commanding officer at Butterworth, is seated third from left. (*Derek Eley*)

Terry leaving the church in Lihue after his marriage to Joan Milner. (*Joan Peet nee Milner*)

One of 110 Squadron's Sycamore Mark 14s at RAAF Butterworth around the time that Terry served there. (*Derek Eley*)

A Sycamore of 110 Squadron landing on HMS *Albion* during the Borneo crisis. Terry was among the first pilots on detachment to Labuan when the crisis developed. (*Derek Eley*)

Troops waiting to be airlifted by a
110 Squadron Sycamore in Malaya.
(Derek Eley)

Wing Commander Derek Eley, the former
commanding officer of 110 Squadron who
praised Terry's 'sheer guts' and put him
forward for his Queen's Award for
Valuable Service in the Air. (Derek Eley)

Ares Klootwyk (holding pole) crossing the Congo River with members of 6 Commando shortly before Terry's arrival to join the Force Aerienne Congolaise in 1965. (*Ares Klootwyk*)

Ares Klootwyk (left) and Charlie Vivier with trophies at Bumba in 1965 shortly before the lax refuelling incident that almost cost Vivier his life. (*Ares Klootwyk*)

Ares Klootwyk sitting on the wing of a T6 'Harvard' holding a Uzzi sub-machine gun with two South African colleagues and a French armourer. (*Ares Klootwyk*)

Three of the first non-Cuban mercenary pilots recruited for the Force Aerienne Congolaise (FAC) pictured with one of the T6 'Harvards' being refuelled at Bumba in 1965. The pilots are (left to right) Bob Brannon, Kevin Bell and Ares Klootwyk. (*Ares Klootwyk*)

Bob Brannon (left) pictured with pygmies of the Ituri Forest when he and Terry were at Faradje with General Mulamba shortly before Mobutu's coup in November 1965. (*Bob Brannon*)

Kevin Bell standing on the wing of a Force Aerienne Congolaise (FAC) T6 'Havard' in Northern Congo in 1965. When the rebellion against the central government started the aircraft were hastily armed with four 7.62mm machine guns and six ground-attack rockets. (*Ares Klootwyk*)

The MiG 17 flown by former RAF pilot John Palliser after a forced landing south of Port Harcourt when it ran out of fuel. The limited range of the aircraft made flying them on interdiction missions hazardous. (*Ares Klootwyk*)

The Hiller FH-1100 flown by Terry to Calabar from Lusaka to join the UNICEF airlift. Joan's pet calf is lying under the tail. (*Terry Peet*)

Leighton and Jane Mishou (left) with Terry and Terry Tindall about to board the Beechcraft for a trip to Elizabethville with CIA station chief Larry Devlin. The Mishous treated Terry like a son. (*Terry Peet*)

Dwyer's downed helicopter just visible in the mangroves. The attempt to recover the engine nearly cost another helicopter. (*Terry Peet*)

Ares Klootwyk with the Bell 47 equipped with floats that was flown by Terry out of Albertville after he was transferred to the CIA-controlled 22 Wing. (*Ares Klootwyk*)

Terry during the failed attempt to recover the engine from Dwyer's downed helicopter in the mangroves on the Cameroon–Nigeria border. (*Terry Peet*)

Terry with Clarq and McClaughlin during the failed operation to recover the engine from Dwyer's downed helicopter. *(Terry Peet)*

Terry gives McClaughlin the thumbs up to try lifting Dwyer's downed helicopter engine from the mangroves on the Cameroon border during the UNICEF operation out of Calabar. *(Terry Peet)*

Terry in a 22 Wing T28 during operations against Schramme's mercenary mutineers. (*Terry Peet*)

One of the two operational B26s of 22 Wing at an unidentified field. This was one of the aircraft that Terry was encouraged to hijack for an attempt against Mobutu. (*Bob Brannon*)

Swede Pelle Ornas servicing Terry's 'Bubble' Bell 47 at Albertville. Note the litters for carrying casualties on each side and the WIGMO emblem emblazoned on the fuel tanks. *(Terry Peet)*

Terry with the CIA-controlled, converted nose-wheel Beechcraft in which he was charged with flying General Mulamba on arrival in the Congo. *(Bob Brannon)*

Terry (right) with Bob Billings in Kauai. Billings was the United Airlines pilot who accompanied Terry on the epic helicopter delivery from Tel Aviv to Calabar and was later his best man in Hawaii. (*Terry Peet*)

Colonel Robert 'Barney' Brook-Fox and Ambassador John Cotton being greeted by Mobutu in Leopoldville. (*Julian Brook-Fox*)

Commandant Pierre Noel of the Force Aerienne Congolaise (FAC), who placed Terry under open arrest after Sadler's outburst accusing him of taking risks by turning into a dead engine. (*Bob Brannon*)

22 Wing T28s on operations out of Kindu against the Katangese following their mutiny at Stanleyville in 1967. *(Bob Brannon)*

A 22 Wing B26 undergoing maintenance checks between operations out of Albertville. *(Bob Brannon)*

Terry standing in a 22 Wing B26 cockpit at Albertville in 1966 after delivering the aircraft from Leopoldville. The Cuban pilots had adopted the rampant bull emblem of Makasi beer as their own. (*Ares Klootwyk*)

Ares Klootwyk and Bob Brannon with a 22 Wing T28 at Albertville in 1966. (*Ares Klootwyk*)

Ares Klootwyk standing in the cockpit of a MiG 17 with Nigerian Air Force ground personnel at Port Harcourt in 1969. (*Ares Klootwyk*)

Ares Klootwyk (centre) with Mike Thompsett (left) and Charlie Vivier (right) and Nigerian Air Force personnel with a Jet Provost in Benin City in 1968. (*Ares Klootwyk*)

Pierre Berthe (left) and Ares Klootwyk with a MiG 17 at Port Harcourt in 1969. Frenchman Berthe was reputed to be the last helicopter pilot out of Dien Bien Phu and Terry thought him 'one of the bravest men I knew'.
(*Ares Klootwyk*)

A 22 Wing B26 being refuelled and rearmed, probably at Albertville. (*Eugenio Popotti*)

Terry on the day of his release from Bristol Prison on 27 April 1972. (*Terry Peet*)

stronghold further north. Chinese-supplied arms shipments and Cuban-trained fighters were regularly crossing Lake Tanganyika at its narrowest point under cover of darkness. Che Guevara was reportedly leading the training and according to the CIA's intelligence, the arms traffic exceeded an average of thirty tons a day. To combat this, Devlin had created a small naval task force with air support from Albertville. The aircraft line-up comprised a B-26K, six T-28s and a Bell-47G helicopter that could be fitted with floats for work on the lake if necessary. On the ground, 5th Commando was facing stiff opposition from insurgents under one of Guevara's star pupils, a young gold smuggler and bandit named Laurent Kabila.[4]

WIGMO had commandeered the former *Hôtel Palais* in the heart of the town to house its personnel. This was a two-storey building around an open quadrangle. It fronted onto the muddy, pot-holed main road. Terry was assigned a room on the first floor next door to the air operations officer, a tubby, jolly man named Earl Myers, who liked to be addressed as colonel, although there is no evidence he ever held that rank. This would be home for the next two months. During the thousand-mile flight from Leopoldville, Houke told him something about the gruelling casevac schedule that he had been running single-handedly for the last month.

'The rebels here are much better armed and trained,' he told Terry. 'They're using mines and heavy machine-guns and they don't run away as soon as the T-28s appear overhead.' He explained that 5th Commando had been calling for air strikes and casualty evacuation or reconnaissance support on an almost daily basis.

A day after arriving in Albertville, Terry performed the first of what would become more than twenty life-saving missions before returning to Stanleyville to do the same. His radio call sign in the helicopter was 'Cucaracha' – the Spanish for cockroach. When *Cucaracha* took to the air it was usually an emergency.

> A lot of the casevacs out of Albertville were wounded mercenaries; there were plenty of those. But I also had ANC troops and civilians who'd been shot or stepped on land mines.

One of the things that Terry packed in his parachute bag when he left Tern Hill was a compact, pocket-sized RAF survival pack of the kind he carried on jungle operations in the Sycamores. 'It was something I'd kept and took with me because I thought it might come in handy.' This proved to be the case when he was evacuating a missionary from a settlement at Fizi, a few miles south of the rebel stronghold at Baraka.

He'd been shot and lost a lot of blood and for some reason that I can't remember now I had him in the cockpit with me rather than in a litter. On the way back to Albertville he was literally falling all over me.

From the way he moaned, Terry could tell that his passenger was in serious pain.

So with my spare hand – and you have a lot of those in a helicopter – I reached for the survival pack in the top pocket of my flying overalls, tore it open with my teeth, found the small morphine syringe that it contained and plunged the needle into his leg. He calmed down immediately; in fact so quickly I thought I'd killed him.

When they landed in Albertville, nuns were waiting to rush the man away and Terry heard later that he survived. 'He's probably an opium addict now.'

The rebels had another fortress on Lake Tanganyika closer to Albertville at Yungu. A small landing zone had been cleared in the forest nearby at Bendere to ferry in supplies to ANC ground forces trying to contain infiltrations from the lakeside refuge. One morning Terry responded to a call for help in evacuating wounded civilians and soldiers after a fierce fire fight to free a remote mission. The approach to the LZ was across heavily wooded, hilly terrain, which rebels frequently penetrated. Even in daylight their presence was difficult to spot from the air, although a comparatively slow-moving helicopter with nothing but a Plexiglas bubble to protect its pilot was an easy and vulnerable target from the ground unless flying high. To minimize the risk of being a sitting duck as he approached the LZ, Terry flew as low as he dared, utilizing the valuable lessons he learned flying in and out of the treacherous Bongsu cul-de-sac in Malaya. 'I had to thread my way through these high trees with the rotors snatching at the branches. To be honest, this kind of thing was a lot easier in the lightweight Bell than the Sycamore.'

On spotting the LZ, Terry swooped in to hover over the roughly prepared clearing. 'You could be reasonably sure that it was safe to land if there were people around. Rebels always stayed out of sight. The first you knew of their presence was when they shot at you. That was scary.'

On this occasion the presence of a few nuns and mission workers with Congolese soldiers milling about under the trees at the edge of the clearing reassured him. Seconds later he was on the ground with two mission workers suffering from serious gunshot wounds loaded into the litters.

They were blood-soaked and in a pretty bad way but there were also some walking wounded ANC guys and I knew that if I didn't take the worst of them as well, there'd be hell to pay. So I put two of them inside the chopper, although it was then very overloaded and would be difficult to fly out of such a confined space.

As Terry took a deep breath and prepared to take off, an angry shouting match broke out between one of the soldiers inside the aircraft and another outside, who was being carried piggy-back by one of his colleagues and insisting loudly that his need was more urgent.

'What's wrong with you, then?' Terry shouted to him.

'I've got a broken heart and he's only been shot in the leg,' the man pleaded with a straight face.

'Well don't worry, I'll be back with your girl friend later,' Terry yelled as he opened the throttle and pulled up on the collective.

I revved up to the maximum to haul this heavy beast out and over the trees and then dipped down into a river bed to get up to flying speed and head back to Albertville. I laugh about the incident now but it could so easily have turned ugly with those soldiers forcing me to take their broken-hearted chum and leave the mission workers behind to die. They'd have thought nothing of doing that.

Notes

1   The C-46 started life as a civil airliner but served as a military transport in almost every theatre of the Second World War and then later in the Korean War and the early years of the Vietnam War. During the Second World War it was most famous for flying 'The Hump' the air route across the Himalayas to supply Chinese nationalists.

2   An RAF flight lieutenant's average pay in 1965 was around £95 a month ($266 at the exchange rate at the time). An air commodore's average pay was £280 per month ($784). $2,000 in 1965 would be worth around $13,000 at today's values based on the consumer price index but more like $24,000 in terms of income comparisons.

3   A U-2 reconnaissance aircraft piloted by Gary Powers had been shot down over Russia in May 1960, creating one of the Cold War's earliest diplomatic confrontations.

4   Three decades later Kabila overthrew Mobutu after a five-year struggle costing three million lives. He was assassinated soon afterwards and his taxi-driver son became president in 2007 in a UN-supervised election – the first in the Congo since independence.

Chapter Fourteen
Cucaracha's Crusade

Being stationed in Albertville offered few attractions. There was a beach on Lake Tanganyika close to the airstrip where pilots and WIGMO ground crews could sunbathe, swim and water-ski in off-duty hours. In the evenings they could choose to sit on their verandas at the old *Hôtel Palais* with an ice-cold Prima or Makasi beer in hand or drink in the well-stocked bar adjacent to the dining mess downstairs. For a change they might clamber into a minibus and drive a short distance out of town up a hillside to the *Chemin de Fer*, a former country club in what was the wealthy residential area during colonial heydays. When he had time Terry did most of these things, often in the company of Brannon once he arrived to fly T-28 combat missions. They were then firm friends. Pelle Ornas, a Swedish engineer who looked after Terry's helicopter, also became a regular drinking partner. Through him Terry was friendly with some of the other WIGMO maintenance personnel, including a young armourer named Trevor Bottomley. Later in the year Bottomley's cold-blooded murder by a member of 5th Commando would cause an outcry and strain relationships between the mercenaries and WIGMO. However, that was still in the future as Terry continued the intense round of casevacs and refugee rescues out of Albertville, clocking almost 125 operational hours of flying over two months.

Several missions took him back to the LZ at Bendere. He remembers one in particular. An elderly Belgian priest with a nicotine-stained, grey beard was waiting for him at the clearing when he set down to pick up a badly wounded victim of a rebel attack. The priest apologetically informed Terry that the casualty was being carried out of the forest but would not arrive until early the next morning. At his suggestion, Terry agreed to spend the night at the nearby mission. That evening he joined the old priest and three of his fellow brethren for dinner at a long wooden, refectory table with hard benches down each side.

> We had a very tough piece of chicken and some dry, starchy manioc root after interminable prayers. To make it worse, the fathers smoked

these foul-smelling cigarillos all the way through the meal, probably to disguise the revolting taste of the food.

As he ate and sucked on his cigarillo between chewy mouthfuls, the old priest regaled Terry with what he insisted was a miracle.

'Only a month ago at this very table we were eating like this when we heard shooting from the lavatory and then six heavily armed rebels burst in here. We could tell from their crazy stares and behaviour that they were drugged to the eyeballs,' he related.

The rebel leader looked no more than fourteen years old. He was in an excited state and yelled belligerently that they were going to kill everyone. The priest looked at him closely and recognized him.

'Jacob, I know you. You were in my confirmation class only a few weeks ago. Why do you want to kill me?' he challenged.

'I won't kill you, Father; my friend here will,' he replied pointing to another of the young rebels.

'In that case, Jacob, may we please pray first?' asked the priest.

As the priests knelt, clasped their hands and began to chant a prayer in unison, the ancient generator, which supplied the only electricity, began to stutter. The lights dimmed and flickered on and off briefly and then came back on as the generator roared back to life.

'When they saw this, Jacob and his young friends fell to their knees and begged God for forgiveness. They promised not to harm us and ran away,' grinned the old priest.

Later, he took Terry outside to the lavatory at the rear of the building and showed him the blood-stained wall.

'Unfortunately, Father Pierre was attending to a call of nature when the rebels arrived and they killed him here, God rest his soul,' he explained, while crossing himself and lighting another cigarillo, adding, 'Come on, let's go and have some communion wine.' Terry lay awake all night with his nine-millimetre pistol in hand and M-15 rifle on the bed. 'Sleeping in rebel-controlled areas wasn't my preferred way of life and I was very happy to take off with the casualty in the morning.'

In early April Terry was relocated to Stanleyville. One of the first men he ran into at the WIGMO headquarters in the old *Hôtel Victoria* was Brannon, who had already returned there from Albertville. 'He told me that Klootwyk had also been transferred to WIGMO and they were flying a lot of missions in the T-28s.' The indications were that 22 Wing was gradually absorbing 21 Squadron. A number of the Cuban pilots had returned to America after completing their tours and reaching the qualifying period to apply for naturalization. Once they became American citizens, of course, they were *persona non grata* as combat pilots in the Congo.

Within days of returning to Stanleyville, Terry accompanied Brannon on an armed reconnaissance flight to Pontierville, around seventy-five miles to the south along the Congo River upstream of Stanley Falls. During the last decade of Belgian rule, this was the town immortalized by John Huston in the 1952 epic *The African Queen*, starring Humphrey Bogart and Katherine Hepburn. There was nothing cinematic about its appearance after being in rebel hands until only a month earlier, when it was finally recaptured for the central government by a mixed force of mercenaries and Katangese soldiers led by Major Jean 'Black Jack' Schramme, a Belgian planter turned warrior who had fought for Tshombe in the aftermath of independence. However, although the town was back in government hands, the surrounding area remained infested with *Simbas* who melted into the forest and continued to terrorize remote communities. The story was the same to the north and east of Stanleyville, where the towns of Banalia and Bafwasende had just been re-secured but their hinterlands were still far from safe. The ongoing struggle ensured a continuous need for life-saving evacuations. Day after day Terry answered emergency calls, sometimes flying perilously close to the limit of the Bell-47's range and often exceeding its official payload.

On one of his early missions to Pontierville, the new American consul to Stanleyville, a man named 'Jungle' Jim Farber, asked if he could go along for the ride. Farber explained that he wanted to familiarize himself with the area. With only one casualty to retrieve, having a passenger on board for the short flight presented no problem and Terry readily agreed to take him. After leaving Stanleyville they headed south, flying low over the slow-moving, muddy swathe of the Congo River, which slid northwards like an oily slick in the dense green of the jungle canopy. Not long after taking off they flew over Stanley Falls, where the swirling, white maelstrom of water plunging through rock-strewn banks of eddying foam marked the end of the navigable stretch of river starting from Stanley Pool at Leopoldville. Terry's eyes greedily scanned the heavily forested riverbanks for any hint of rebel activity.

> I normally flew quite high to stay out of trouble but Farber asked me to show him the scenic route and I wasn't too worried because there hadn't been any recent reports of rebels along the river.

About ten miles south of the falls, where the river was filled with wooden-stake fish traps built by the Wagenia tribe, Farber suddenly unclipped his harness and reached behind the seat for Terry's M-15 rifle.

'What the hell do you think you're doing?' yelled Terry, his hands full flying the helicopter, his eyes still scanning the shores for any signs of potential trouble.

'Look, they're rebels,' shouted back Farber, pointing to a canoe crossing the river as he started to climb out onto the skid with the rifle in hand. Terry had already seen the vessel, one of the famed forty-feet-long, wooden dug-outs, in which the tribe's men folk were renowned for shooting the rapids at Stanley Falls. Heavily loaded with women and children and baskets of vegetables, the canoe's freeboard was dangerously low. Two men worked hard to paddle it across the river. Terry had dismissed any threat. 'They were obviously just villagers going about their business.'

Before Terry could stop him, Farber opened fire on the canoe. 'He had the gun set to full automatic and he raked the boat from end to end. I screamed at him to stop shooting but he didn't listen.' Instinctively, Terry pushed the cyclic lever sideways and pulled on the collective as he opened the throttle to swoop right and gain height, spoiling Farber's line of fire and throwing him off balance so that he fell backwards into the cockpit.

'Are you fucking mad? They're not rebels,' Terry remonstrated. 'Can't you see?' He was furious and uncharacteristically lost his temper. 'I wish now that I'd gone left and chucked him off the sled. I don't know if he actually killed anyone but there were people in the water splashing about and I felt sick.'

In Pontierville they collected an elderly mission worker who was suffering from severe malnutrition after living rough for months to evade rebel capture. According to Terry, Farber lamely used the old man's plight to justify his unprovoked assault on the Wagenia canoe and continued to insist that its occupants were rebels. But once back in Stanleyville, Terry filed an official complaint. Whether this was responsible is unclear but Farber was recalled soon afterwards.

By then what those around Terry were learning was that in his personal crusade, he would go anywhere and do anything in a Bell-47, just as one of his superiors in the Far East had said of him when he was flying Sycamores. Most of the time he flew alone, knowing full well that if he came down in the jungle the only other helicopters were hundreds of miles away in Leopoldville and Albertville, making the chance of rescue extremely remote. 'I didn't think about it too much if I could help it.' Sudden changes in the weather and mechanical failure were the two major risks. Pre-flight checks on the Bell were much the same as with the Sycamore. Terry was always meticulous about going through them, although he had every faith in the WIGMO engineers.

Everything seemed routinely fine when he took off one morning to go in search of a Congolese Roman Catholic schoolteacher and two young children. They were reported to have escaped from rebels near Bafwasende. Fighting to oust *Simbas* from the town had only recently ended. Spearheaded by Spanish mercenaries, units of Katangese troops were still in the process of clearing enemy enclaves along the Ituri Road leading to Stanleyville from Bafwasende. Terry followed the road by air before turning off to find the village where the young female teacher and children were said to be waiting. Once he reached the locality he started searching. 'Remember in those days you had no accurate map co-ordinates with GPS to guide you in. It was a compass and eyeball exercise.'

Customarily he set himself a search pattern going on whatever landmarks he could use as co-ordinates. One of the Congo River's many tributaries crossed the Ituri Road at Bafwasende and Terry used this to help delineate the search area. 'I soon found the village and flew over it a few times to see what sort of reception I was going to get.' Satisfied that it would be friendly, he landed. The teacher had been sexually abused repeatedly. The children, both small boys, had witnessed their families' massacre. Terry quickly helped them into the helicopter and prepared to take off. On the ground he was at his most vulnerable. Stanleyville was about an hour's flying time from Bafwasende but only a few minutes into the flight the Bell's turbo-charged Lycoming, six-cylinder 288-horsepower engine started misfiring and then stopped. 'When the engine quits it's not like suddenly losing a tail rotor. It's a straightforward case of using auto-rotation to land – something you practise in training.' In Terry's case it was also something he had done for real at Tern Hill and in Malaya. Driven by the airflow over its blades, the rotor keeps turning as the helicopter starts to lose speed and height. Even so, landing by auto rotation requires skill on the pilot's part. Any heavy-handedness with the controls can cause a phenomenon known as flying through the flare. 'If you make this mistake you end up in a bloody great heap of nuts and bolts.'

Luckily, Terry was following a dry river bed when the engine stopped. Without too much difficulty he landed the Bell gently in soft sand and radioed for help. If they had been over thick jungle they would probably have been killed and no trace of them found.

'*Cucaracha* to *King Twelve*,' he transmitted two or three times before the radio at Stanleyville crackled in response.

'*Cucaracha*, this is *King Twelve*, come in.' Terry recognized the voice of Leighton Mishou, who had recently arrived to relieve Big Bill as air operations officer.

'*King Twelve*, the engine's quit and I'm down with three passengers. There's no damage and no injuries but you need to get us out of here,' he explained.

'Okay *Cucaracha*, we'll send someone out to look for you. This is *King Twelve* out,' reassured Mishou.

Terry decided that it would be safer and cooler to wait hidden in the undergrowth rather than remaining in the helicopter with the sun burning fiercely through the Plexiglas bubble, making the interior hotter than a sauna. With the teacher and children following close behind, he started crawling into the forest.

Suddenly I came nose to nose with this animal. I have no idea to this day what it was but I remember thinking at the time that I was about to be swallowed whole by a mountain gorilla and I beat a hasty retreat pushing the others in front of me.

Fortunately, the animal, whatever it was, had also had a nasty surprise and disappeared in the other direction. Terry told the teacher to stay hidden in the undergrowth with the children while he returned to the helicopter. He off-loaded a survival pack containing a small inflatable dinghy, secured this to his back and started climbing into the trees.

The top of the jungle canopy is so thick you can virtually walk on it. When I got up there I inflated the dinghy in the treetops. It was bright orange and I knew it would be easy to spot against the green of the jungle.

Back on the ground, he decided to try and discover why the engine had cut out. The obvious starting point was the fuel feed.

When I began draining the filters the problem was immediately apparent. All that came out was water. I kept pumping and draining until eventually some fuel started coming through again. By then I could hear an aircraft engine in the distance and I called on the radio but got no response. Afterwards I learned that they'd sent a couple of Cubans who were busily searching the next valley along and claimed they couldn't hear me calling them on the radio.

With only an hour or so until nightfall, Terry decided to try and start the Bell's engine. After a few misfires it burst into life. He beckoned the teacher and children to leave their shelter under the trees and climb aboard. An hour later they were safely in Stanleyville. Mishou greeted Terry with a hearty slap on the back and then reminded him that he had the only helicopter anywhere within range of making a rescue.

'I'm not sure how we'd have got you out even if we'd found you, so well done,' he shrugged. Several weeks afterwards Terry flew over the site of his enforced landing. 'There was my dinghy in the treetops bright as a beacon and it was still there months later. It stood out like a bloody sore thumb and I don't know how those Cubans missed it.'

Mishou was a short, chubby, round-faced man with fleshy jowls and a loud personality. People either liked him or loathed him. An ex-USAF pilot who served in the Pacific theatre in the final months of the Second World War and then in Korea afterwards, he resigned his air force commission in 1962 to join a Fort Lauderdale, Florida-based company called Aircraft Ferry. The company specialized in delivering new and used aircraft to customers throughout the world as well as finding aircraft and aircrew for contract work. In this role it developed a lucrative working relationship with the CIA and had been hired by the agency to operate a Catalina flying boat in the waters round Cuba. As a cover the company had a legitimate contract to collect practice missile parts from the Gulf of Mexico, but the CIA's longer-term aim was to familiarize the Cubans with the flying boat's radar signature so that it could be used later to infiltrate undercover teams into Cuba and spirit defectors out. Years later Mishou would learn that his boss at Air Ferry – Charles Gabeler[1] – was a CIA aviation legend, although he was unaware of this in August 1964 when Gabeler introduced him to a CIA case officer looking for air operations officers for the Congo.

As Mishou recounted it, he was on secondment by Air Ferry as a DC-6 flight instructor with United Arab Airlines, the forerunner of Egypt Air, when he was approached to join Operation *WITHRUSH*. He had the necessary air force experience and flying credentials and jumped at the opportunity to be part of the CIA's new paramilitary adventure, arriving covertly in Leopoldville via Nairobi in Kenya and Bujumbura in Burundi. After being involved in the Stanleyville hostage-rescue operation, he worked continuously as one of the field air operations officers, often alternating with Big Bill in Stanleyville. From the outset he was frustrated by not being allowed to fly, believing that it undermined his authority with the Cubans with whom he frequently found himself at loggerheads.

He greeted the arrival in 22 Wing of pilots of the calibre of Terry, Brannon and Klootwyk as a welcome improvement. He would make Terry his particular protégé and in time identify him as a potential CIA stay-behind asset.

Notes

1   Charles Pierce Gabeler was the brainchild behind Air America, the CIA-owned airline used to support the 'secret war' in Laos. A former US Navy pilot, Gabeler went on to become head of the CIA's Air Wing. He died in 1998 of pneumonia aged seventy-six.

Chapter Fifteen
Rescues and Ransoms

Weekend breaks to enjoy the social life in Leopoldville had become a rarity for Terry since joining 22 Wing. The constant round of casevacs and refugee recoveries left little time for anything more than 'a few drinks with the lads before hitting the sack for a decent night's sleep'. This kept his mind off the guilt he sometimes felt about the way he had left Tern Hill. Earlier, after first arriving in the Congo when his flying schedule was less demanding, his spirits often sank as his mind turned to his children and parents. More than once he was tempted to write home to his mother as these black moods overwhelmed him. What stopped him was the thought that if he broke his cover he would never hear from WIGMO, risking his entire *raison d'être*. That was why he had lied to Brannon about what brought him to Leopoldville. He felt bad about that too. Characteristically, Terry usually said nothing rather than lie if there was something he wanted to hide. He would admit the truth if confronted but avoid the confrontation if he possibly could.

The other person who was never very far from his thoughts was Joan Milner, the Audrey Hepburn look-alike he had met on the way to Brussels. The trouble was that she was on the other side of the Atlantic in Canada and, anyway, he was under the impression that the liaison they had enjoyed together had probably been nothing more than an impulsive fling, on her part at any rate. He felt differently but presumed that she would most likely want to forget it ever happened. He wrote to her without expecting a reply. Later, after joining WIGMO, he also wrote to Oscar Koksa, enclosing the thousand francs he owed him. This was a point of honour. He had only accepted the money on the understanding that he would repay it when he could afford to.

Partying with Brannon and linking up with the Sabena air hostesses had been welcome diversions but Terry wanted something more meaningful than a succession of one night stands. This was particularly true when he was feeling down. For this reason he was buoyed by the arrival of a new woman in his life. Just before being summoned by Weber he had been invited to an American Embassy party and introduced to one of the new secretaries in the ambassador's office, a lively brunette named Terry Tindall. They hit it off immediately. 'When I met her she said, 'Hi, I'm Terry,' and I replied, I'm Terry too. From then on we referred to each other as Terry One and Terry Two.' She was drawn to his good looks, English accent and suave manners. He enjoyed her witty, outgoing personality. He also liked the idea of a close relationship with an embassy insider and somebody he felt he could confide in.

After getting to know her, Terry sent his new admirer chatty missives from Albertville and Stanleyville in the embassy pouch whenever he could. Knowing his fondness of Chivas Regal, she responded with gift-wrapped bottles that arrived on the liaison transports by return. On one of his brief visits to Leopoldville she invited him to dinner and he stayed the night, although it would be some time before she allowed him to share her bed. However, once they were lovers he usually stayed at her apartment in the *Building Royale* in the heart of Leopoldville whenever he returned to the city. The arrangement was informal and for appearances sake Terry kept his room at *Le Residence*. It was the gentlemanly thing to do.

> We became very close and she was very special but she never invited me to move in. In those days that would've been a bit infra-dig for an embassy secretary. We've remained friends and I still think of her fondly.

On another rare trip back to Leopoldville for a routine medical check-up at the end of May, Terry was staying at the apartment when he heard that ex-prime minister Kemba and three members of his former cabinet, who had all been deposed in Mobutu's coup, had been found guilty by a drumhead court martial of plotting against the president. Mobutu ordered a public hanging as an example. By coincidence, Terry was waiting for the result of his medical at a building with a balcony overlooking the stadium where the executions were taking place. 'A huge crowd filled the stadium but they weren't yelling for blood, in fact I sensed that they didn't particularly like what was being done.' The hangings were clumsy, leaving the corpses writhing and twitching.

> Kemba was very popular locally. When they came to hang him the crowd surged forward and a massive flock of black birds flew over, darkening the sky. This was a very bad omen and the spectators started running away. Mobutu didn't make any friends that day but he proved who was in charge.

Terry was disgusted by the spectacle but he was beginning to understand that big, bullying gestures carried a lot of weight in the Congo where people were indoctrinated with their traditional role as the underdog. As a result of his own schoolboy experience, he hated anything that smacked of bullying. Since arriving in Leopoldville he was witnessing it all too frequently.

> The Congo was a place that bred bully boys like flies. ANC officers treated their soldiers like dirt and in turn they took it out on ordinary people. Anybody with any power or authority used it like a chicotte.[1] It wasn't just the Africans either. A lot of the mercenaries behaved like thugs too.

An environment like this bred distrust, hatred and paranoia. Rumours of plots and counter plots circulated as freely as stolen goods on the black market.

One rumour that gathered some serious currency concerned an alleged coup being planned by Tshombe from his exile in Spain. Word of this had been picked up by the CIA and one of Mishou's tasks in Stanleyville was to check out suspicions that Colonel Bob Denard,[2] the leader of the French-speaking mercenaries of 6th Commando, might be implicated. Mishou asked Terry to keep an eye out for anything suspicious whenever he flew Denard on reconnaissance and liaison trips.

> I didn't see or hear anything to support the idea of Denard hatching a plot. He wasn't a stupid man. As a professional mercenary he knew that he could never expect another contract anywhere if it ever got out that he'd turned on his employers.

Denard was every bit the hard-bitten, ex-Foreign Legionnaire. He habitually drank a lethal, bright green cocktail of pastis mixed with crème de menthe, nicknamed perroquet after the colour of a parrot, just as a mixture of pastis and grenadine was called a tomat. Terry always thought that paraquat, after the herbicide, would have been more appropriate. 'It was a pretty foul mixture and Denard enjoyed challenging me to compete in knocking the damn things back shot for shot.' This was a contest that Terry wisely avoided if at all possible. All the same, he liked Denard. 'I respected him as a soldier and for the most part found him agreeable company, except that he picked his nose a lot.'

On one mission with Denard they were flying back from Buta with a Belgian mercenary casualty in one of the litters when they nearly wiped out. Denard had insisted on making a low-level pass over a village where rebels were suspected of hiding. Although Terry thought this was asking for trouble, he swooped in over the surrounding treetops in order to surprise any gunmen and give Denard the close look he wanted. With the Bell's nose down they scorched along the course of a mud track leading between flimsy mud-daubed wooden and corrugated iron shacks with palm-thatch roofs. Flying not much higher than the rooftops, a cloud of swirling dust and debris forced up by the downdraught followed them like a small tornado. It ripped through the shacks on each side shaking them violently and tearing chunks of their roofs off. Suddenly the aircraft lurched sharply and strands of flailing wire started lashing the Plexiglas canopy furiously, accompanied by deafening, whiplash cracks like overhead thunder.

'Shit,' shouted Terry above the infernal din. 'We've flown into some sodding telephone cables or something. I'm going to have to put down.'

'*Merde*,' echoed Denard, leaning across to yell into Terry's ear. 'Okay, land in the road away from the houses if you can.'

Within seconds Terry chose a spot on the road with a view back to the village where he could touch down. They landed in a protective cocoon of roiling dust. The rotor blades were still turning as Denard leapt out with his machine gun in hand to stand guard while Terry clambered up to the rotor hub to inspect the damage.

There was this huge ball of telephone wire wrapped round it with several loose ends hanging down. The wires had obviously been strung across the road and I'd flown into them without knowing they were there.

While Terry worked feverishly at unwinding the choking tangle that would soon have downed them, Denard stood over his wounded compatriot, ready to rake anybody daring enough to emerge from the huts nearby with a deadly burst from his gun. The wires were wound tightly into the hub with jamming, riding turns, complicating the laborious task of unravelling them.

I don't remember how long it took me to get the hub clear, maybe twenty minutes, but it seemed like hours. When we got back to Stanleyville I kept quiet about the incident because I'd committed the cardinal sin of a helicopter pilot, 'Thou shalt not fly into cables'.

A week or two later Terry's engineer – Pelle Ornas – came up to him after doing a major service inspection. He handed him several inches of wire.

'Here, you must have flown into something,' Pele said.

'Can't have been much if I didn't know anything about it,' Terry shrugged.

With permission from Weber to undertake non-operational flights, Mishou asked Terry to train him on the Bell-47. He would be the first of many pupils. Unlike at Tern Hill, instructing in the Congo was very much a part-time activity squeezed between the real challenges of operational flying. The need for more helicopter pilots had not changed despite Terry's arrival. Apart from himself and Houke, the only other active pilot was Pierre Berthe, another Frenchman with the distinction of having been the last helicopter pilot out of Dien Bien Phu.[3] With three Bells in service, the three of them were working almost round the clock. Moreover, the Alouettes were still expected at any time. This increased the pressure to have more pilots available and so Klootwyk, who had trained on helicopters some years earlier, agreed to convert so that he could be called on when necessary. He needed nothing more than a refresher course with Terry. 'Ares could fly anything; he might as well have been born with wings.'

Mishou's training and Klootwyk's conversion were interrupted by one of the most concentrated series of back-to-back rescue missions Terry undertook. The first involved the immediate evacuation of a badly wounded soldier from Buta. Terry had scheduled to take Mishou through a series of confined-space manoeuvres when the report of the casualty came in. Instead, he found himself flying over 'miles and miles of endless cabbage' crossed by just a couple of rivers to help with navigation. The journey involved a round trip of 350 miles.

When I arrived in Buta I found the mercenary medic there had tried open-heart surgery and been pumping this guy's heart all night to keep him alive. I think he was dead before they put him in the litter, poor sod; he certainly was by the time I got him back to Stanleyville.

Terry always experienced a feeling of failure when he brought back a body rather than a live evacuee. What drove him to take the risks he did was the gratification of saving lives, a sensation he first experienced in Malaya and one that added immeasurably to his sense of purpose and self-esteem. Although a futile journey, like the one to Buta, left him temporarily down, it also served to reinforce his determination to carry on.

The following day he was all set to resume the confined space training manoeuvres with Mishou when a call for help with more evacuations from Pontierville came through. When Terry arrived at the pick-up point there were nearly a dozen mission workers, mostly Congolese nuns with some small children waiting for collection. 'The nuns were in a shocking state: habits torn, covered in insect bites and half starved by the look of it. I didn't dare think what they'd been through.' He took four on the first return flight and then went back twice for the others. 'They were wonderful; there was no arguing or pushing. I just pointed to the oldest or youngest, smallest or heaviest and over they came and climbed aboard.' He was about to take off from Stanleyville to collect the last of the refugees when Mishou appeared.

'Hey, I'm coming with you,' he announced. 'I want to see if I can find anyone there with some better intelligence on where the rebels are hiding out than we've got at the moment.'

'I thought you weren't allowed to fly operationally, Mish?' Terry said. 'And anyway, I need all the space there is in the chopper.'

'You can leave me there if you have to, but I'm coming,' he insisted climbing into the left-hand seat and clipping on the harness.

As Terry swooped back down to the landing area in Pontierville it was late afternoon. To his horror there were four nuns huddled together with the priest in charge of the evacuation, two more than he had been expecting. Mishou announced that he was going to talk to the priest and see what he could find out, leaving Terry to grapple with how to pack everyone on board for the return trip. The sun was already dipping below the tree line, casting long, deep shadows across the landing area. Terry shepherded the four women across to the Bell, ducking them under the slowly whirling rotor blades. He squashed the three smallest into the cramped space behind the seats. 'I put the fourth into the left-hand seat and then sat myself in the centre with a buttock on each seat and the pilot's collective lever between my legs.' This meant that when Mishou squeezed in on the right-hand seat he would have to operate the cyclic lever.

'Come on Mish,' Terry yelled. 'This thing's not set up for night flying. We've got to get out of here while we can.' As the chubby air operations officer shoved his backside onto what remained of the right-hand seat and pulled the door shut, Terry said: 'Right, we're flying this dual; we've got no bloody choice. You've got the cyclic and just do as I say.' Mishou nodded obediently as he gripped the directional lever with his right hand.

'Okay, here goes,' shouted Terry, opening the little Bell's throttle to maximum revs and then tugging on the collective. The turbo-charged engine raced as if it sensed the urgency of the occasion, lifting the helicopter clear of the ground as Terry asked Mishou to go into forward flight. 'There were no trees in the immediate area and we had plenty of room to reach flying speed otherwise we'd have never stayed airborne. I dread to think how much over the payload we were.'

They headed for the river. Being right on the equator there was virtually no twilight. The sun had set as they lifted off and darkness swallowed its lingering radiance within minutes. In the soft, early-evening starlight the river's surface gleamed like a silver ribbon. It was also an essential guiding beacon.

I was flying at night, which I shouldn't have been; I was flying with Mishou, which I shouldn't have been; and I had four nuns in the helicopter as well, which I shouldn't have done. When we landed in Stanleyville people watched the Bell empty like a bus. I didn't think much of it at the time but looking back now that was a pretty big moment.

One or two of the nuns he pulled out that day were European and Terry thinks it may have been one of them who wrote to his mother later.

Another routine casualty evacuation from a settlement at Isangi the next day completed the consecutive three-day tally of rescue missions and Terry was glad for a break when Mishou asked him to be his co-pilot for a few circuits in a new tail-wheel Beechcraft that had just been delivered. Their first touchdown nearly forced the undercarriage through the fuselage.

'Christ, I landed that like shit from a tall cow,' confessed Mishou as they bounced along the runway. A close relationship between the men was now developing. Mishou started hinting that Terry may be of as much use to the CIA gathering intelligence as he was in flying.

'According to Bouzin, the new Alouettes are going to arrive before long. He wants you to be put in charge of them when they do and that means you'll be flying Mobutu and most of the Congolese high command around. It could be very useful having you in that position,' Mishou explained.

'From what I've heard the Alouettes have been due *any day now* for ages. Anyway, if they ever materialize, I'll be glad to help out,' replied Terry, 'but let's cross that bridge when we come to it.' He was being deliberately cool, although privately he was excited about the prospect of heading the helicopter unit, flying the president and being a spy.

On one or two occasions Colonel Brook-Fox came to Stanleyville on intelligence-gathering forays and pumped Terry for information. He also asked him to report anything that he might hear about the fate of a British missionary who had been among eleven mission workers taken hostage from a village ninety-five miles south-east of Stanleyville in November 1964. Miss Winifred Davies, a fifty-one-year-old, Welsh-born nurse had worked in the Congo for over twenty years and adopted a small Congolese orphan. Although nine of the Belgian mission workers seized with her were subsequently murdered, there were reasons to believe that a Dutch priest and Miss Davies were still alive and had been moved by their *Simba* captors to the Bafwasende area. Understandably, the British Government was keen to secure Miss Davies's release.

Brook-Fox was quietly letting it be known that a £2,000 ransom would be paid for her safe return. Earlier, the Greek Government had secured the release of hostages in return for ransoms.

> He wanted me to keep my ears and eyes open for any word of the poor woman. I really couldn't think of anything worse than being a *Simba* hostage but I never heard anything at all about her whereabouts until a year later when the old Dutch priest was freed and she was found dead.

Her *Simba* captors slashed her throat and shot her in the head fifteen minutes before an ANC unit could free her. 'It was sickening and absolutely tragic.'

After less than a year in the Congo, Terry was well aware that tragedy, like bullying, was endemic. While he did his utmost to concentrate on what he did best, flying helicopter search and rescue missions out of both Stanleyville and Albertville with occasional breaks back in the capital, the curtain went up on a drama of Shakespearean proportions. In Leopoldville Mobutu lavished money on extravagant independence-day celebrations. Following this example, his thuggish army chief in Stanleyville went completely overboard on spending for a family wedding. Yet the Katangese units who provided the backbone of the Congolese army went unpaid and were to be disbanded and replaced by newly trained ANC troops from tribes more acceptable to Mobutu. When the Katangans resisted, they were brutally punished. In the end they retaliated. First they seized control in Bukavu. Then they did the same in Stanleyville, after murdering their free-spending commander. Terry's old boss Mulamba, then in his last months as prime minister, intervened personally to secure a brief ceasefire but the stage was set for another round of internecine warfare. Rumours that the mutiny was part of a Belgian-orchestrated attempted coup to reinstate Tshombe merely worsened the crisis and precipitated ruthless revenge in which Terry would be caught up.

Notes

1 A hide whip used to administer lethal beatings in King Leopold's brutal state.
2 Denard gained notoriety for his involvement in numerous sub-Saharan coups. He died in October 2007.
3 The major French defeat in Indochina.

Chapter Sixteen
Nothing but Murder

Terry was back in Albertville continuing with casevacs for 5th Commando when the Katangese mutiny triggered a panic in 22 Wing. With the mutineers in command of Stanleyville, they controlled the airport there and with it 22 Wing's aircraft and personnel. They refused to allow any of the aircraft to leave, causing a flap for Johnson back at headquarters in Leopoldville. He sent Ken Weber with a negotiator to try and strike a deal. After some tense discussion, the mutineers allowed Mishou to fly out the B-26 then at Stanleyville providing it was disarmed first. The Cuban pilots and WIGMO personnel were permitted to leave with Weber. In return the CIA promised not to launch air strikes against the mutineers. As insurance, the T-28s were to be left behind guarded by men of Denard's 6th Commando. Despite the earlier suspicions about him, Denard remained resolutely loyal to the central government.

The last thing the CIA wanted at that juncture was any let up in operations to eradicate the remaining rebel strongholds in the north-east and east of the country. However, with a shooting war in Stanleyville between the ANC and the mutineers, and the city's airport closed, they had little choice. Moreover, the threat to the stability of Mobutu's regime made resolving the Katangese problem a pressing priority. This highlighted another potential difficulty. The operational strength of 22 Wing was already considerably lower than it had been at the height of the rebellion. Many of the Cuban pilots were by then back in America or preparing to leave. In order to keep the air support programme going, the CIA was drafting in all other available pilots to man the T-28s and B-26s. As a result Terry was called on to participate in combat missions. Although he had not gone to the Congo with the intention of flying offensive operations he accepted the need to do so.

I basically had no choice. If I wanted to carry on doing the helicopter rescue work I also had to fly the T-28s and B-26s, simple as that. Had I refused I would have been asked to leave, no doubt with a message to London to the effect that I was no longer required.

Initially, the sorties involved attacking and strafing rebel positions. By then most of the former FAC pilots were also playing combat roles with 22 Wing. In addition to Brannon and Klootwyk, the non Cuban line-up included Klootwyk's close pal, Charlie Vivier, as well as the chain-smoking Kiwi, MacDonald; a feisty Belgian named Léon Libert; a newly recruited former Italian air force and Alitalia pilot named Eugenio Papotti, and the taciturn French Indochina war veteran, Pierre Berthe. They increasingly took over from the Cubans as the principal attack pilots operating out of Albertville.

Berthe alternated with Terry flying the helicopter when necessary. Despite being a big man with a tough-guy appearance and close-cropped hair, Berthe was quiet and unassuming. He and Terry became close friends. 'He was one of the bravest men I've ever known. He didn't say much but you knew instinctively that in a difficult spot he wouldn't let you down.' Another man who made a big impression on Terry was the Italian newcomer, Papotti. He was a few years younger and had given up his Alitalia job to go in search of something more exciting than ferrying people around in 707s.

> I knew the first time I flew with him that he was a complete professional. I took off in a B-26 with him as my co-pilot. A couple of minutes after getting airborne he handed me a note with the ETAs for the whole route. That sort of thing was unheard of in the Congo. His flying was just impeccable.

Although Terry and some of the other surviving pilots now have real qualms about their role in air attacks, at the time most felt that rebels were fair game. Pounding their positions with fifty-calibre machine-gun fire and rockets was a pretty unequal struggle given their lack of anti-aircraft weapons. Yet they were hardly a chivalrous enemy and, anyway, well-directed small arms ground fire could be lethal, as Brannon had discovered. On a rescue mission in the Bell-47 near Bukavu a bullet nicked Terry's tail rotor. As it happened the damage was inconsequential but it could easily have been catastrophic. One of the Cuban pilots had even returned with a poison-tipped arrow embedded in the fuselage just behind the cockpit. Nonetheless, as Terry is the first to admit, air attacks on rebel positions were usually nothing short of slaughter.

> They'd never seen anything like it. With eight machine guns and thirty-two rockets in a B-26 you were a force to be reckoned with. If

you were on the ground with that lot aimed at you, it was going to do a lot more than make your eyes water.

The only problem was that strafing targets in the remote hinterland on the basis of what was often unreliable intelligence undoubtedly led to countless innocent, civilian casualties. There were no observers to verify the nature of the targets and rarely any body counts. These were not considerations that troubled the Congolese Government or the CIA and its pilots at the time. However, for Terry and some of his comrades this changed when they were ordered to attack fleeing Katangans after their mutiny was crushed. 'I just couldn't do it. It would have been nothing short of murder.'

The mutiny and occupation of Stanleyville by the Katangans lasted about two months. As ANC forces laid siege to the city, operations against rebels in the surrounding area came to a standstill. Rebels reoccupied a town in the north and brutally massacred the population. Eventually, however, the disgruntled Katangese capitulated in the face of overwhelming odds and promises to repatriate them to their southern homeland or absorb them into new ANC units. Although some accepted one or other of the options, a body of around 1,500 men, many with their wives and children, chose to disappear into the bush and try to make their own way home. They distrusted the government's pledges, not least since most of their leaders had been arrested and taken off to an uncertain fate in Leopoldville. As this column of dejected and defeated soldiers and their families headed southward, orders were given for their elimination. This task fell to 22 Wing.

By then a man named Jim Lassiter had taken over from Earl Myers as air operations officer in Albertville. He was nicknamed 'the cayman' because of an unfortunate alligator-like protruding front tooth and an ice-cold demeanour to match. He had been a pilot with the Flying Tigers ferrying supplies 'over the hump' in C-46s to nationalist Chinese forces during the Second World War. Attacking the Katangese became his responsibility. Terry was flying a B-26 with instructions to search for the dissident column. When he reported that he had found it, Lassiter relayed an order from Washington: 'Wipe them out'. Terry flew over the slow-moving trail of people. 'They didn't try to run or hide. They were crammed into the backs of open trucks, waving, cheering and laughing. They were sitting ducks. I just couldn't do it.' His radio kept repeating, '*Slingshot*, go ahead and attack'. But Terry had already decided that this was an order he would not obey.

I called Washington directly on my HF set – frequency 14323 – got the duty officer out of bed at three in the morning and told him the mission wasn't feasible. He yawned and said, 'Roger *Slingshot*. Return to base. We'll be in touch.' I then called Lassiter.

'Sorry, mission aborted, the weather's too bad. *Slingshot* out,' he transmitted, turning away and heading home.

Later, Lassiter decided to try again with a flight of T-28s. Brannon was one of the pilots to be involved. After the briefing he took Lassiter aside.

'Listen Jim, I'm sorry but I'm not prepared to do this. These people are just trying to go home. They've got their families with them,' he told him.

'I'm going to pretend I didn't hear that. Now I'm going to step outside and if you're still here when I come back you can pack your bags and be on the first plane back to South Africa,' Lassiter answered. Brannon held his ground. The flight left without him but Lassiter withdrew his threat to terminate Brannon's contract. He knew that most of the other pilots could be relied on to do the job and in the end the fleeing Katangese were eliminated by air attacks and ground forces.

Eugenio Papotti still has sleepless nights about his part in the killing.

They were going down the road to Katanga and we had orders to stop them. Much later on I realized that they'd suffered really bad treatment, they'd been cheated and then killed. I feel a little bit responsible for that. I don't know why because I wasn't responsible but I do feel real regret. It's difficult to understand the African reality and for me at the time it was absolutely new. I was just a young, ignorant boy looking for some adventure. Knowing what I know now and at my age, I wouldn't do it again.

Although Brannon did not participate in the attacks on the Katangans, he shares a sense of remorse for his involvement in many other air strikes.

Looking back now I realize that most of our missions in the T-28s and B-26s were no different to what the Americans and their allies have done or are doing more recently in places like Iraq and Afghanistan – killing women and children and excusing it as collateral damage. That's what it was all about. We were ordered to go and attack schools, hospitals and even churches. Well, I refused to attack churches but I did attack the other targets because that's where the enemy would always be. Probably we killed a few of them but we also killed a lot of innocent people – just like what's happening now. I mean we used rockets and they were absolutely lethal.

One of the key figures responsible for heightening tension at the time of the Katangan mutiny was Major John Peters, the man who had taken over from Hoare leading 5th Commando. Peters was a thirty-nine-year-old one-time street fighter from Leeds in Yorkshire. A former National Service NCO, he enjoyed his new-found rank as a mercenary major and liked to toy ostentatiously with his officer's baton. Terry loathed him. 'He was just a ruthless thug. Discipline in 5th Commando went to pot under his command.' Brook-Fox found him 'conceited and swaggering'. In an early despatch he complained that increased indiscipline in the ranks of 5th Commando under Peters had brought the unit into considerable disfavour and risked giving Britain a bad name.

Peters was on leave in South Africa when news of the Katangan mutiny broke. He immediately returned to Leopoldville and went to Mobutu with what he claimed was intelligence on a well-developed plot to overthrow the president and bring back Tshombe.

Peters later repeated the same story to Brook-Fox at the British Embassy, bragging as he did that he had more clout with Mobutu than any of the UK Government's representatives. He asserted that he had travelled to Rhodesia at the request of his former second in command, Alistair Wickes. At a meeting in Salisbury he claimed that Wickes offered him £15,000 to lead 5th Commando in a *coup de main* to seize Elizabethville and towns in the east of the country so that a triumphant Tshombe could return and proclaim himself president. Belgian business interests, including the powerful Union Minière[1] in Katanga, were supposedly behind the plan. In truth it appears that Peters set out to ingratiate himself with Mobutu by heavily embellishing what may have been little more than a contingency plan on the part of Union Minière in response to growing anti-Belgian sentiment whipped up by Mobutu. If so, he succeeded. Mobutu rewarded him with immediate promotion to colonel, something that appealed to Peters' inflated ego. The President also ratcheted up his anti-Belgian rhetoric and implicated the Katangan mutineers in the alleged plot. A number of white mercenaries who had been attached to the Katangan units were summarily shot dead in the ensuing frenzy.

Terry claims that he came across Peters in a disturbing incident shortly after the crisis provoked by the mutiny. On a flight out of Albertville he landed at Baraka on the shores of Lake Tanganyika in the Bell-47 to refuel. A 5th Commando troop leader told him that a dozen rebels had surrendered under an amnesty and were being held in the custody of a Belgian officer. Terry immediately relayed the information to Lassiter, who agreed that the captives should be interrogated. 'I split up the rebels so that I could question them individually. One by one with the help of a Swahili-speaking interpreter I got them to sit down and write out their life stories.' With the confessions and a search of the men's belongings, a clear picture of their communist training began to emerge. Some had been trained in Tashkent, others in Peking and Cairo. They possessed training manuals with instructions on sabotage and guerrilla warfare tactics.

I wrote a fairly comprehensive report, got all the material into the Bell and flew back to Albertville with a recommendation to Lassiter that the men should be brought down for further interrogation.

'Oh, I don't think that'll be necessary,' Lassiter told Terry.

Shortly afterwards Terry was back in Baraka when he saw a signal from Lassiter to Peters at 5th Commando headquarters. It read: 'Dispose all twelve yellow packages'. Alarmed by this, Terry immediately went in search of the prisoners. He found them being led by armed mercenaries to a boat on the shore of Lake Tanganyika. It was a Swift Boat of the type used by the US Navy in Vietman. Devlin had acquired two to patrol Lake Tanganyika at the height of the insurgency when Baraka and the surrounding area was a rebel stronghold. Armed with a 50-calibre mounted machine gun, they were originally manned by crews of Cuban exiles. Peter was waiting on board as the prisoners arrived.

'What's going on? These men have surrendered under the amnesty. We need to take them back for further interrogation,' Terry demanded.

'We're taking them by boat,' Peters grinned back. 'You can come along if you like.'

The boat headed off into the middle of the lake. At first Terry thought that the men were being taken towards the Tanzanian shore to point out the place from which they had originally made their crossing. 'One of the guys who spoke some English told me that he knew they were going to be shot and I tried to reassure him. He just smiled at me.' When the Congolese shore was nothing more than a distant smudge, the boat slowed down and stopped. Peters emerged from the cabin and shot one of the prisoners, whose body was unceremoniously bundled overboard. The others were then machine-gunned to death as they made to jump overboard or when they surfaced struggling for breath. Terry knew that if he said a word or moved a muscle in protest he would join them.

Peters treated the shooting like a bit of afternoon sport. When I got back to Albertville I tried to make a stink about it but all that came back from Washington via Lassiter was: 'What are you talking about? It never happened.' He told me that I'd done a bloody good job, was being promoted and should go back to Leopoldville because the first of the Alouettes had finally been delivered.

The arrival of the new helicopters was the best news Terry could have had. Back in the capital he started conversion training with a French pilot named Onde from Aviation Sud who arrived with the first aircraft. The Alouette III was a:

> ... great big, heavy beast on wheels. Converting to it from the Bell was like moving from a Morris Minor to a modern, large truck. It was noisy and the jet engine was so versatile it could run on anything from avgas to petrol. In fact, I once used paraffin from village lamps to get me home. It was very up-to-date. The Bell had been around much longer and was like an egg beater and just about as sophisticated.

As it happened, only three of the five new aircraft would ever become operational. Clumsy Congolese stevedores unloading the aircraft at Matadi managed to wreck one before it reached the shore. Another lost its entire tail section while being inexpertly manoeuvred on the ground by a trainee Congolese pilot who decided to have a go at taxiing it without Terry present to supervize. These setbacks were compounded by a refusal on the part of Aviation Sud to supply WIGMO with the maintenance manuals because the CIA front was not an accredited customer. While the wrangling went on the surviving helicopters stood idle. Common sense eventually prevailed and Tluszez and his crew at Ndjili received the necessary information. They would do the same sterling work keeping the sophisticated Alouettes airborne as they had with the primitive Bells.

The first Alouette arrived on almost the first anniversary to the day of Terry's arrival in the Congo. He knew that with its delivery, Bouzin and the CIA would start positioning him to become Mobutu's pilot. He was by then reconciled to the reality that search and rescue flying was becoming less of a priority and he was not really in a position to object to other roles. Flying the President and spying on him at the same time seemed an attractive enough alternative. His first solo flight in one of the new helicopters was a fly-past as part of a lavish ceremonial to celebrate the first anniversary of Mobutu's rule. The extravagant partying in Leopoldville had barely ended when WIGMO faced its next major flap.

This time for once, the drama was not of Congolese making. In the early morning of 19 December, Peters' second in command at 5th Commando shot and killed a young WIGMO armourer in cold blood in the WIGMO mess in Albertville. Terry was on temporary assignment as the CIA field agent in Stanleyville, the only non-American ever given such a role, when he heard the news. 'It was horrific and the balloon really went up. Devlin and the whole CIA high command rushed up there to find out what had happened.'

What they quickly discovered was that Trevor Bottomley, the young armourer who Terry counted among his drinking friends, had fallen foul of Major Samuel Cassidy after going to the defence of an elderly Congolese retainer. Bottomley was drinking with two other British WIGMO employees at the *Chemin de Fer* club. Cassidy was there with one of his men. When the old retainer called last orders, Cassidy's companion started abusively manhandling the old man. The WIGMO men tried to stop this and Bottomley challenged Cassidy directly.

'You're a big man when you know you've got a gun, aren't you?' he said pointing to Cassidy's concealed firearm.

'Mind your own fucking business and don't meddle in military matters,' Cassidy replied.

The three WIGMO men then left and returned to their mess at the *Hôtel Palais* to contine drinking. Shortly after midnight Cassidy walked in with his companion of earlier and several other mercenary friends. He was wearing a holstered, nine-millimetre automatic Browning. Walking up to Bottomley at the bar and slapping the holster he said:

'I'm not hiding it now. Do I still look like a big man?'

'You're in our mess now. Check your gun at the desk,' Bottomley countered.

Cassidy responded by pulling the gun and pointing it at Bottomley. He pushed the barrel part of the way into Bottomley's left nostril and pulled the trigger, blasting the back off Bottomley's head. Klootwyk was standing next to the twenty-five-year-old armourer, whose lifeless body collapsed at his feet in a pool of blood. Cassidy waved the Browning over his head menacingly, yelling at Bottomley's companions, 'Have you anything to say now?' Then he looked at Klootwyk and the other WIGMO men and shouted: 'Anyone who doesn't like it can get the same.' At first nobody moved. Cassidy then pointed his gun at the most senior WIGMO man in the mess, Jack Irwin, the engineering manager from Nottingham in central England.

'Come on Sam; don't be silly we've known each other for years. Put your gun away and have a drink,' Irwin coolly said as he looked down the barrel. Cassidy nodded and one of the Swedish mechanics quickly poured him a beer. As he swallowed it, Klootwyk crept out, rushed upstairs to Lassiter's room and reported what had happened.

Lassiter urgently pulled on his clothes and raced down to the bar. With nerves of steel 'the cayman' walked up to Cassidy, who was still in an agitated state, and without speaking held out his hand for the gun.

'I guess I've fucked up this time, eh Jim,' acknowledged Cassidy as he handed the weapon over, butt first. He then left quietly with Lassiter, who took him back to his 5th Commando quarters. Shortly afterwards, helped by some of his men, Cassidy escaped by motorboat. He headed across Lake Tanganyika. At daybreak two 22 Wing T-28s took off to search for him. Two more joined the search later and found the motorboat abandoned on the lakeside near the Zambian border. The CIA quickly arranged with the Zambian authorities to track Cassidy down and he was spirited back to Leopoldville to face a Congolese military tribunal. After what British observers described as a 'well conducted and fair' trial, Cassidy was sentenced to death. However, Britain had just abolished the death penalty and the British ambassador, Sir John Cotton, was ordered to plead with Mobutu for Cassidy's life, a task his subsequent communiqués suggest he found deeply distasteful. After additional Foreign Office intervention, Mobutu commuted the sentence to one of life imprisonment.

Cassidy was a twenty-eight-year-old, Glasgow-born thug who had been in the Scots Guards as a national serviceman and never made it to NCO. He had a civil conviction for assault and had been guilty of numerous military offences before being discharged. In the Congo he was suspected of murdering a fellow mercenary and reputed to have been part of the inner sanctum of mercenaries guarding the gold at Watsa who amassed a small fortune for themselves. On his return to the Congo from the UK, where he was on leave at the time of the shooting, Peters characteristically but unwisely threatened to kill CIA station chief Devlin if he did not use his influence with Mobutu to have Cassidy released. This only served to worsen what had become a very strained relationship between 5th Commando and WIGMO. Bottomley, who was from Royston in Hertfordshire, was buried in Kalima cemetery in a leafy suburb of Leopoldville. Owing to his role in Stanleyville, Terry was unable to join the thirty or so WIGMO mourners who attended the funeral, along with Brook-Fox representing the British Government. To his disgust he later heard that British consular officials regularly took food, including a sumptuous Christmas dinner, to Cassidy in the cell he shared at Camp Kokolo with some of the Katangan mutineers. What he did not know was that Bottomley's killer was paying for this with money sent by his South African girlfriend. Even if he had, it would not have made Terry feel any better about it. 'He should've been left to rot for what he did.' He was even more incensed when Mobutu later freed Cassidy to go and live in South Africa. Devlin was convinced that the stolen Watsa gold enabled Cassidy to buy his way out of jail and Terry agrees. 'Money could get you anything in the Congo.'

Notes

1   Union Minière Haute Katanga was founded in 1906 and controlled the vast mineral resources of Katanga Province. It supplied the uranium for the atomic bombs dropped on Japan to end the Second World War. The Belgian-owned company backed Tshombe's secession after independence. Mobutu nationalized it at the end of 1966 and shortly afterwards production collapsed.

Chapter Seventeen
Another Storm Brewing

One of those closest to Mobutu in the early years of his presidency was an American doctor by the name of William T Close. He was Mobutu's personal physician and widely suspected of being a CIA plant, although he always vigorously denied this. Terry met him quite soon after arriving in Leopoldville and they became friends. In the course of a routine flying medical, Close diagnosed Terry with hypertension and started treating him for it, something for which he remains profoundly grateful. 'Bill Close was probably one of the best doctors I've ever known. Mobutu wouldn't go anywhere without him. I flew him on many occasions and taught him how to fly a helicopter.' Close, the father of the Hollywood actress Glenn Close, was equally complimentary about Terry. He was still practising medicine at a clinic in Wyoming until shortly before his death in early 2009. 'The best words I can use to describe Terry are that he was a gentleman warrior,' he then recalled. Close knew nothing about Terry's past but said quite categorically that even if he had known the whole story it would not have changed how he felt. 'None of what I learned later made any difference. My memories of him are all very positive. He was a great teacher and a great guy.'

Close, who was both a surgeon and general practitioner, spent his early childhood in France before being educated at Harrow School in England, where he and his brother were known as 'the little frogs'. Back in America in 1943 aged nineteen, he enlisted in the US Army Air Corps, serving first in France after the Normandy landings and then in Berlin following the occupation of Germany by Allied forces. After graduating from medical college he was drawn into the Moral Re-Armament (MRA) movement. This was what took him to Africa. Shortly before the Belgian Congo's independence he participated in a six-week MRA missionary assignment to Leopoldville, where his fluent French was a significant advantage. In the end he stayed for sixteen years. At one time he was the only qualified surgeon in the Congolese capital. He lived through all the turmoil. When he left he had been responsible for entirely renovating the city's general hospital and played a crucial role in combating the first deadly Ebola outbreak to afflict the country. He had also become one of Mobutu's most trusted confidantes. Whether a CIA agent or not, he was also certainly close to Devlin.

Mobutu was still an army colonel when Close first met him. He became his doctor after being appointed chief medical officer to the Congolese army in January 1962. Over the next few years their relationship developed. After Mobutu seized power he installed Close and his family in a large house in the paramilitary compound above Stanley Pool, only a stone's throw from the presidential residence. He also appointed him an honorary lieutenant colonel in the army and often sought his advice on non-medical matters. As the communist-backed rebellion started being brought under control, Mobutu warmed to a proposal from Close to organize a relief operation for villagers in pacified areas. More than two-thirds of the country had been in rebel hands at times. As a result the economy was devastated with starvation and disease claiming as many lives as the fighting. Close persuaded Mobutu to offer food and medicine to rebel supporters who surrendered under an amnesty. They called the plan Operation *Survival*.

Terry's working relationship with Close began in March 1966 when he took over from Houke flying him in the Bell-47 on some of the earliest Operation *Survival* missions out of Albertville. On these flights Close filled the space behind the seats in the bubble with cartons of Belga jaune cigarettes, the cheapest available. He threw these out over known rebel villages as the helicopter swooped across at treetop height. Leaflets promising food and medicine if the people evacuated to open spaces and flew white cloths on bamboo poles to denote their surrender, accompanied the cigarettes. When Houke made the very first of these flights he guarded against any treachery on the part of surrendering rebels by flying with a box of hand grenades between his legs. In Terry's words it was 'his insurance'.

Despite limited success, Close persevered with Operation *Survival*. Terry started flying him again in September, this time in the tail-wheel Beechcraft visiting towns in the Kwilu province where the rebellion originated under the leadership of Pierre Mulele, Lumumba's former minister of education. By then Mulele had fled across the Congo River seeking refuge in Brazzaville. Later he would accept an amnesty from Mobutu and pay the price by being viciously tortured, having his ears and eyes ripped from his head before being killed. Savagery in the Congo knew no bounds. The war left the surviving people in affected areas destitute. What the rebels did not take the army did. Their food crops were destroyed and their game killed or driven away, leaving them struggling to live on patches of soil sown with peanuts. Most of the children suffered from kwashiorkor, the disease caused by protein deficiency that cruelly shows itself in empty, swollen pot bellies. In one village Close found a path lined by wooden stakes topped with human skulls, a hideous echo of Conrad's description of the approach to Mr Kurtz's trading station in Leopold's Congo.

Close, of course, had qualified as a fixed-wing pilot in the Army Air Corps. In January of 1967 Terry checked him out on the Beechcraft so that he could continue Operation *Survival* flying himself. Later still, he taught him to fly one of the new Alouette III helicopters. 'Mobutu insisted on it. I don't know why, but he refused to let Bill fly in a helicopter with him unless he learnt to fly it first.' For Terry the opportunity to work with Bill Close was a godsend. It not only meant that he was still doing some humanitarian work but it also introduced him to Mobutu. He recalls returning from an Operation *Survival* trip and sitting with Close on the edge of Mobutu's bed talking about the plight of his people. In the villages, they had taken Polaroid photographs of starving women and children to show him. In one village an old woman with a claw of a hand came out of a mud hut and told them that the people needed help. When they responded by saying that that they would tell the authorities she said: 'We don't need it tomorrow or later. We need it now.' All this they related to Mobutu. Watching and listening to the thirty-six-year-old president's reactions, Terry felt that he gave the appearance of being 'genuinely interested in his people and his country'. From what he said, Mobutu seemed to want to do the right things. 'The trouble was that the country was so big, so ungovernable and so full of different factions that it was a heck of a lot to ask of anyone, let alone a man so young who started life as an army sergeant.'

Although in the end it did not amount to much, Terry's involvement in Operation *Survival* was an important personal morale booster. It reaffirmed his belief that he had done the right thing in going to the Congo. More than a year after faking his death to disappear he still suffered 'many heartwrenching moments alone in the night' when he thought about his children. There were times when he wavered and thought about going back to England, although he worried that 'being cleared all the way' did not mean being off the hook. So long as he was working with the CIA he presumed he was safe. But if he threw in his lot and went home what sort of reception could he really expect? He could not be sure but he did not intend to find out unless he had to. Anyway, the end what really stopped him from returning was his exposure on almost daily basis to 'an even worse case of cruelty or suffering'. As the rescue missions dried up, working with Close convinced him that he was still needed more where he was than at home. 'I was confident that my children were being looked after well and that many of the Congole kids I came across needed me more.'

As Terry waited to start his new role flying the President, he spent a increasing amount of time working alongside Mishou. By this point had been given his CIA cryptonym of W I Mossie and was being asked do more 'spying' and less flying. Klootwyk sums him up during the period as 'more of a gentleman intriguer than a gentleman warrior'. It probably a fair assessment. Brannon disliked and distrusted Mishou are thought less well of Terry for getting so close to him. Of course, what did not understand because he did not know the truth about Terry presence in the Congo, was that Terry saw the relationship as an essenti requirement. Photographic reconnaissance flights and eavesdropping of conversations between senior Congolese army officers whenever he fle them became run-of-the mill assignments. The rebellion may have bee losing its momentum but Mobutu was still whipping up anti-Belgi sentiment and rumours of a Tshombe-inspired counter coup to topple hi continued to do the rounds. In this atmosphere every move by anyoi with any political or military muscle had to be monitored. One of the m Terry had to keep a close eye on when flying him was the arm commander in chief General Joseph Bobozo. He was a big, stupid bru who only held on to his position through having the right trib connections and the good fortune of having been Mobutu's mentor wh the President first joined the army. Terry rather enjoyed the idea that t bullying old fool had no idea he was being so closely watched.

Meanwhile, new faces started to appear at the FAC base at Ndolo. O of them was a red-headed, thirty-five-year-old English pilot nam Desmond 'Ginger' Parker. Terry checked him out on the T-28s and fle with him a couple of times. Then one morning Parker collared Terry his way to the crew room.

'Hey Terry, what speed do I have to be doing to do a loop in a T-28?' asked.

'Don't,' replied Terry firmly. 'The T-28 is the most unforgiving, fuckin thing you'll ever fly.'

'What about 240 knots?' Parker persisted.

'Just don't do it you stupid bastard,' Terry told him.

That evening in the bar of the *Hôtel Regina* a man named Peter Wickstead approached Terry. He claimed to be ex-RAF and wanted to know how he could join the Congolese air force.

'Depends what you can fly,' Terry told him.

'I can fly just about anything,' Wickstead bragged.

'Well, I wouldn't let the other pilots hear you say that. But if you're here first thing tomorrow I'll introduce you to the commandant and you can take it from there.' Terry was as good as his word. The following morning he took Wickstead to see Henry Laurent, who had replaced Noêl as commandant. Laurent was stocky, full of confidence and a good pilot, unlike his predecessor. He agreed to check Wickstead out in a DC-3 later that afternoon. The ex-RAF man was hanging around in the crew room waiting when Parker appeared in full flying gear.

'I'm going for a spin in a T-28. Fancy coming for the ride?' he is reported to have asked Wickstead, who agreed enthusiastically. They never returned.

When Terry arrived back at the airport after lunch he was told that one of the T-28s was missing. He immediately jumped into a Beechcraft and started a search, criss-crossing the jungle for miles around. After two days of fruitless looking he was called away on a more important job. One of the other pilots eventually found a small hole in the jungle canopy, at the bottom of which lay the crumpled wreckage of the T-28 and the remains of Parker and Wickstead. Terry knew full well that Parker had ignored his advice and attempted to loop the loop with fatal consequences. In trying the manoeuvre he had obviously experienced reverse control. 'At first the joy stick is solid and cannot be moved. Then the aircraft's controls reverse. At this point the pilot has to be able to do the same and reverse his instincts if he is to survive. It's like having a split personality.'

Towards the middle of the year Terry received an unusual communication from Léon Libert, one of his former 22 Wing comrades who had returned home to Belgium. In his message Libert said he had an important proposition to put to Terry. He could not be more specific in writing but would reveal all if Terry flew to Belgium for a meeting. Terry immediately took the missive to Mishou.

'I think I'd better go and find out what this is all about, don't you?' he suggested.

'Yeah, I smell a rat of some kind here,' agreed Mishou. The next day Terry flew to Brussels, hired a car and drove to Liège, where Libert lived. They had agreed to meet at the railway station because Terry would have no trouble finding it and the bar there stayed open all night. Libert was waiting near the station entrance with Roger Bracco when Terry arrived. Bracco was another former 22 Wing pilot who had been sent home after being responsible for the loss of two T-28s. Terry witnessed him crash one of them spectacularly at Albertville and knew he was lucky to have survived.

After warmly greeting Terry, the two men escorted him to the station bar. They ordered beers and exchanged pleasantries.

'Okay, what's this important proposition then?' asked Terry when they had exhausted catching up on their news.

'I want you to think about stealing one of WIGMO's B-26s,' said Libert cautiously. 'Actually, both of them if you can,' he added quickly.

'Don't be so bloody stupid, Léon. Why would I want to do that?' replied Terry, grinning in disbelief.

'Look, things are going to change in the Congo and when they do you'll be on the wrong side,' answered Libert urgently. 'Terry, you are one of the best pilots there. We want you and Klootwyk with us. And we want the B-26s out of the way.' Terry could hardly believe his ears but he let Libert finish and then asked him to explain exactly how he and Klootwyk were supposed to take the aircraft.

'It'll be really easy,' Libert laughed. 'All you have to do is take them on a routine training flight. Nobody will think anything's unusual. You'll use the call signs *Coca* and *Cola* and we'll radio you and tell you where to bring the planes. *C'est tout.*' Libert paused and swallowed a gulp of beer before continuing. 'You'll be well paid, very well paid,' he assured.

'How well paid?' asked Terry.

'Like you can go on a very long holiday, well paid,' answered Libert with a Gallic flourish.

Terry was completely taken aback by the audacity of the scheme. Yet he knew it would be as simple as Libert said to steal the aircraft. By the time anyone realized what had happened they would be gone. Their absence would make a big hole in WIGMO's firepower just as the whole air support operation was being wound down.

'Okay, I'll think about it,' he responded. 'Have you spoken to Klootwyk yet?'

'No, we want you to do that when you get back. If you're both in agreement, telephone me at home here,' answered Libert.

'One last thing, when's all this suppose to happen?' Terry asked.

'We can't say yet,' shrugged Libert.

Back in Leopoldville Terry reported the whole conversation to Mishou.

At the time he said nothing to Klootwyk. What seemed clear was that Libert and Bracco were either privy to a plot to overthrow Mobutu, or had dreamed up the preposterous idea of stealing the B-26s in order to take the plan to Tshombe supporters in exchange for a handsome pay off. For a while the proposed *Coca-Cola* heist jangled nerves. It looked as if another storm was brewing. Then Tshombe,[1] who had been sentenced to death for treason in the Congo *in absentia*, was kidnapped and taken to Algeria after his aircraft was hi-jacked on a routine flight from mainland Spain to Majorca. Most observers accused the CIA of being behind the hi-jacking, although it has never been proved.

With Tshombe conveniently out of the way, the immediate panic subsided. Terry told Mishou that he wanted to take a spot of leave and go to the United States to take his commercial pilot's licence. He was still seeing Terry One in Leopoldville but had heard from Joan in Montreal and knew that she was keen to resurrect the fleeting relationship they had enjoyed in Brussels. Mishou secured the agreement of Weber and Johnson to Terry's request. He had not taken any leave since arriving in the Congo twenty-one months earlier.

'Off you go. You deserve it. You've earned it,' Mishou told him. 'Just make sure you stay in touch, that's all.' Terry made plans to fly out of Leopoldville in early July. By then Klootwyk had returned to South Africa after narrowly surviving a crash that killed one of his passengers in one of the Bell-47s. Before leaving, he had told Terry that he also wanted to take his commercial licence. Terry called him and they arranged to make the trip together. Klootwyk flew into Leopoldville from Johannesburg en route for Paris on a UTA flight on the evening of 5 July. As agreed between them, Terry boarded the aircraft to join him. They travelled first class and joked about how easily they could have carried out Libert's *Coca-Cola* theft had they wanted to.

The timing of Terry's departure was extraordinary. On the day he chose to go on leave the majority of the remaining white mercenary units in the Congo mutinied. When the news reached Leopoldville all flights in and out of the country were suspended. The evening UTA flight to Paris was the last one out. At the time there were no more than two hundred mercenaries left in the Congo. All the same, they were more than a match for the ill-disciplined, cowardly ANC and Mobutu knew it. The country was plunged into another crisis. Whites everywhere became targets, sparking more wholesale evacuations. At the airport in Leopoldville a group of fifteen mercenaries who were leaving the country and could not possibly have been involved in the mutiny were arrested. Later they were summarily executed in the ANC para-commando compound on Mobutu's orders. So, too, were three British, former mercenaries who were languishing in jail for civil offences at the time of the mutiny.[2] According to a witness, the men were called by name one by one at fifteen-minute intervals and shot by an army captain, presumably after being tortured. Later three vehicles were seen driving away towards the Congo River to dispose of the bodies. Amazingly, the vile Cassidy survived this senseless butchery.

Notes

1   Tshombe was imprisoned and then held under house arrest until he died of a heart attack in 1969.
2   The fifteen mercenaries executed without trial were six Belgians, four Frenchmen, two Spaniards, two Italians and one South African. The Britons were men by the name of Graham Pahl, Joseph Larkin and Nicholas Van Staaden who were serving sentences for theft.

Chapter Eighteen
From Friend to Foe

Word of the mercenary uprising reached Terry and Klootwyk the moment they arrived in Paris. Terry telephoned Mishou immediately. The CIA man told him not to change his plans. The situation was far from clear and extremely dangerous. For the time being at least, the best thing for Terry to do was proceed on leave and keep in touch. In the course of subsequent communication the full story of what had happened emerged. The mutiny appeared to be part of a well-orchestrated plot to overthrow Mobutu and secure Tshombe's release and return. This must have been what Libert and Bracco were alluding to in their attempt to persuade Terry to get together with Klootwyk and hijack the two B-26s. Surprisingly, Denard was in on the plot. He had the support of Schramme and what remained of his Katangese commando.[1] Apparently, the original idea had been for their men to take over Stanleyville and Bukavu on 5 July.[2] They would then steal whatever aircraft they could at Stanleyville and launch an attack on Leopoldville two days later.

After a promising start, the plan went hopelessly wrong. A handful of mercenaries thrashed the ANC battalion in Bukavu and briefly occupied the town before mysteriously melting away again. However, after initial success in Stanleyville, fierce fighting broke out later in the day and Denard suffered a serious head wound. A number of his men were also wounded. He commandeered an Air Congo DC-3 and forced the crew to fly himself and the other casualties to Rhodesia for medical treatment. Schramme assumed command of the remaining mercenaries and a tense stand-off followed with most of the town and airport under their control. The mercenaries stole a FATAC DC-3 and sent it to Angola with a number of WIGMO hostages on board. They also appropriated two T-28s to be flown by Libert and Bracco, who had secretly reappeared in the country. This created even more of a flap for the CIA than the Katangese mutiny a year earlier.

After an uneasy ceasefire and Red Cross evacuations of ANC wounded, Schramme eventually withdrew from Stanleyville and headed southwards towards Bukavu, inflicting more heavy casualties on the ANC as he did. He knew that his small force could hold out almost indefinitely wherever he chose provided he was not attacked from the air. In Stanleyville the ANC resorted to its favourite pastime of looting and raping the defenceless civilian population rather than pursuing Schramme. Foreign embassies, with the notable exception of the Americans, started making urgent plans to evacuate their nationals if necessary. There were still some 17,000 European and other foreign nationals scattered throughout the country. Meanwhile, Mobutu and his army heads seemed preoccupied with organizing a planned visit by heads of state for an Organization of African Unity meeting and attending medal-giving ceremonies. Reporting on events to the Foreign and Commonwealth Office the British ambassador started a tongue-in-cheek communiqué, 'herewith another gripping instalment in the absorbing serial we are running on the Congo'. He referred to a 'shattering defeat of the ANC' at Bukavu while 'Mobutu and his ministers continue to behave like a lot of Walter Mittys'.

While all this was going on, Terry and Klootwyk arrived in Montreal. Terry rented an apartment in Sherwood Street near the city centre close to where Joan lived with two women flatmates. He and she quickly rediscovered the mutual attraction that had drawn them together on the cross-Channel ferry and in Brussels. What was then an impromptu, whirlwind romance settled into a more well-defined relationship. After almost a month together enjoying what Montreal had to offer, they were what people today would call 'an item'. Klootwyk, who all the girls loved, was not short of admirers either. At the beginning of August the holidaying ended and he and Terry headed off to Dallas to do their fortnight-long commercial pilot's course at Fort Worth.

Mishou kept Terry regularly updated on developments in the Congo. Securely ensconced in Bukavu, Schramme had offered to negotiate with Mobutu. The stalemate continued. What remained of the CIA air force was not mobilized against Schramme and all the FAC's mercenary pilots had left the country. Their departure followed a dramatic confrontation between commandant Laurent and Mobutu. When they heard about the arrest and subsequent execution of the fifteen departing mercenaries on the day after the uprising, Laurent and his pilots went into hiding in a house in Leopoldville. Their pay was months in arrears and they feared for their lives given the rampant anti-white hostility in the streets. Marauding ANC soldiers had raped several white women in Leopoldville for the first time since the immediate post-independence chaos. As Terry heard later from Laurent himself, the commandant eventually went to Mobutu's headquarters. 'He somehow bluffed his way into Mobutu's office and found him sitting at his desk.' Laurent took out his nine-millimetre pistol and laid it down in front of Mobutu.

'If I was on the wrong side I would have killed you by now,' he calmly told the startled President. 'But don't worry I'm on your side and so are my men. What I'm here to say is that we don't intend to be butchered like the other guys. All we want is to be paid what we're owed and allowed to leave.' Mobutu immediately summoned an aide.

'Arrange for Major Laurent's men to receive their money and then have them escorted to the ferry for Brazzaville without delay,' he ordered. All flights in and out of the country remained temporarily suspended.

Just before Terry and Klootwyk were due to leave Fort Worth, an urgent message arrived from Mishou asking him to telephone a number in Washington. Terry immediately made the call. A telegram had arrived from Mishou asking him to return to Leopoldville without delay. He was needed to lead a new group of Cuban pilots who had been recruited to reactivate the air support programme against Schramme. Mishou warned that the situation was dangerous and that Terry would have to be careful in returning. If he was prepared to accept the assignment he should go back to Montreal. The American consul there, a man by the name of Jeff Gould, would provide money and air tickets. This was just the kind of summons Terry liked. It went to the heart of his *raison d'être*. Nothing made him feel better about himself than being needed, whether by the women in his life or by the people for whom he was working. This was what made helicopter rescue work so addictive. He thrived on being indispensable. What drove him to the Congo may have been misplaced idealism and the attraction of covering himself in glory airlifting nuns to safety. However, over time a healthy sense of realism kicked in. What he craved most was opportunities to prove himself and then being recognized for what he could do. The cause was secondary.

Terry found Gould in the midst of Expo '67, the world fair hosted by Montreal as part of Canada's centennial celebrations.

'Wow! This really makes my day. This is the first time I've ever had to deal with one of you chaps,' he told Terry, obviously enjoying his first taste of cloak and dagger work. There was no ticket for Klootwyk. As a South African he had become *persona non grata* in the Congo. Mobutu's Government had raised stink at the UN over the uprising by the mercenaries and succeeded in winning support for a complete international ban on their recruitment and use in African conflicts. As the principal recruiting ground, the apartheid regime in South Africa became the focus of hostility. Ironically, however, the 187 mercenaries allegedly involved in the uprising and named by the Congolese in an arrest warrant were mainly Europeans, including one Briton. Klootwyk's specific exclusion from Mishou's summons was an added fillip for Terry. He, Terry, was needed and he alone. How more indispensable could he be?

He bade Joan farewell, promising to write regularly. For the first time, he told her that he felt a real attachment to her. Mishou was at Ndjili to meet him off his flight and spirit him away before any Congolese officials could be heavy handed. He took him straight to *River House* to brief him. The Cuban pilots were due a day or so later and Terry was to meet them and then start checking them out without delay. He and a detachment of pilots would then take the Alouettes and T-28s and meet up with Ken Weber, who would be directing operations. Mishou explained that the CIA was stepping in to end the uprising because Congolese efforts were a shambles. Mobutu had reacted to the uprising by trying to rid himself of white support. He asked the Ethiopians for a squadron of jet fighter-bombers and hired a Turk named General Suat Eraybar to head the FAC with a bunch of fledgling Congolese pilots. The Ethiopian planes had arrived and parked at Kamina, where they remained on the ground. Meanwhile, Eraybar had crashed two T-28s himself and the Congolese pilots had managed to destroy two others. Anyway, they refused to fly below 10,000 feet for fear of being shot down. 'The situation was a complete joke. No wonder they wanted me back.'

Terry met the Cubans as instructed. He used the usual technique to get them away from the airport without being harassed by Congolese officials and headed off to *River House* with them in two minibuses. Foolishly, a Cuban driving one of the buses tried to jump an army road block. They were stopped and arrested by the irate soldiers, who prodded them threateningly with the barrels of their FN FAL rifles. Terry was under no illusions about what might happen if he did not secure their release quickly. By then he understood that what the Congolese rank and file feared most was wrath from their bullying superiors.

'We're here at the invitation of your president. I wouldn't want to be in your shoes when he hears about this,' he told the young officer in charge. 'If you release us now you have my word that I'll say nothing. But if you keep us much longer somebody is going to come looking for us and Mobutu is bound to hear.' The officer conferred with a colleague and shortly afterwards Terry and his men were freed. As it happened his bluff turned out to be nearer the truth than he thought. Within a day or two he was summoned to see Mobutu.

The plan originally agreed between the CIA and Bouzin to have Terry installed as Mobutu's helicopter pilot had finally come to fruition. He was given a new car and the rank of colonel in the Congolese army. He expressed his delight in one of his first letters to Joan after returning.

> I now have three helicopters available and I'm the only one able to fly them in the whole of the Congo, which I think is wonderful. Mobutu has given me a Volkswagen for myself as his personal pilot ... and I'll want you with me when it's a calmer atmosphere here and Schramme is out of the way – but for the moment I will be off in the interior with the helicopters and the fighters, not always in Kinshasa.[3]

This was the first time that Terry alluded to a future together with Joan but it became a constant theme in his subsequent correspondence. At the same time he never hid his interest in other women without ever being specific. For example, writing from Albertville, where he was stationed in late September, he complained 'all the white girls have left – it's called enforced faithfulness'. Later he bemoaned missing a Thanksgiving ball in Leopoldville, writing 'Alas the girls will have to do without the pilots because we are all about a thousand miles away – we all got invites but that's too bad I guess.' What he conveniently neglected to mention was his continuing relationship with Terry One.

Based in Albertville with Weber, Terry started leading regular reconnaissance flights over Schramme in Bukavu. They represented a show of force while negotiations for a peaceful withdrawal continued. However, this did not stop Schramme's men from shooting at the T-28s. Writing to Joan, Terry described the situation. 'They fired at us like crazy. My wing man, a Cuban, got a hole in his wing. They didn't get my aircraft but they tried pretty hard. We'll be back again tomorrow but we're not firing back at them at the moment, not until we know the results of the negotiations.'

In a subsequent mission Terry's aircraft was hit. A bullet pierced a fuel tank and fractured an all-important hydraulic line. Terry managed to get the hydraulically controlled landing gear down and open the cockpit canopy before the oil leaked away and prayed that there would be enough left to operate the brakes after landing. 'There was, just. I was bloody glad it wasn't an explosive round or it would've been a wing off and curtains for me.'

After a while the shooting stopped to be replaced by radio communication. Libert and Bracco knew the old 22 Wing frequency.

'Hey, Terry, this is Léon,' Libert announced as Terry's T-28 flew overhead. 'We need your help old friend.'

'Okay Léon. So what do you want?' Terry answered.

'We need you to get us passports with Rwanda visas so that we can go across the border. Can you do that for us?'

'I don't know, but I'll see what I can do,' Terry told him.

He reported the request to Weber and it became part of the official negotiations. He also told Joan in another of his letters describing day-to-day developments.

> They also told me where their hospital is and I told them where to stay in Bukavu to be safe – so we have a good relationship with Schramme and his men. Sounds just crazy doesn't it? Still that's the way it goes here. We call each other by our Christian names and enquire about families and children – most amusing when you think about it.

The phoney war ended abruptly, however, when a mercenary force mounted an invasion from Angola. In early November an ill-equipped band of 112 men led by Denard crossed the border into Katanga. Terry and his Cuban pilots were hastily relocated to Kamina and sent off to find the invaders. To Terry's astonishment they were ordered to attack anything moving on the Benguela railway.[4] They took off at dawn one morning and attacked and destroyed two trains, eight lorries and a fuel dump. Then they followed the railway to the Angolan border, where in Terry's words 'the Cubans came into their own by deciding to attack the wrong country'. The Cubans' habit of chattering non-stop on their radios had always exasperated Terry. On this occasion it infuriated him as he tried vainly to prevent them strafing a church parade of Portuguese troops at Dilolo.

'Stop. Get out of there, get out of there,' he remonstrated on the radio. But the Cubans had their transmit buttons down and 'there was just a stream of hysterical Spanish and it was too late'. In spite of American attempts to hush it up, the incident provoked an angry Portuguese complaint at the United Nations. Meanwhile, Denard's force quickly retreated back across the border after suffering five dead in a skirmish with Congolese troops. The general belief was that Denard mounted the cursory invasion as a token morale booster for Schramme. He probably also wanted to ensure that he would not have his throat slit when he ran into mercenary friends angry about being left in the lurch in Stanleyville when he encountered them later in bars in Europe.

If the foolhardy invasion attempt had done anything to boost Schramme's spirit, it quickly backfired by provoking an air attack on him. Terry returned to Albertville with the T-28s, where Weber and Mishou were both waiting. They were listening to propaganda radio transmissions by Schramme's force when Terry joined them. As he listened to the broadcast he heard a clock chiming in the background.

'There's only one clock in Bukavu like that,' he suddenly told the others. 'It's in the American consul general's house. That's where the buggers are broadcasting from.' Terry recognized the chime because he had been a frequent visitor at the house on trips to Bukavu, which had once been the Riviera of the Congo. Situated on the mountainous shore of the placid Lake Kivu some 1,500 metres above sea level, the town had been one of the most populace and prosperous of the colonial era. It was where the wealthy went to breathe fresh, highland air and escape the fetid heat of Leopoldville in the days *'avant'*, Belgian shorthand for 'before independence'. Although few of the town's elegant buildings had been damaged as a result of the war, they were mostly empty, giving the place what one writer at the time described as a 'sense of chilling desolation'. Schramme and his men shared the streets with stray dogs and abandoned vehicles.

'Okay,' said Weber in response to Terry's identification of the mutineers HQ. 'Now we mount an attack. Take the T-28s in there tomorrow and frighten the backsides off that lot. This waiting game's gone on for long enough.'

Early the following day Terry led a flight of four T-28s over Bukavu. As they roared across the rooftops Terry's radio crackled.

'English, English. What the hell is going on?' It was unmistakeably Libert's voice.

'It's me Léon,' said Terry. 'Listen, I've got orders to attack you.'

'Ah, Terry, why are you attacking us?' Libert pleaded.

'Listen Léon, I'm not attacking you personally but I have to attack somewhere, do you understand? I know you're in the consul general's house so where do you want me to attack?'

'Hit the brewery. We were there before but not now,' Libert suggested.

'Okay, but while we go and do that you'd better clear out of where you are because I'm coming back to put a few rockets through that house next, is that clear?'

'Yes, yes. Okay Terry, no problem, no problem,' Libert assured.

After attacking the deserted brewery, Terry and his fellow Cuban pilots returned to the other side of the town and swooped to strafe the consul general's house. Terry fired two rockets through it and then broke off the attack and ordered the planes home. The Cubans failed to follow his instructions. 'Once again they did me proud. They decided to attack the wrong country again and went off and shot up the bridge leading into Rwanda.' Much later in Leopoldville at an American Embassy function, Terry encountered the Bukavu consul general's wife.

'It was you, you bastard,' she remonstrated. 'You destroyed all of my grandmother's linen and all my child's toys. You had no right to do that.'

'Listen Madam, forgive me but I had every right. More to the point, I was following American orders. I'm sorry about your linen and toys but Schramme was using your house as a propaganda base,' he retorted. 'Now if you'll excuse me I have some friends to see.'

As the stand-off with Schramme continued, Terry's own frustration mounted. His letters to Joan convey his growing disenchantment with the Congo and the Congolese. 'Today they captured a European up there (Bukavu) but the soldiers ate him I think – we've asked them so many times not to do that.' Then he describes visiting the general in charge of mounting an ANC assault on Schramme before Red Cross negotiations could succeed in having him and his men evacuated to Rwanda.[5]

> He showed me his plan to destroy Bukavu. He asked me to stay with him as advisor throughout the campaign to fly the helicopter and control the troops. He offered me money, whiskey and even his best girl. Can you imagine General Westmoreland running a campaign along those lines? We flashed all that off to Washington when I got back. The hot wires are buzzing like crazy just now. I expect a heap of US-type advisors here to take my place. Anyway I'm certainly not going back up there. His plan is foolhardy and amateurish.

Later he wrote: 'I am attached to the Presidency but not uniquely, so that is the first problem. I wish a unique place.' However, the last thing he wanted was to be under Congolese control.

Mishou had indicated that once Schramme was dealt with, the CIA's involvement in the Congo would be minimal. Devlin and his entire team were going to Laos where a much bigger, even more secret war was under way to stem the flow of arms and men into Vietnam along the Ho Chi Minh trail. Mishou was probably going to be directing clandestine air operations from neighbouring Thailand. Terry would be on his own with Mobutu. In saying all this, Mishou reiterated what Terry had already heard from Weber about his having been cleared with London. Although Devlin claimed he could not remember whether this was done, he conceded that it would have been standard practice where intelligence was to be shared.[6] Terry would have his unique place but the problem was for how long? After two years in the Congo he knew that the only certainty was uncertainty. He started worrying about whether the job would last and what he would do if it did not. 'I'm still reading that book about how to make a million – it's not doing very much good though. I'm afraid I'm still not a millionaire,' he wrote to Joan.

While he was fretting like this in the middle of the continuing crisis over Schramme, he received a summons from Mobutu. The President wanted to be flown by helicopter to his steam yacht on the River Congo. Terry hopped on an American C130 transport for the thousand-mile trip to Leopoldville from Albertville to give Mobutu his first ever ride in a helicopter. 'He was like a child with a new toy,' he recounted to Joan. 'Madame Mobutu went next for ten minutes.' Terry ate breakfast with the President the following morning. He decided to make the most of the situation for as long as he could.

Notes

1 In his memoir Devlin stated that Denard was not part of the plot. However, according to eye-witness testimony from evacuees from Stanleyville, he openly admitted his involvement to twelve visiting journalists trapped in the city by the uprising.
2 Jerry Puren is reported to have arrived in Stanleyville by light aircraft from Angola on 5 July, pointing to the existence of external co-ordination and Portuguese complicity.
3 Mobutu had embarked on a programme of Africanization the previous year, changing the names of all the major towns. Leopoldville became Kinshasa; Stanleyville became Kisingani; Elizabethville became Lubumbashi. Later the country's name was changed to Zaire.
4 This provided a vital link between the copper belts of Katanga and the Angolan port of Lobito.
5 In the end the negotiations succeeded in achieving Schramme's withdrawal to Rwanda from where he and his men were eventually repatriated to their home countries.
6 Under a secret post-war 'five eyes pact' the major English speaking countries – America, Britain, Canada, Australia and New Zealand – agreed protocols for an intelligence sharing arrangement.

Chapter Nineteen
Too Dangerous to Stay

Being Mobutu's helicopter pilot while heading up the remnant of 22 Wing meant that Terry was constantly commuting between Leopoldville and the field stations at Albertville and Kamina. Invariably, these trips produced their surprises. Taking Mobutu's helicopter back to Kamina on one occasion, Terry landed en route to refuel. While he was doing this a scruffy-looking soldier walked up.

'Whose helicopter is this?' he demanded, leveling his automatic rifle at Terry.

'It's President Mobutu's,' Terry answered.

'Here I'm the president and Mobutu is nothing,' the soldier insisted threateningly.

'Okay, *Monsieur le President*, what would you like to do with your helicopter?' Terry responded without hesitation.

'I'd like to fly around my village to show everyone who's their boss,' he said quite seriously. With that, Terry put him in the Alouette, took off and flew him several times round the village at little more than rooftop height. The man grinned like a child, waved at everyone as they flew overhead and told Terry he was free to leave when they landed. 'I buggered off without waiting for him to change his mind.'

Quick thinking in a tight spot was one of Terry's strengths. It saved him from life- threatening situations and awkward ones too. On a visit to an ANC unit with Mobutu, he was waiting in the Beechcraft while the President inspected a company of soldiers.

My co-pilot was Pierre Berthe and I remember that there was an Air Brousse twin-engine charter plane and a FATAC DC-3 parked nearby. As Mobutu made his way between the ranks of men, an ANC officer approached us in the Beechcraft. He had a baboon on a lead bouncing along beside him, biting at his legs. Eventually, he arrived beside us. We had the cockpit doors open because it was so hot. The officer stood there with this bloody baboon jumping up and down beside him.

'The President says you must take this baboon in the aircraft with you,' he explained.

'I'm sorry Colonel, I'm afraid I can't do that,' Terry answered. 'I have strict orders to protect the President at all times. I cannot allow him to be in the aircraft with a dangerous animal.'

To Terry's surprise, the officer swivelled round without any argument and marched off with the baboon following, continuing to snap at his heels. Mobutu was still in the middle of the ranks as the poor man chased after him with the animal. Eventually, he caught up with the President and whispered in his ear. Terry saw Mobutu pull a face and stamp his foot and the man came scurrying back with the baboon in tow.

'The President insists that you take the baboon,' he announced firmly.

'I've told you I can't take it,' repeated Terry. 'You must tell the President that I'm very sorry but this animal is dangerous and the President cannot be exposed to risk for the sake of a monkey. He is more important to the country than a baboon. You should order the pilot from Air Brousse to take the animal.' The infuriated Colonel then trailed back to Mobutu with the leg-biting baboon and whispered in the President's ear again. Mobutu stamped his foot again. However, this time he sent the man and animal off towards the Air Brousse aircraft. Terry and his friend Berthe chuckled with mischievous delight.

Whenever he could, Terry wrote to Joan. He usually managed one or two letters every week, documenting events in the country and his own exploits. Many of the letters describe the country's rapid economic collapse as Mobutu ramped up Belgian hatred and nationalized the major mining operations.

All the Europeans are leaving – I have never seen such an exodus, with good reason too … Food is scarce and very expensive when available. The restaurants are prohibitive … Mobutu is going to flood the market here with goods to combat rising prices. God knows where he's going to get the goodies from and who is going to pay for them in the first place … There are robberies going on all the time, mostly hold-ups in the street for girls' handbags. People are getting desperate for lack of food and money and they are collecting flying termites to eat. When I get served those I'll call it a halt.

In lighter moments he described going on game-hunting expeditions 'about the last bastion of my experience I've yet to fulfil' and braving crocodiles to dive in Lake Tanganyika, 'mind you, I'm so skinny now no self-respecting croc would be interested anyway.'

He concluded an account of one hair-raising adventure with the supreme understatement, 'so the day was not without interest'. Early one morning Terry left Leopoldville in the President's Alouette heading back to Kamina. Pelle Ornas, his WIGMO-employed Swedish engineer, accompanied him. They planned to land and refuel twice on the marathon eight-hour, thousand-mile flight. At each stop the helicopter would be at the extreme limit of its three hundred-mile range. Terry had put extra cushions on the seats because he knew they would have sore backsides by the time they reached Kamina. He also took the precaution of carrying a two hundred-litre drum of spare fuel. As always in the Congo, navigation was by compass and eyeballing the land below for identifiable features. Their first scheduled refuelling stop was to be at Kikwit, a provincial capital about two hundred miles east of Leopoldville. When their flying time and fuel gauge told Terry that Kikwit should be looming into view, all that stretched out below was the interminable, featureless jungle canopy. Terry knew immediately they were in serious trouble and he anxiously searched the endless carpet of treetops for any recognizable landmark.

Eventually, the fuel-gauge's red warning light started blinking ominously. Now scanning the landscape with added urgency, Terry eventually identified the River Kasai. He concluded that they were at least a hundred miles north-east of where they should have been with no hope then of making it to Kikwit without refuelling. The explanation was that their gyro compass was malfunctioning and they had been flying way off course. The most worrying consequence was that they were over an area where some of Mulele's rebel enclaves were known to be holding out. Spying a large sandbank in the centre of the Kasai, where he felt sure they would be secure from any attack, Terry decided to land and refuel from the spare drum. With luck, he thought, they could then reach Kikwit. However, not knowing exactly where they were and without the help of the compass, Terry knew this was not going to be easy. He headed off in what he thought was the right direction but when the fuel warning light started blinking again he began looking for another likely landing place.

He spotted what he thought might be a mission station with a rough clearing nearby on a plateau overlooking a deep, heavily forested valley.

It was the only place I could see where we could land safely and I decided to put down and wait for the cavalry. We were so overdue I knew that they'd start looking for us. Anyway, I called base on the radio and asked for a fuel drop giving them my best estimate of where we were. The truth is, by then I didn't have a clue.

His instincts told him to expect the worse when they touched down and nobody appeared. 'Normally when you landed a helicopter where the people were friendly they swarmed out from behind every tree and bush.' He and Pelle climbed out of the aircraft and tied down the rotors. They were finishing when a lone man appeared at the edge of the clearing. 'He made an extraordinary sight dressed immaculately in a collar and tie and suit in the middle of the jungle.'

'What are you doing here?' he asked Terry after approaching the Alouette.

'We're taking the President's helicopter to Kamina and we've run out of fuel. They're sending an aircraft with some for us now,' Terry answered.

'Come and sit here while you wait,' the man insisted, pointing to a shady clearing under a large tree. 'My people will bring food and drink and we can talk.'

As Terry and the blue-eyed, blond-haired Swede nervously followed the suited man several villagers emerged from the trees carrying some rickety, old deck chairs and a makeshift table. Their host motioned for the two airmen to sit down. Someone produced a fresh pineapple and bottles of home-brewed rice wine.

'I think we've been invited to lunch,' Terry joked to Pelle. The slightly built Swede nodded unhappily as one of the village men hacked the pineapple into large chunks with a few deft strokes of a fearfully sharp machete and the man in the suit began pouring the wine into filthy chipped, white enamel mugs. But before the feast could begin, Terry recognized the distant drone of a DC-4 approaching. He had been told on the radio that the American Embassy aircraft was ferrying the entire foreign diplomatic corps to Elizabethville for a conference. The pilot was a good friend and offered to look for the missing Alouette on his way southward. He made a low pass over the plateau and waggled his wings to indicate that he had spotted the helicopter. Terry raced to the radio as the aircraft made a long turn to swoop back overhead. As it approached along the valley a burst of machine gun fire crackled not more than half a mile away.

'Christ, they're shooting at him,' Terry yelled to Pelle, who was already running towards the helicopter, hotly pursued by the man in the suit. 'Come on, we've got to get the hell out of here.'

'That's not gunfire, that's the plane's engine backfiring,' insisted the man in the suit.

'My friend, for an African in the middle of the jungle dressed in a suit and tie, you're very well informed about aircraft engines. But that's gunfire and we're leaving,' retorted Terry, climbing quickly into his seat while Pelle released the rotor blades.

Starting the Alouette's jet engine required a particular sequence on a new-fangled, revolutionary computer-like control panel. In his anxiety and haste, Terry fumbled it. His battery was low and he worried that the power would cut out before he could complete the second start sequence. But the engine burst into life and the rotor started whirling as Pelle scrambled to get on board. By then two or three other men had joined the man in the suit. They surged towards Pelle. Three of them grabbed hold of his legs and started trying to pull him out of the aircraft.

'Lift off Terry. Just go,' he yelled as he gripped the doorframe and tried kicking his legs. The men tightened their grips in response. As the Alouette became airborne they were lifted off the ground, hanging from Pelle's legs. First one fell and then another and then, when they were about twenty feet up, the man in the suit. Pelle has never forgotten the experience. 'If you'd never shat your pants before, you would have that day.' It remains the most scary moment of Terry's life.

As they flew off the red fuel-gauge warning light flashed urgently. Terry knew they were going to have to put down again quickly or face the prospect of a crash-landing. He wanted to get as far away from the scene of the shooting as he could but not so far that the aircraft being sent out with spare fuel would not find him. After a few minutes he found a valley where the forest gave way to swathes of tall elephant grass. Very gently he lowered the Alouette. The thick grass bent and parted under the force of the down draught as the aircraft neared the ground. Terry grabbed his 9mm pistol as he and Pelle left the helicopter to hide nearby. 'We stayed there with our hearts pounding for a long time. Then this C-46 flew over and came back low to drop a drum of fuel.' It exploded when it hit the ground. Terry ran to the helicopter and radioed the Cuban pilot.

'Look, it's no good dropping full drums. They'll all burst. You need to take a third of the fuel out and try again or you're wasting your time,' he told him. Later the aircraft returned and successfully dropped two half-full drums. They rolled down a steep slope, leaving Terry and Pelle to manhandle them uphill and then hand pump as much fuel as they could manage in their exhausted state.

'That's going to have to do. Let's get out of here,' Terry finally said to Pelle. Twenty minutes afterwards they landed in Kikwit.

Later, back in Leopoldville, Terry met the American pilot of the DC-4.

'God, am I glad to see you,' he beamed at Terry. 'Those bastards shot the shit out of one of my engines.'

'Well thanks for showing up when you did. Any later and I don't think we'd have got out,' Terry acknowledged.

Shortly afterwards Terry picked up Mobutu to fly him to his yacht. As they headed out over Stanley Pool towards the vessel, Terry recounted the incident involving the compass failure and the last-minute escape from what was clearly one of Mulele's rebel enclaves.

'My friend, those people weren't inviting you for lunch,' grinned Mobutu. 'They were inviting you to be lunch.' Then he roared with laughter. But Terry knew he meant it.

Terry had recognized the first signs of what would later become Mobutu's notorious despotism very early on, when he tested the Learjet that the President considered buying for himself shortly after his coup. Subsequently, as his helicopter pilot, Terry learned something about what drove Mobutu's lust for ostentatious wealth. The President decided to take his steam yacht on a cruise up the Congo River from Stanley Pool to Stanleyville. Terry was required to accompany him with the Alouette III parked on the yacht's afterdeck. Inevitably, Dr Close was on board as well. Mobutu's wife, Marie Antoinette, and their children were also present with some visiting dignitaries, who included Egyptian president Abdul Nasser's daughter. Terry was awed by the extravagant luxury of everything on board. Even the tooth mug in his deluxe cabin was Baccarat crystal glass. Champagne flowed freely and there were three choices of wine for dinner every evening. The stewards were all recruited from the first-class section of *Maritime Belge*. As Terry wrote to Joan, the trip was 'an absolute must for the old colonialists and I suppose we're doing it now in equal style'. There was certainly no hint of concern for the wretched poverty of the people who gawped from the riverbanks.

One evening Terry was on the bridge talking with Close when Mobutu joined them. The conversation turned to Operation *Survival*. Close reported on some of the most recent suffering he had witnessed and then bravely asked Mobutu a simple question.

'*Mon President*,' he said, 'how can you justify going up here in your big yacht when the people, your people, all along the banks have nothing?' Mobutu looked at him and sighed deeply. He looked exasperated rather than angry.

'You still have so much to learn about Africa my friend,' he answered. 'If someone came behind me with a bigger boat and more gold, he would be president. That's why I'm doing what I'm doing.' Mobutu understood only too well that the Congo was full of men waiting to take his place. He surrounded himself with acolytes and rewarded them with wealth to ensure their loyalty.

One of these men was Bobozo, the bullying army chief. He resented anyone being close to Mobutu.

'I see you're still with us,' he remarked to Terry one day. 'You must be careful. Men like you who spend too long in the Congo always die here. If you stay you will die here too.'

'Well, I've no intention of doing that but it would be very rude of me to leave just now. I've got an air force to prepare for you,' Terry answered. By then he was immersed in a pilot training programme at Kamina. Apart from Congolese candidates he was also instructing a small group of Ghanaians at Mobutu's request. One of them was a man named Obeng. By one of those quirks of fate, being Obeng's instructor would save Terry from a tricky predicament less than a year later.

With December coming to an end, Terry was given a month's leave. He arranged for Joan to fly out so that they could go on holiday together. After going to South Africa and staying with Brannon and his family, they flew to Spain. Terry had bought a small apartment in Fuengirola on the Costa Blanca with the proceeds of his bonus for going back to lead the air group against Schramme. He completed the transaction by post and had never seen the place but was pleasantly surprised by what he found. By the end of the holiday he was talking of inviting Joan to join him in Leopoldville. He told her that he was sure Dr Close could find a role for her there. She was entranced by her first taste of Africa, although Terry warned her that the Congo would be nothing like South Africa. She still had no idea that he was married with two children back in England.

When Joan flew home to Montreal, Terry returned to Leopoldville. Terry One was at Ndjili to meet him. He had arranged to take her on holiday to South Africa as well. Terry was now so deeply into his double life that he simply did not know how to extricate himself. He felt unerringly in love with Joan but did not have the courage to tell Terry One. 'I was getting my friends to tell me which one I should marry' is how he jokingly explains his duplicity. Yet the truth is that his lifelong fear of confrontation was haunting him again. He kept telling himself that something would happen to sort it all out. That was how he dealt with personal problems. He was having the same conversation with himself about not writing to his mother. After all, he had been 'cleared all the way' so there was no risk in breaking his cover any more. Even if he did not plan to return to England, there was really nothing to stop him writing home. However, he convinced himself that he would cause even more hurt by admitting that he was alive than by maintaining the charade of being drowned. The extraordinary thing is that even when the truth finally came out, all the people affected would forgive him. They all looked beyond his flaws to the big-hearted, charming gentleman warrior who Dr Close remembers.

The long-suffering Brannon family hosted the two Terrys at their Cape Town house. Brannon was still under the impression that Terry's first wife and children had died in an air crash. However, he never spoke a word about it to Joan or Terry One, who had heard the story in Leopoldville, although not from Terry. She never mentioned the subject to him either. When she arrived back in Leopoldville with Terry, he was arrested at the airport. He just had time to give her the baggage tags and ask her to let Weber or Mishou know what had happened before being hauled away to the prison at Kokolo. On arrival there he was dragged in front of an officer who was examining his passport studiously.

'What's this all about?' he demanded. The officer ignored him. Terry decided to invoke the fear-of-wrath-from-above technique again.

'You realize, of course, that I'm the personal pilot of President Mobutu,' he said.

'Oh, you're a liar,' the officer replied.

'Call him. You're the big boss, give him a call. Surely you're not afraid to do that?' Terry taunted. The officer leaned across his desk and picked up the telephone. Eventually he was put through to one of Mobutu's aides. Terry could hear the man confirming that he was indeed the President's pilot and ordering his immediate release.

'Okay. You can go,' the officer said brusquely handing him his passport.

Terry went straight to the American Embassy and found Johnson.

'Look, I think you're time here's up,' the CIA paramilitary chief told him. 'There's somebody in the Congolese hierarchy who's out to get you and frankly there's not much we can do to protect you now. I suggest you call it a day.'

'That clown Bobozo warned me that I'd die here if I overstayed my welcome, so I guess I'd better go,' Terry answered. He had no idea who his particular enemy was but supposed it was one of the new Congolese air force officers who resented his proximity to Mobutu. They had disposed of their Turkish boss Eraybar by shooting him in a roadside ambush and Terry had no intention of suffering the same fate. He sent a telegram to Joan saying that he was on his way to Montreal. However, instead of flying straight to Canada he risked returning to England first.

The immigration officer did not look at him twice when he arrived at London's Heathrow Airport. Relieved, he checked into a luxury room at the Hilton Hotel in Park Lane, flush with a bonus from Mobutu and his CIA pay off. 'I was tempted to call my mother but considering all the heartache I knew I must have caused I eventually decided against it.' That evening he went to the Playboy Club. As he was leaving he bumped into one of his former RAF colleagues from Tern Hill on the stairs.

'Hi Terry, you're looking well,' the RAF man said.

'Smithy isn't it?' said Terry. 'I'd love to buy you a beer but I'm just leaving. Good to see you again.'

Convinced that Smith would report the sighting, Terry brought forward his departure and flew out to Montreal via New York first thing the following day. 'I remember flying into New York and looking down at the Statue of Liberty and thinking: 'You've got no job; you've got no prospects; what the hell are you going to do now?'

Chapter Twenty
Destination Calabar

Living with Joan in Montreal, Terry's moods fluctuated from characteristic ebullience to sullen withdrawal. He was fretting about where his next pay cheque was going to come from. As usual he bottled up his anxiety, refusing to share his thoughts with Joan. Fortunately, her training as an occupational therapist enabled her to accommodate his ups and downs with equanimity. All the same, however much she tried she could never encourage him to reveal his inner feelings to her. As the gloomy winter months dragged on Terry grew increasingly morose. He started a course to obtain a commercial helicopter air transport licence in the hope of landing a job in Canada but he was suffering severe depression after the real challenges and excitement of the Congo. Without Joan's reassuring presence there is no telling what he may have done. At one of his lowest moments he even considered returning to the UK and going cap in hand to the RAF. Then, out of the blue, in early March a life-saving telegram arrived from Ares Klootwyk. It read: 'PLEASE COME IMMEDIATELY STOP EXPENSES WILL BE REIMBURSED STOP NIGERIAN GOVERNMENT NEEDS YOU TAKE OVER HELICOPTER SQUADRON STOP ARES.' Klootwyk and several more of Terry's old Congo comrades, including Charlie Vivier, Pierre Berthe and Henry Laurent, had gone to Nigeria as mercenary pilots soon after the start of the brutal civil war against breakaway Biafra.[1] Just like the chance meeting at Tern Hill that led Terry to WIGMO, the telegram from Klootwyk would change everything and open an extraordinary new chapter of his secret life.

The summons could not have come at a more crucial moment. Terry had been hoping to hear from Mishou or Weber calling him to Laos, where Devlin and almost his entire CIA team from the Congo were then heavily engaged in the so-called 'Secret War'.[2] He felt that he had done enough to prove himself to them and the CIA prior to his abrupt exit from Leopoldville. Weber had told him that he would try and get him into Air America[3] if he possibly could. However, the subsequent lack of any contact understandably left him feeling abandoned. His sense of rejection was heightened by the conviction that in spite of the promise that he had been 'cleared all the way' he had, in fact, burnt his bridges by faking his death. All this made the telegram from Klootwyk as ecstatically welcome as winning the lottery. Terry was packed and ready to go before Joan returned from work. 'I didn't need a second invitation. I flew out with Air France the next day.' Before leaving, he promised Joan that he would send for her as soon as he settled in. By then, a well-orchestrated public relations campaign highlighting the plight of Biafran refugees was just beginning to arouse worldwide sympathy for the breakaway regime. In the face of this, Joan had mixed feelings about Terry working for the Nigerian Federal Military Government (FMG) against the beleaguered Biafrans but she wanted to be with him and she wanted to go to Africa, so she agreed.

Charlie Vivier was at the airport at Ikeja near Lagos to meet Terry when he arrived. He and Klootwyk were then flying Russian-built MiGs supplied to the FMG by the Egyptians. They were the first Westerners to do so with Soviet approval in the midst of the Cold War.[4] Vivier was the chief mercenary pilot in the embryonic Nigerian Air Force (NAF). The odious Colonel Peters, who, after quitting the Congo, briefly succeeded in finding himself a new role as a recruiting agent in Africa's newest conflict, had hired him and the other Congo veterans.[5] There was to be no clandestine CIA air force in this war but, nevertheless, mercenary pilots would play a significant role on both sides.

Vivier welcomed Terry effusively. 'Bloody good to have you back, man,' he said, shaking his hand vigorously. 'This lot have got as much idea about flying as the Congolese but they want you to train some of their chaps on some old Sikorsky S-55 choppers they've got. When was the last time you flew one of them?'[6]

'Never, Charlie,' answered Terry laconically. 'But I don't suppose that'll be too much of a problem.'

Vivier drove him to the nearby *Ikeja Arms Hotel* where all the NAF's mercenary pilots were then billeted. He dumped his bags, quickly washed and changed and then went back to the airport with Vivier. They drew up alongside one of the hangars where a row of five Sikorsky S-55s was neatly lined up under heavy tarpaulin covers. The ancient aircraft were in the sole care of a former Royal Navy engineer named Cliff 'Yorkie' Grimes, who Vivier then introduced.

'Can any of these old heaps actually fly?' Terry asked Grimes as he surveyed the cocooned aircraft.

'I think we can probably get one of them going,' replied the phlegmatic Grimes.

'That's good, because your new boss wants you to give a demo flight in an aerobatic display later today,' laughed Vivier, looking at Terry. He was serious. The air force chief was the brother of Lieutenant Colonel Yakuba Gowon, the head of Nigeria's FMG. He was due to give a demonstration flight in a Czech-built L-29 Delfin jet fighter and wanted Terry to show off one of the S-55s.

> At the third attempt Grimes and I managed to get one of them started. I gingerly air taxied it about until I got the feel of it, then flew it a short distance, did a circuit and a couple of tender auto-rotations at the end of the runway and then landed, relieved that it stayed in one piece.

Accompanied by Vivier, Terry went to meet the air force chief, who handed him a letter confirming his appointment as the NAF's chief helicopter and twin-engine, fixed-wing flying instructor. Terry was elated to be working again. He was to be paid $1,000[7] a month and have a rank equivalent to that of a squadron leader. With Grimes's help, he soon ensured that all the helicopters were operational again and then began familiarization flights. He wanted to get to know the machines and the country.

By the beginning of May, Terry had the training programme in full swing. 'I used to take the choppers to a small clearing by a nearby beach where I was well out of the way of the civilian traffic.' However, he quickly encountered the same lack of discipline and frustration that was all too familiar from the Congo.

> The course was a text-book copy of what I'd been doing at Tern Hill, basically the RAF Central Flying School training programme right down the line to the lectures. I had six pilot students who turned up when they wanted to. Sometimes they didn't bother to show up at all. In the end I managed to get some of them to go solo but god knows what happened to them after that.

Joan arrived to join him at the end of June. They moved into an apartment in one of Lagos's smarter suburbs and joined the swanky Lagos Country Club. As Joan recalls it, life was 'very social with gatherings of friends at the apartment or at a hotel or restaurant most nights'. She found a job working at the military hospital rehabilitation centre in Lagos and travelled around the country visiting casualties while soothing Terry's mounting frustrations over doing circuits with unwilling pupils. He needed a new challenge but resisted overtures from his Congo pals to join them flying combat sorties in the MiGs.

By then the war had reached a virtual stalemate with Biafra blockaded. Haunting images of refugees, especially children bloated with kwashiorkor, fuelled a mounting international outcry over the resulting humanitarian crisis. The International Committee of the Red Cross (ICRC) and separate church groups, which later co-operated under the title Joint Church Aid, began an emergency airlift from the islands of Fernando Pö and São Tomé[8] in the Gulf of Guinea. Every night under cover of darkness their aircraft ran the gauntlet to an improvised airstrip at Uli in Biafra, heavily laden with desperately needed medical and food supplies. The mercy flights went on for over a year and became the largest airlift since the Soviet blockade of Berlin in the aftermath of the Second World War.[9] Terry knew that his friends had been ordered to interdict the flights but were actually hoodwinking their NAF paymasters with what amounted to sham intercepts and attacks. They often joked about it over drinks. Even so, he wanted no part of that game.

After seven months in Lagos without a break, Terry decided it was time to take some leave. His initial contract was coming to an end in any case. He made arrangements to take off the whole of October so that he and Joan could include a visit to the Olympic Games in Mexico. However, a couple of weeks before he was due to fly out, he encountered an energetic, nattily dressed and smooth-talking American named Robert Robards at Ikeja. This would be another chance meeting with dramatic consequences. Robards was supervising the unloading of two white-painted Sikorsky H-19s with United Nations Children's Fund (UNICEF) markings from a giant C-97 'Guppy' cargo aircraft of the kind then normally used to transport Saturn rocket sections. They had just been flown in from San Francisco. In conversation it transpired that Robards was a helicopter charter entrepreneur from Dansville, New York, who had been contracted by UNICEF to operate an emergency helicopter airlift out of the coastal town of Calabar in the extreme south-eastern corner of Nigeria. An estimated 250,000 refugees were crowded into the humid mangrove swamps and forests of the surrounding Cross River Delta. In what was to be the first American team to join the relief effort, Robards had assembled a group of eight volunteers. They included a salesman from the *New Yorker* magazine, a financial analyst from General Dynamics, a United Airlines pilot and a mechanic who had built his own helicopter aged sixteen. All had responded to a convincing heart-felt appeal by thirty-five-year-old Robards on a late night television chat show.

'Well, I'm familiar with the route to Calabar and know the people down there,' volunteered Terry. 'I'd be happy to come along if that would be any help.' Robards jumped at his offer. 'I instinctively knew he would. He was standing there in his fancy suit looking lost and confused with no idea what to do next.'

'That'd be great. You can fly with Brandt in the lead chopper.'

Former US Navy pilot and financial analyst Brandt Beck greeted Terry enthusiastically, no doubt glad to have his company for the six-hour flight across unfamiliar terrain. With Terry navigating from the co-pilot's seat, they led the way to the staging post where they were to refuel for the remainder of the trip. The H-19 had the same engine as the S-55 but different controls, including a device for making the fuel mixture leaner. Terry noticed that Beck seemed to be running the engine too rich once they were in flight.

'Look, you're the pilot and they're your aircraft, but you're using a lot of fuel and I don't think you'll be doing the engine much good running it this rich,' he remarked to Beck.

'Well, I don't know. It seems okay to me,' he replied.

After arriving at the staging post they were air taxiing towards the control tower when the helicopter's engine abruptly cut out. Beck reacted too slowly and the aircraft, still a few feet above the ground, dropped onto the tarmac like a deadweight. The undercarriage came up through the floor and it rolled onto its right side in a crumpled mess. Terry and Beck emerged unscathed but it was an inauspicious start to the relief effort and Robards was understandably furious over the loss of one of his machines. 'The truth is that he'd bought the choppers on the cheap from a dealer in Texas and they were in a shocking state. The floor of the one we were flying in had been rotted by spilled battery acid.' The following day Robards went out to survey the wreckage, followed by Terry and the other members of his team. The machine was a write-off. Robards reacted by grabbing a screwdriver and feverishly punching a hole through the oil filter.

'It's obviously been shot at,' he announced with a conspiratorial grin.

'Not here. You'll be in big shit if you try to claim that,' responded Terry.

Media interest in the incident was fuelled by Robards' outrageous assertion that the helicopter had been fired on by Nigerian troops. Later he quietly dropped an audacious attempt to claim compensation from the

FMG when an investigation correctly attributed the accident to fuel starvation.

The affair should have set alarm bells ringing about the sort of opportunist and unscrupulous character that Robards really was. Instead, what Terry saw was the potential to get involved in the relief operation, something that really appealed to him. Consequently, he did everything he could to make a favourable impression. It clearly worked. Six weeks later, when Terry was in New York about to board a flight back to Nigeria after his holiday in Mexico, he received an urgent message from Robards asking him to go to the UN building.

> I don't know how he tracked me down but he did. I was put in a chopper at JFK, flown to downtown Manhattan and then driven to a top-notch hotel next door to the UN headquarters. Later I was taken to a big building alongside the UN, known affectionately by UN people as 'the heap', and asked if I would take charge of running the UNICEF helicopter relief operation in Calabar.

He was told that Robards had managed to procure five Sikorsky H-34s[10] from the Israeli military. Would he please put together crews and go to Tel Aviv to complete the transaction and then fly the aircraft to Calabar and lead the enlarged mission?

Terry could scarcely believe what he was being asked to do. The Arab–Israeli Six Day War had ended only months earlier. How was he going to deliver five Israeli helicopters across Arab northern Africa? And even if he could plan a route avoiding potentially hostile airspace, where was he going to find pilots and engineers for such a crazy undertaking? He soon discovered that Robards was already well ahead with planning for the operation. An ambitious flight plan was in the process of being cleared with relevant governments through the UN. It involved following the European coast westwards along the Mediterranean and then skirting the West African coast southwards, before tracking across the Sahara Desert to Nigeria. Also, experienced helicopter pilots who had volunteered for the mission in response to advertisements in American newspapers were waiting to be interviewed. What Terry then had to do was make it happen and take charge of the whole operation when he arrived in Calabar.

He started by selecting the pilots. As he whittled down the shortlist of applicants he learned that only two helicopters were going to be available rather than the original five. The volunteers who made the final cut were Bob Billings, a United Airlines pilot awaiting his turn for promotion to the co-pilot's seat, and Joe McGinity, a senior executive with Chase

Manhattan Bank in search of excitement. They were both former US Navy men with direct experience of flying H-34s. One of the secretaries in the UN building put forward her husband Jerry Gauntlett, an ex-RAF mechanic, for the role of engineer. With the team complete, Terry then focussed on checking and amending the flight plan. By the standards of the day it was an extremely hazardous undertaking, entailing numerous long legs of up to four hours of non-stop flying – about double what was normal – for much of the 4,500-mile journey. Without any back-up and the absence of anybody monitoring their progress, they would literally be on their own.

By early November, Terry was satisfied that everything was in order. He left for Tel Aviv, flying first class with TWA. Joan, who had arrived in New York to join him, followed on an El Al flight with Billings, McGinity and Gauntlett a few days later and they all settled into the *Hilton Hotel* in the Israeli capital. After a week of familiarization and test flights, Terry agreed to take possession of the two aircraft, insisting first that every sign of their Israeli origin was removed. Then, on 21 November, they left Tel Aviv for Rhodes. For this first leg, Gauntlett accompanied Terry with Joan. Billings flew the other aircraft with McGinity as co-pilot. They carried extra fuel tanks for the long flight but when Billings switched across to them, he found to his consternation that there was no feed. He radioed Terry, who immediately decided to divert to the then British island of Cyprus. Terry had originally planned to avoid landing there at all costs because of the large RAF base on the island. They dropped to sea level and raced across the wave tops to provide the aircraft with additional lift and eke out the little fuel Billings had left. Once safely on the ground in Larnaca, Billings sensed that Terry was extremely uncomfortable and anxious to get away, although he had no idea why.

> I wouldn't find out until years later just how much of a risk Terry had taken in landing there. As it happened the air force people couldn't have been more helpful. We sorted out the problem on my aircraft, refuelled and carried on to Rhodes.

The next leg to Athens brought another surprise for Billings. Towards the end of it they were flying at night after a later-than-planned start when the gyro providing his artificial horizon malfunctioned. 'Terry was leading and I was flying in loose formation on his lights when I realized that I was steadily losing altitude.' He called Terry.

'What's your altitude?' he asked.

'I'm steady at 10,000 feet,' came the answer.

'Well, I'm flying on your wing and I'm descending at 300 feet a minute,' Billings told him. He then understood that he must have lost his horizon and was flying below Terry while thinking he was level with him. Terry sympathized with his predicament. 'It's a really hairy feeling. Without a horizon you're completely disoriented and don't know which way is up or down. Bob did a great job of sticking with me and getting down safely.' By this stage, however, McGinity had decided that he had already experienced more excitement than he had bargained for when he volunteered to leave behind the comfort and security of his leather-padded Wall Street desk. He told Terry that he would only continue as far as Rome, where he wanted to visit the Vatican before going home. Joan also left them there in order to visit family in the UK.

Good luck was an uncannily repetitive feature of Terry's life. The next stop after Rome was Marseilles. Without realizing it, Terry flew beyond the main civilian airport and landed at an adjacent military base, which turned out to be the main servicing station for Aviation Sud, which built H-34s under licence.

We walked into this hangar that was teeming with mechanics and dripping with spares for aircraft like ours. It was a complete godsend. I arranged to have both our choppers fully serviced while we went off for three days' R and R. When we returned they were good as new and after paying the bill with a UN cheque, we went on our way.

After stopping briefly in Malaga for more R and R at Terry's apartment at nearby Fuengirola, they started the long haul down the West African coast. They hopped successively from Casablanca to Agadir in Morroco, and then on to El Ayun, Villa Cisneros and Nouhadhibou in Western Sahara, before turning inland to head across the desert. Flying mile after mile over blistering sand, they made stopovers at Kaedi in Mauretania, Bamako in Mali and then Bobo Dioulasso in Upper Volta, all without incident. Gauntlett alternated between accompanying Terry on some legs and Billings on others.

On 4 December, almost two weeks after leaving Tel Aviv, they flew across the border into Ghana and approached the northern town of Tamale to refuel. Terry was surprised when he called the control tower and, instead of being greeted with the usual welcoming recognition, received a blunt refusal for permission to land.

I said, look, we're UN helicopters going to Nigeria to do relief work and we're coming in. You should have full details because our flight's been cleared through the UN. But all I got back was, 'No, no, it's not possible, you do not have permission.' So I said we were coming in anyway.

Immediately after landing, Terry, Billings and Gauntlett set about the customary job of greasing the rotor heads when jeeps laden with police and armed soldiers skidded to a halt beside them. The soldiers surrounded both aircraft while the policeman in charge approached Terry.

His uniform was immaculate, like something out of a Hollywood film set, and so were his English and manners. I found this reassuring after the sort of thuggish behaviour I was used to in the Congo.

'Good afternoon, sir. Would you mind coming with me please?' the police officer asked Terry.

'Certainly officer, I'd be glad to. I'm sure I can explain everything to your satisfaction,' he replied.

After completing a lengthy written report, Terry was politely informed that he and the others would be placed under house arrest while further investigations were made. They were taken to an officer's quarters under armed escort.

Gauntlett was shitting himself but, in fact, we were treated very courteously. Even so, there were eight guards posted on the room so there was no mistaking we were prisoners and not going anywhere fast.

'Are you here to stop us escaping or to protect us,' Terry joked to the young sergeant in charge, who smiled wanly. 'Would you mind very much asking the officer of the day if I could have a word?' he added. He had suddenly had a brainwave. One of the men he trained in the Congo was the Ghanaian named Obeng. It was a long shot, but if he was still in the air force, he just might be able to help clear things up and get them released.

The officer of the day duly arrived to see Terry as requested.

'I understand that you'd like to have a word,' he said.

'Yes, as a matter of fact I would just like to mention that not so long ago when I was working in the Congo I trained one of your air force officers to fly a helicopter. Look, I have his name here in my flight log,' he said, pointing to the relevant entry.

'My God, he's our air force commander in chief,' observed the startled young OOD.

'Well, perhaps you would be kind enough to telephone him with my compliments,' suggested Terry.

'Yes sir, of course, right away,' agreed the young officer. Half an hour later he was back.

'Sir, he remembers you very well,' he confirmed. 'He's instructed us that you and your men are to join us in the officers' mess tonight. We have cold beer and we also have a film: *Lawrence of Arabia*.' As he said it, Terry roared with laughter.

'We've just flown halfway across the Sahara and now you're going to show us *Lawrence of Arabia*. I hope that beer's really cold,' he grinned.

The following morning Terry was told that he was to take the helicopters to Accra where Obeng would be delighted to see him again. They flew to the Ghanaian capital accompanied by armed guards who escorted them to the air force headquarters building on arrival. The floor had obviously just been repainted. Obeng was waiting to greet Terry in his office.

'Welcome to Ghana, my friend,' he announced proffering his outstretched hand.

'Thank you, but you really didn't need to paint the floor for me,' Terry replied. Obeng laughed.

'We couldn't find a red carpet,' he quipped, adding, 'look, I'm sorry about what's happened. There's obviously been a breakdown in communication from our people at the UN. Anyway, you're free to continue to Nigeria.'

The arrival of the two helicopters with their armed escort had created quite a stir. When Terry went back outside he found an RAF officer named Squadron Leader Price standing on the tarmac surveying the hubbub. Price, who was tall, slim and slightly balding with a long face, knew Terry from the Far East and Tern Hill. They recognized each other immediately. 'He and I never did get on. Anyway, there he was larger than life, the British air attaché in Ghana. As soon as he spotted me he came striding over.'

'Hello Peet, you seem to have lost weight,' Price sneered.

'Yes, it must be all this good living I'm enjoying,' flashed back Terry. 'Now, if you'll excuse me, I really must be going. I'm delivering these helicopters for the UN and we're running late.' Price, clearly taken aback, nodded without saying another word. Terry waved nonchalantly and climbed aboard his H-34. 'I left him standing there, mouth agape and off we flew to Lagos and then on to Calabar.'

Price immediately reported his sighting of Terry to the RAF high command. Even if they did not know for certain where he was prior to this, they undoubtedly knew then. A loose minute in Terry's service records written by a Squadron Leader G G Callaghan confirms that in February 1968 an unidentified Ghanaian air force officer, almost certainly Obeng, had reported meeting Terry in the Congo to the British High Commission in Accra. According to Callaghan, the British defence advisor there at the time had undertaken to do all he could to verify the accuracy of this report. In fact, a quick telephone call to the British Embassy in Kinshasa would have been all that was required. However, this simple procedure was not followed. In another loose minute dated 10 December 1968, shortly after Terry's sighting by Price, Callaghan reported:

> I have just received a reliable report through diplomatic channels that Flt Lt Peet is presently employed flying a helicopter on operations for UNICEF in Nigeria. Evidently he had to land at Accra where reasonably positive identification was made and where the United Nations Resident confirmed that he was on a properly sponsored mission.

If the RAF had seriously wanted him back for desertion at that point, it would have been easy enough to alert the British High Commission in Lagos. With a little diplomatic pressure it would then not have taken much to have Terry returned to the UK to stand trial. In the event, no attempt was made to contact him, let alone apprehend him. Nor was his family informed that the RAF then knew that he was definitely alive and working in Nigeria.

Notes

1   The Nigerian Civil War, also known as the Biafran War, had its roots in the ethnic and religious divisions of the Federation of Nigeria after independence from Britain in 1960. In the aftermath of an election riddled with fraud and a failed coup attempt in 1965, the civilian government was replaced by military rule. In July 1966 the predominantly Muslim north staged a counter coup placing Lt Col Yakuba Gowon in power. Subsequent massacres of Christians led to the secession of the eastern region as the Republic of Biafra in May 1967 under Col Odumegwu Ojukwu. Gowon's Federal Military Government launched the war against Biafra two months later. The conflict continued until 1970 and claimed an estimated 1.5 million lives. Britain and the USA backed the FMG but maintained an arms embargo (only partial in Britain's case) forcing the FMG to turn to the Soviet bloc for aircraft and heavy armaments and leading to an ironic, unholy alliance in the midst of the Cold War. France and Portugal supported the Biafran cause, covertly assisting to supply arms and munitions.

2   A covert US campaign in pursuit of the 'Domino Theory' to prevent Laos falling to the communists and to deny supplies to the Viet Cong in Vietnam along the Ho Chi Minh trail.

3   A CIA owned and operated air force founded to support covert operations in Southeast Asia between 1950 and 1976. Its aircraft were primarily civilian transports, including a substantial helicopter fleet. All of its pilots were American, usually ex-military personnel.

4   In fact, Klootwyk and another South African mercenary pilot named Jimmy Webb had secretly trained on the Nigerian MiG 17s without Russian approval. Until then the MiGs were flown exclusively by Egyptian pilots but they proved totally ineffective.

5   Peters was involved in various ventures after his role in the Nigerian civil war, notably a company called Coastal Surveys. He died of a heart attack in 1986 at Miami International Airport while waiting to board a flight to Taiwan when working as a salesman for a Florida-based fitness equipment maker.

6   Also known as the H-19 Chickasaw, the S-55 was a multi-purpose US Army helicopter, which started operational flying in 1950. It was also built under licence by Westland Aircraft in the UK and known as the Westland Whirlwind. Attempts were made to arm it as the first helicopter gunship but it was too underpowered for this role.

7   Around $6,000 at today's values.

8   Fernando Pö was then a Spanish possession and São Tomé one of Portugal's African territories. Later ICRC flights were also made from Cotonou in what was then the former French West African territory of Dahomey, now the Republic of Benin.

9   Illicit arms flights were also being made from these places, as well as Libreville in the former French territory of Gabon, in some cases by the same contractors flying relief supplies. This understandably angered the FMG who controversially attempted to interdict all the traffic.

10 The H-34 was a larger, more powerful turbine-engine aircraft that supplanted the H-19 (S-55). It was widely used by the US Navy for anti-submarine warfare. The British version used by the Royal Navy was known as the Westland Wessex.

Chapter Twenty-one
The Relief Operation

Calabar, an ancient slaving centre near the border with Cameroon, had been captured from the Biafrans only months earlier after a concerted drive by the FMG to occupy oil-rich Port Harcourt and the surrounding coastal area. The town remained the closest large settlement to the fighting against what was then land-locked Biafra. Terry and Billings were sharply reminded of this as they flew in with the H-34s and a fifty calibre machine gun opened up at them from across the front line. Most of Calabar was in ruins after being comprehensively ransacked by victorious federal soldiers. Virtually nothing functioned. The harbour had been blocked by the Biafrans as a defensive measure prior to them being ousted. It had to be cleared and dredged before lighters laden with relief supplies of salt cod and powdered milk could reach the dockside. UNICEF's helicopters often provided the only feasible means of then distributing the food to the tens of thousands of refugees in the interior on the federal side of the front line. Heavy rains meant that roads were frequently impassable. They were mostly unfit for heavy vehicles anyway. With hardly any infrastructure in place, only rudimentary communications and nothing in the way of a support team, running a successful helicopter airlift required a superhuman effort. Terry seized the challenge with indefatigable resolution. He had never felt more needed. This was an opportunity to demonstrate helicopter rescue work at its best and he relished the chance to prove that he was up to the task.

Initially, his reception from the earlier arrivals was frosty.

They were all Americans and now here was this Brit coming in to take charge. The chief among them up to that point was a burly, rough and tumble Irish-American from Connecticut called Jack McLaughlin who'd been a Marine recruiting sergeant for Vietnam and really didn't take kindly to my presence. Worse than being a Brit so far as he was concerned, was the fact that I was English. Anyway, I realized that I had to pull things together pretty quickly.

Terry rustled up some cases of cold beer and called the pilots and engineers to a meeting.

I explained that I wasn't there to give orders or teach them how to do their jobs. They were all experienced enough at what they did. My role was to make sure they had everything they needed to accomplish what they'd volunteered for – to feed and save starving refugees. That would mean working round-the-clock as a team to get as much food and medicine as we could off the docks and into the interior. There were to be no prima donnas and I'd give them all the support I could. Also I'd make sure they were paid.

The promise of pay cheques quickly changed the atmosphere, as the tough guy McLaughlin, who cut his shirt sleeves off at the shoulders exposing hirsute, muscle-bound arms, interjected that Robards had not sent any money for at least a month.

'Well, that's all going to change,' assured Terry, producing his UN cheque book. 'From today you'll be paid every week on the dot.'

They had three serviceable helicopters at their disposal: the surviving H-19 from San Francisco and the two H-34s that Terry and Billings had flown from Tel Aviv. There were also two old machines that Robards had ostensibly acquired from the NAF. Neither was airworthy and they were stripped to provide a stock of spare parts. Apart from Billings, 'the squat, ugly Gauntlett' and McLaughlin, the other team members were a US Navy lieutenant commander named Brett who left almost immediately, Joe Dwyer, Karl Timms, Roger Nastau and Denny Clarcq. Dwyer was another burly figure like McLaughlin, a New Yorker and also an ex-US Army pilot. He immediately asked Terry if he could share his room with a black girlfriend named Lilac. Timms was a San Franciscan, lantern jawed with gingery hair and hands like plates. He towered well over six feet tall and had left a job as an oil company executive to join the relief team. Nastau was another giant with a barrel chest and a shock of black hair. A Bostonian insurance company financial director, he joined the team as its loadmaster, a job he did very well. Even so, he is best remembered for incorrectly guessing the weight of yams and so overloading one of the helicopters that it flew the length of a football pitch before getting airborne. Clarcq had originally teamed up with Robards back in Dansville. He was the prodigy who built his own helicopter at the age of sixteen. In this respect he was the complete opposite of Gauntlett, who in Terry's opinion thought being a mechanic was about 'taking things apart and then trying to reassemble them, usually unsuccessfully'. By contrast, what Clarcq did not know about the mechanics of a helicopter could be written in capital letters on the back of a small postage stamp. He almost single-handedly worked miracles to keep the UNICEF helicopters flying, even when later in the operation the availability of spare parts became a pressing problem.

Over the next six months, Terry and this eclectic group of men were responsible for ferrying well over two thousand tons of food aid to crude helipads at Uyo and Akpap in the Cross River Delta. The helicopters carried up to a ton per flight and between them sometimes managed to deliver as much as ten or twelve tons a day. At times the men worked tirelessly for days or weeks on end without a break, flying between two and six return trips during daylight hours whenever the availability of supplies and weather conditions permitted. They made a crucial contribution to UNICEF's entire aid programme in Nigeria, which altogether delivered over 20,000 tons of food and medicine to both sides during the conflict at a cost of over \$95,000[1] a month. As Terry recalls, the pilots 'were often so exhausted that all they wanted to do in the evenings was collapse with a few cold beers and then sleep.' He 'bust his butt' to make sure that they always had their beer.

The team members lived in a dilapidated former schoolhouse at the bottom of a hill near the river. They spruced it up the best they could and nicknamed it 'the palace'. The brown, sun-scorched grass of the disused playground provided a convenient parking place for the helicopters, as well as enough storage space for the scores of forty-gallon fuel drums needed to keep the aircraft flying. A storeroom became an improvised workshop. Terry lived apart from the others in a spartan room in the crumbling remains of a cement factory until Joan joined him. They then shared a former colonial government mansion known as *Trenchard House*[2] with Calabar's British harbour master and his wife, Ron and Margaret Clark, and their two young children. The house commanded the top of the hill above 'the palace' with a spectacular view across the mouth of the Calabar River. It had been assigned to the Clarks when they arrived from Lagos immediately after Calabar's capture. At the time they were among only a handful of white faces in the town. Even after the UNICEF team's arrival and then a Red Cross relief mission shortly afterwards, there were fewer than twenty expatriates.

In the early days of 1969, Terry ensured that one helicopter was always on standby at 'the palace' so that all the foreign nationals could be evacuated at a moment's notice if necessary.

We were not that far from the fighting and you couldn't really be sure of the situation from one day to the next. I also wanted an aircraft immediately available for search and rescue in case of an accident.

In the event, the closest the shooting war came to Calabar was one night at the end of January when the Biafrans staged a 'bombing' raid. They then possessed two DC-3s, which were used primarily to augment mercenary-flown, gun-running operations. The aircraft were all that remained of what had been a rudimentary air force, including a number of helicopters and two old B-26 bombers, most of which had been crashed or destroyed by NAF ground attacks. On the night that the two DC-3s arrived over Calabar, Terry was lying in bed reading when he heard a succession of loud bangs. Seconds later the houseboy ran up the stairs shouting urgently: 'Douse de lights, de enemy done come.' From a spacious upstairs veranda, Terry and the other occupants of *Trenchard House* watched the aircraft lumber overhead towards the airfield.

Now, this sounds so bloody funny that you couldn't make it up: they were dropping crates of beer bottles that they'd refilled with kerosene and then lit as they pushed out, like giant Molotov cocktails. Some fell quite close to us and one succeeded in making a crater about ten feet across in the runway at the airport.

Although the raid was more laughable than serious, the threat of some kind of Biafran attack remained real enough. As a result, the Nigerian navy fired wildly at anything that moved on the river at night. On one occasion, Terry with some of his team and harbour master Ron Clark were the targets. They were returning by barge after an abortive attempt to recover the engine from one of the H-34s crashed by Dwyer in neighbouring Cameroon. Dwyer had disappeared in the aircraft early one morning after stealing out before the others and taking off alone. To maximize the number of daily mercy flights, Terry had established a simple routine. At the end of every flying day the helicopters would land by the docks or at a heavily guarded, disused plywood factory converted to store incoming relief supplies. After being filled to their maximum payload they flew back to 'the palace' and refuelled, ready to take off for the helipads at Uyo or Akpap at first light. 'Sometimes we'd have to wait for a morning mist to clear before leaving but depending on where we were going and how quickly the ground crews loaded and unloaded, we could manage anything up to six round trips a day.' The morning of Dwyer's lone departure was thick with an unusually heavy mist. The charitable explanation is that he was anxious to get started and followed the regular compass bearing to the helipad at Uyo, expecting the mist to clear before he arrived there. Terry has his own alternative theory about where he was actually going. What is not in question, however, is that he arrived back over Calabar at around seven o'clock in the morning, when the town was still shrouded in mist. Neither of the other helicopters had been able to take off.

As was more often the case, the radio-direction finding beacon at the airport was switched off. Dwyer flew backwards and forwards over 'the palace' but had no idea where to land. Terry and his teammates could hear the urgent, chattering whir of his helicopter overhead. They tried vainly to reach him on the radio so that they could talk him down. 'We couldn't get him to answer and eventually he headed off in the direction of Cameroon. When the mist cleared later in the morning I flew off to look for him. I spent the best part of a day searching as far as the border but there was no sign of him.' Then two weeks later Terry received a message that Dwyer was being held in the town jail.

> Apparently, he'd flown into Cameroon and crashed among the mangroves after running out of fuel. Natives who found him, paddled him back to Calabar by canoe hoping for a reward. His helicopter was wrecked but we took a barge down and tried to save the engine.

Clarcq managed to free it from its mountings. Terry then joined McLaughlin in the other H-34 to try lifting the engine aboard the barge.

> The damn thing was just too heavy. McLaughlin tried like hell to hold it but I could tell we were going to lose it. Between McLaughlin's legs there was a pedal to release the cable but he didn't want to hit it; he wanted to work at it and see if he could lift the engine across bit by bit. I could see it wasn't going to happen, so I reached across and pushed the pedal. The engine went down in the river just before we lost another chopper.

With only two helicopters remaining, Terry could no longer afford to keep one on standby. He put both to work flying supplies round the clock. Dwyer returned home with Billings, who had been recalled by United Airlines. After his escapade, Dwyer was not much of a loss but Terry was genuinely sorry to lose Billings who he valued both as a pilot and trusted friend.

Although he had already witnessed a lot of suffering in the Congo, Terry was deeply affected by the pathetic condition of many of the refugees he saw in Nigeria.

> It was the gaunt kids with their swollen stomachs and fly-infested sores who really broke my heart. Once I found this abandoned, half-starved little girl with a huge goitre on her neck. I brought her back to Calabar in my chopper and then sent her to hospital in Lagos to be treated. Shortly afterwards I got a stinking cable from the UN bollocking me for what I'd done because of the potential legal ramifications.

That sort of red tape and petty bickering from UN officials in Lagos angered and frustrated him. So did rampant corruption among Nigerian officials in Calabar who enriched themselves by creating bureaucratic obstacles unless they were permitted to steal aid supplies and vehicles for sale on the black market. Keeping the operation running was a logistical nightmare without these added problems. Food and grocery supplies, as well as fuel and spare parts for the helicopters, had to be flown in from Lagos, but what arrived often bore little resemblance to what was ordered. All the same, Terry persevered. For Margaret Clark, he was the hero of the moment. 'Almost anyone else would have simply given up and walked out. But Terry had so much determination that there wasn't any challenge he wouldn't take on and fight to the end.'

Both Mrs Clark and Joan made efforts to help at the refugee camp in Calabar itself. A steady stream of starving people arrived there daily, crowding into an old factory – a long, narrow building that was damp and dark – fronted by a muddy compound and surrounded by a low, stone wall. Joan found going to the camp heartrending.

> There were so many children just milling about – lost, shocked, hungry, lonely and abandoned – and fewer adults, many of them ill and traumatized, all homeless and without families doing their personal best to survive, eating donated foods that were strange to them, like dried cod and powdered milk. Usually when I got there I'd see dead bodies lying against the surrounding wall. That's where those who died in the night were left for disposal. It broke my heart. And then I'd go home to food and laughter, the Clark's healthy children who had toys and books and nice clothes and plenty of love. It was tough.

Going to the hospital, where she also tried to help, had the same devastating impact. She cut the long sleeves off her dresses and shortened all her skirts so that she could use the material to make clothes for orphaned babies. 'When these infants we'd worked so hard to save died, the heartbreak was so painful I had to give it up. This was the most difficult lesson for me to learn about Africa and life in a war-torn country.'

The man primarily responsible for the Red Cross contingent in Calabar was a wiry, blond-haired volunteer from the British Special Air Services (SAS) Regiment named Terry Crawley. He and Terry decided to work together rather than draw distinctions between their respective efforts. In the process they became firm friends and Crawley is another of Terry's committed admirers. 'I took to him straight away. In those situations you meet all kinds of people, good and bad. I liked Terry from the word go. He told me at the outset about how he'd left the RAF but that didn't make me change my view at all.' At the height of the famine created by the war, the Red Cross had over 100,000 refugees in two camps in the Cross River Delta area. Crawley acknowledges that without UNICEF's helicopters the death rate would have been much higher.

> The helicopters were absolutely vital; we simply couldn't have got the relief out without them. No question, they helped to break the back of the famine. We had new trucks capable of carrying thirty tons but the roads were treacherous and often impassable and they couldn't take thirty-ton trucks. So we often used Terry's helicopters to shift our supplies. He was working for UNICEF but in those days we all mucked in to help each other. All that mattered was getting the job done, not who did it and took the credit.

Like Terry's UNICEF operation, the Red Cross mission in Calabar was dedicated to relief work on the Nigerian side. Nonetheless, both were often involved in rescuing Biafran children who strayed across the front line. Crawley recalls that:

> Terry and his guys would sometimes pick them up and fly them in and we'd often pick them up in our trucks and bring them back. I remember at one time we must have had a hundred Biafran kids at various points of starvation in the camp at Calabar. It's amazing how hardened you get and how you adjust to seeing misery like that on a daily basis. Our doctors and nurses tried to save as many as they could but a lot of them were beyond help. That's just the way it was. You could kill them just as easily by giving them too much food too quickly as by not getting enough to them.

In the middle of February, Terry heard from Robards that he had bought a replacement helicopter for the aircraft crashed by Dwyer – a Fairchild Hiller FH-1100.[3] The only problem was that it was more than 1,500 miles away in Zambia. Terry immediately flew to Lusaka to collect it. He arranged for Joan to join him there briefly, as well as encouraging her to go to South Africa to see the Brannons and to the Congo to stay with Belgian friends. 'I wanted her to see white-run South Africa as well as the independent African countries so that she could understand the reality that Africa was a lot more complex than the idealistic view portrayed by her friends at the University of Montreal.' Meanwhile, Terry flew the red-painted FH-1100 across Zambia into the Congo and on to Calabar by way of Gabon and Cameroon, making refuelling stops after every five hours or so of flying time. It was another epic flight involving considerable risks and calling on all his nerve and charm.

> They threatened to arrest me if I landed in the Congo but I knew where the old fuel dumps were and took my chances. At one place in Gabon they were out of fuel when I arrived. I had to persuade the villagers to sell me all the paraffin they used in their lamps and I filled up with that. The FH-1100's good old Allison engine would run on just about anything.

Back in Calabar, Terry alluded to the possibility of marriage to Joan for the first time since their meeting. In her diary she noted: 'I'm still not able to believe he really means to go through with it but just talking about it was pretty elating. He could keep me going like this for years.' Other than hinting at marriage, Terry was no more forthcoming about his thoughts or longer-term plans and Joan still knew virtually nothing about his past. He was, of course, still legally married at the time, which explains his reticence. She wrote: 'I'm always up in the air. There seem to be so many things I want to find out but I just don't know where to begin. He won't discuss anything at all with me.' Nevertheless, he found them a place of their own to live and bought her an Amazon Green parrot for her twenty-eighth birthday. She named the bird Sparky and it enjoyed snuggling on her chest while she stroked its neck. Amusingly, it would also sit on the rim of Terry's beer mug and drink from it. A little later Joan also adopted a stray calf, which often escaped from its enclosure of empty fuel drums to run amok in 'the palace'. These were the homely diversions that helped take her mind off the death and suffering that otherwise surrounded them.

As the relief operation continued, the serviceability of the three helicopters started becoming a major issue owing to a persistent lack of spares. To

Terry's relief, Gauntlett had been replaced by a new Geordie engineer from Newcastle in the north-east of England named Jeff Hooper. With his more able assistance, Clarcq kept the aircraft airborne despite the shortage of replacement parts. Yet Terry knew that the effectiveness of the relief operation was being undermined by Robards's failure to supply urgently needed spares.

> He was charging UNICEF an arm and a leg and coming over and living it up in Lagos but forcing us to do everything on a shoestring. I realized then that, to him, my helicopter mission was just another way of making money. He didn't really give a damn about the refugees.

Robards kept a luxury suite at the *Federal Palace Hotel* in Lagos but seldom visited the operation in Calabar. On one of the rare occasions when he did, he arrived with his wife who wanted to see one of the refugee camps in the delta region. Terry arranged for McLaughlin to fly her out in the surviving H-34. Before they reached the camp, the aircraft's engine seized after swallowing a valve. McLaughlin managed an auto-rotation landing on a school playing field. The first Terry knew that something was wrong was when they failed to return before nightfall. Early the next day he went looking for them in the FH-1100. 'They'd spent an absolutely miserable night in a deserted schoolroom, being eaten alive by mosquitoes. That was the last we ever saw of Robards in Calabar, with or without his wife.' By then the sharp dresser from Dansville had sunk very low in Terry's estimation. On administrative trips to Lagos, Terry was free to use the suite he kept at the *Federal Palace Hotel*, where the wardrobe was filled with expensive clothes. 'I often went up with Terry Crawley. He happened to be about the same size as Robards, so I used to tell him to wear whatever he liked. Robards would have been mightily pissed off if he'd known.'

Notes

1 Well over $500,000 a month at today's values.
2 More recently this was occupied by the Liberian dictator Charles Taylor during his refuge in Nigeria.
3 A fast, lightweight helicopter originally developed as a contender for the US Army's Light Observation Helicopter (LOH) role and not really suitable for the relief airlift.

Chapter Twenty-two
A Bizarre Twist

Around the middle of March, Terry received a summons from the army commander in Calabar saying that he needed to see him about a message from the British High Commission in Lagos. He instantly suspected that the RAF had finally caught up with him. What he found puzzling was why it had taken them so long. He never doubted for a minute that Squadron Leader Price had reported their encounter in Accra more than three months earlier. However, when he heard nothing afterwards he assumed that the powers that be had indeed either 'cleared him all the way' or simply lost interest in him. At any rate, regardless of his identification by Price, he was sure that his presence in Nigeria was no secret. He assumed that the High Commission must have been aware of his earlier role as an instructor with the NAF since any defence attaché worth his title would have kept close tabs on the military activities of British subjects in a country at war. So why the sudden interest in him? 'I went along to see the local army boss expecting the worst and you could have knocked me down with a feather when he told me what the High Commission wanted.'

'Your prime minister is coming to Nigeria on a visit and your people at the High Commission in Lagos want you to help with security,' the commander explained.

'Well, that's not what I'm really here to do,' Terry responded hesitantly, somewhat taken aback. 'But I suppose I don't have much choice, do I?'

According to the commander, the High Commission had sent word to the effect that they knew there was an RAF pilot in Calabar flying helicopters. They wanted him to fly one of them up to Port Harcourt and liaise with the military commander there over security arrangements for the Prime Minister's motorcade through the port city during his forthcoming visit. Terry was told that Prime Minister Harold Wilson was expected to arrive in Lagos on 26 March. After meeting the following day with General Gowon, the FMG leader, he would make brief visits to Enugu, Port Harcourt and Calabar. Although the Royal Navy assault ship

HMS *Fearless* would be in Lagos to provide a secure base for the Prime Minister's trip, the High Commission had requested local helicopter support in Port Harcourt from the Nigerian security authorities.

'They've told us that you're the man for the job,' the officer explained.

'That's nice of them. In that case I suppose you'd better tell them that I'm always happy to be at Her Majesty's service,' replied Terry, relieved at the bizarre twist that had him being asked to hover protectively over the leader of Britain's Labour Government when he had been expecting a summons for desertion. He savoured the irony. 'I thought it was wonderful.' He longed to share his enjoyment of the paradox with Joan when he told her of the request later the same day. That, of course, was out of the question. She was still completely in the dark about his faked death nearly four years earlier.

Here was another paradox. Terry willingly faced all manner of physical risks. He thought nothing of flying with next to no navigation aids. He readily accepted the dangers of spending hours on end alone over jungle that could swallow him without trace or leave him at the mercy of cannibalistic rebels if he crashed. He could blag his way out of trouble when faced with thuggish, armed soldiers who would have thought nothing of killing him. Yet so often his courage failed him in the context of his private life. In this respect, he was what some people might call an emotional coward. Rather than risk confronting unpalatable truths, he would wait until events overtook them. This was what he was doing with Joan: relying on his conviction that at some point fate would intervene so that everything would sort itself out.

Wilson's visit to Nigeria was intended primarily as a public relations exercise. The British Government was desperately trying to head off mounting criticism at home and abroad of its support for the FMG. A chorus of voices attacked the apparent hypocrisy and duplicity of supplying armoured cars, automatic rifles and munitions to the FMG on the one hand while sending relief aid to stem the humanitarian disaster to Biafra on the other.[1] There was a good deal of justification for the criticism. Behind the scenes what the government really hoped for was a quick FMG victory. Publicly, however, it pressed the case for a ceasefire and negotiated settlement. The prime ministerial visit was announced at the end of a gruelling parliamentary debate and cynically projected as a peace initiative, although diplomatic officials knew perfectly well that the chances of achieving anything of the sort were extremely remote at best. The real intention was to deflect attention from Biafra's stunningly successful propaganda about the enormity of the humanitarian emergency and portray Britain's role in a better light.

On the eve of Wilson's arrival in Port Harcourt, Terry flew the H-19 there with McLaughlin and Hooper. Joan went along for the ride. That afternoon Terry went to see the military commander – a politically important figure named Colonel Adekunle and known popularly as the Black Scorpion – to ascertain exactly what he was required to do. 'He instructed me to fly over the crowd along the route of the motorcade with one of their security agents who'd be on the lookout for anything suspicious. It was all very casual.' After his meeting with Adekunle, Terry and the others spent the evening partying with a Czech medical team who insisted on singing the Beetles song *Hey Jude* repeatedly. They were hoarse and hung-over when they returned to the airport early the following morning to prepare the helicopter for the security detail.

Terry hunted around and found an old wicker armchair that he loaded aboard the H-19 and placed by the open doorway. 'We hadn't had time to clean the aircraft and it reeked of dried fish and stale milk powder. The floor in the back was filthy and there was nowhere for the security man to sit. The old chair was the best I could do.' Then, after completing a routine mechanical check, Hooper nonchalantly remarked that he thought the tail rotor bearings were about to pack up.

'That's great,' quipped Terry. 'We're here to protect the Prime Minister and we'll be flying over him with a dodgy tail rotor that could see us crash on top of his motorcade.'

While McLaughlin and Hooper continued final preparations for the flight, Terry escorted Joan to join the crush of pressmen and dignitaries gathered in the airport terminal to watch Wilson's arrival. Joan had her camera slung round her neck ready to take photographs. As Wilson's plane touched down, Adekunle suddenly appeared by her side, dramatically grabbed the camera and wrenched the strap over her head.

'Don't you know this is absolutely forbidden,' he snarled, opening the back of the camera and ripping out the film. 'I could have you shot, you know.'

'Yes, but you won't, not in front of the world's press with the British Prime Minister about to arrive and not if you want me to fly the helicopter for you,' challenged Terry. Adekunle laughed. 'Well, you'd better go and do it then,' he grinned.

As soon as he landed at the end of the security detail, Terry collected Joan and flew straight back to Calabar. Wilson was expected there later the same day. Members of the relief teams based in the town were lined up to meet him. Terry joined them with Joan at his side. As he shook Wilson's hand, he explained that he would again be flying cover in one of the UNICEF helicopters as the Prime Minister was driven to a ceremonial at the football stadium. Wilson thanked him and then asked about his work for UNICEF.

'Is there anything I can do for you?' he offered when Terry finished outlining the relief operation.

'Yes, Prime Minister, there is. You can help us get more helicopters and more medical support so that we can save more lives,' he answered. At that point an aide tapped the Prime Minister on the shoulder and muttered that it was time to be going. Needless to say, Terry never heard anything more. However, the episode had an amusing ending. Terry took Joan with him in the helicopter to accompany the slow-moving motorcade. She remembers looking down out of the cockpit window as they hovered overhead at about five hundred feet. 'The people lining the street were all looking up at us in the helicopter and waving wildly as the Prime Minister's car passed them. So I waved back. They obviously thought Wilson was in the chopper.'

The visit immediately preceded an emergency that kept UNICEF's helicopters working flat out for days on end to help the Red Cross. Crawley appealed for Terry's urgent help to move 35,000, twenty-five-kilo sacks of milk powder conservatively valued at $300,000 that was rotting on the docksides. Some of the powder had been there since December and the remainder for at least a month, owing to a lack of lighters to carry it up river from where vehicles could transport it to the refugee camps. There were also insufficient tarpaulins to cover the huge mountains of sacks stored in the open at two separate wharfs. Soaked by rain and overrun by rats that chewed through the sacks, much of the precious powder leaked into the muddy river water, sending a white ribbon out to sea. With Terry's help, Crawley set out to salvage 60 per cent of the Dutch-supplied powder by airlifting 5,000 bags to Uyo immediately and ferrying most of the rest to the plywood factory for storage until it could be shifted inland.

Rats were not the only scavengers Crawley had to contend with. Local palm nut traders had bags stolen so that the emptied sacks could be used by them to export their crops. This sort of corruption in Nigeria infuriated him. 'Forty years ago, I used to say that I'd never been anywhere in the world so corrupt. Judging by everything I read and hear, today nothing's changed.' In this he echoes Terry's sentiments.

I often reflect on the situation in Africa nowadays and wonder whether I should have been so gullible and done what I did. Well, when I was young I was an idealist and I genuinely thought I could make a difference. And yes, I saved lives, many of them, and that in itself was very satisfying then and still is now looking back. But Africa remains the same – cruel, despotic, corrupt and sad. The ordinary people are often wonderful and I feel sorry for them. I see them like children being led to one disaster after another by self-serving politicians who are like latter day pied pipers, full of false promises.

Important as they were, the UNICEF and ICRC relief efforts out of Calabar were small alongside the massive airlift into Biafra, then close to its peak. The ICRC was managing an average of around five mercy flights a night out of Cotonou and Fernando Pö and the groups constituting Joint Church Aid regularly exceeding twice that number, mostly from São Tomé. During the course of the airlift, they pressed more than a hundred aircraft ranging from pre-war DC-3s to more modern DC-6s, DC-7s, Super Constellations and C-46 Commando transports into use. These would leave at dusk to arrive over the Nigerian coast in the vicinity of Calabar as darkness fell and then make their way to one or other of the two makeshift airstrips in Biafra. The principal of these was the converted road at Uli, which was lit by flares as the aircraft approached. No more than two aircraft could be on the strip at any time and ground crews worked feverishly to unload them in order to let successive flights land. The aircrews were all volunteers, many motivated by genuine compassion for the thousands starving to death in Biafra as a result of the war. That said, they were also well rewarded for the considerable risks they took. In the end twenty-four paid with their lives in accidents on the hazardous approach to Uli and a notorious shooting down.

Terry knew from his former Congo comrades and other mercenary pilots whom he frequently met in Lagos – including another former RAF man named Mike Thomsett – that the FMG high command was getting increasingly alarmed about the extent of the airlift. Gowon and his aides suspected that arms were being smuggled into Uli at the same time as relief. They were probably right. Although the flights were distinct, two of the best-known gunrunners[2] were operating relief flights under contract as well as allegedly smuggling weapons. Differentiating between an aircraft carrying military hardware and another carrying food aid at night was impossible. This was the reason for the Biafran leadership's obdurate refusal throughout the war to allow daytime relief flights. Thanks to the high-profile public relations campaign highlighting the plight of starving Biafrans, they knew that the world had to act. Enforcing night relief flights created the perfect cover for arms shipments, equally vital for Biafra's survival as an independent nation. Efforts to interdict the flights involved bombing the airstrip at Uli as well as attempting to intercept and deter incoming aircraft. Those responsible for doing this were Terry's friends. 'We were a fairly close family and there were no secrets between us. They would happily have attacked the arms flights but they had a lot of sympathy for the relief ones and you really couldn't tell them apart, so most of the time they played a game.'

Henry Laurent, the former FAC commander in the Congo who bravely confronted Mobutu after the mercenary mutiny, piloted a DC-3 infamously dubbed *Genocide One* on nightly raids against Uli. His co-pilot was another Congo veteran named François Reip, known to his comrades as 'rape and escape', and the radio operator-cum-bombardier a South African named Jimmy Calderhead. Terry had a good relationship with them all.

> It was routine for Henry to talk to the relief pilots when they were flying in because the name of the game was to let them land and offload the aid and then attack the airstrip once they were safely out of the way. Jimmy used to say all sorts of threatening things on the radio to make it sound authentic.

Meanwhile, Klootwyk and the other mercenaries flying the MiGs would regularly blame weather conditions and the lack of navigation aids for not intercepting the flights. As Klootwyk recalls, they were also severely restricted by the short endurance of the aircraft before running out of fuel.

> Finding the flights in the dark was a question of chance and our limited range meant that without extra fuel in drop tanks we could be up for no more than half an hour if we wanted to get home in one piece.[3] So we humoured the Nigerians in this way.

The rules changed, however, when the Biafrans acquired a new mercenary air force led by the colourful Swedish aristocratic adventurer, Count Carl Gustav von Rosen. After participating in aid flights, he decided to go a stage further and supplied the Biafrans with six Swedish-built Minicom sports planes adapted and armed by the French to carry out ground attacks. In the wake of a number of successful raids by von

Rosen's so-called 'flying circus', the FMG reacted angrily. The mercenary pilots were threatened with being replaced by Russians if they were not more resolute in ending the airlift. To make matters worse, at around this time, a newly recruited former RAF pilot[4] exposed what he claimed were the sham excuses being used to explain the failure to close Uli and intercept incoming flights. Terry recalls the atmosphere changing as the pressure on his old comrades increased.

> For them the game was up really. I remember the Nigerians wanted Charlie Vivier to put together a team to fly one of their Russian-supplied Ilyushin Il-28 bombers to flatten Uli and the rumour was that he was paid-off by one of the aid agencies not to do it. But their jobs were on the line if they didn't do something.

Just after dusk on the evening of 5 June 1969, a Red Cross DC-7 on its way to Uli was shot down. The American pilot and his three Scandinavian crewmen were all killed. The ICRC immediately suspended all further flights, although the Joint Church Aid relief continued. Terry remembers being shocked but not at all surprised when he heard the news. 'The relief flight guys were getting cheekier and cheekier and collecting bonuses for doing extra flights every night. I suppose you could say that they were pushing their luck. In the end it was bound to get ugly.' The MiGs believed to have been nearest the scene at the time of the shooting down, were flown by Klootwyk and the ex-RAF man Thomsett. Speculation about who was responsible was rife in the bars in Lagos and Terry heard much of it firsthand. 'Everyone said afterwards that it must have been Ares. He was the acknowledged ace. But it could just as easily have been Thomsett. Ares won't talk about it and Thomsett's dead, so I suppose we'll never know.'[5] Klootwyk's reticence is understandable in view of the fury caused by the shooting down of a Red Cross aircraft and the deaths of the four crewmen. He admits that he knows who was responsible but 'would rather not say'.

In spite of the controversy surrounding the incident, the British High Commission was more than happy to see former RAF pilots working as NAF mercenaries if it improved the effectiveness of the FMG's air force. Officials even connived at helping one of them get round a technical breach of the Queen's Regulations in order to remain in the Nigerians' employment. They also encouraged the involvement of a British-based company in training Nigerian pilots 'so long as advertisements recruiting personnel were discreet'. What they meant by this was that the advertisements should not make a mockery of Britain's public stance on the war by highlighting that although the government refused to supply military aircraft, it was not at all averse to providing RAF-trained pilots. A quick military victory by the FMG remained the key objective. In retrospect Terry is convinced that his role on the FMG side, first as an instructor and then flying for the UNICEF sponsored operation, is what ensured that no steps were taken to stop him. 'They knew I was there but they turned a blind eye because what I was doing was useful.'

However, when UNICEF's contract with Robards came up for review, the value of continuing the helicopter airlift was called into question on the grounds of cost. UNICEF notified Robards that the contract would be terminated at the end of June. Accordingly, he had given Terry and the remaining team members – McLaughlin, Timms, Nastau and Hooper – a month's notice. Terry had no idea what he would do next but the furore over the shooting down of the Red Cross mercy flight convinced him that rejoining the NAF was not an option.

Notes

1   At the time Britain had supplied up to a fifth of the FMG's weapons by value, including most of the rifles and bullets. Biafra was succeeding in illicitly importing up to seventy tons a week of arms, a figure that later doubled.
2   Jack Malloch, a Rhodesian sanctions buster who also ran munitions to Schramme after the mercenary mutiny in the Congo, and Hank Wharton, a maverick German-American who flew with the UN in the Congo and later operated a number of 'shady' air freight businesses.
3   The actual operational endurance was only eighteen minutes.
4   Flt Lt John Driver.
5   Thomsett's MiG crashed after running out of fuel on a return approach to Port Harcourt. Before the accident he claimed that he and another mercenary pilot had been offered a huge bounty if they stole their MiGs and flew them to Biafra.

Chapter Twenty-three
Double Crossed

How Robards persuaded UNICEF to award him the relief contract in Calabar remains a mystery. Nothing in the UN archives explains why this small-town boy with big dreams was entrusted with the undertaking. Some simple checks might have revealed the treacherous character of the man and precarious financial state of his Dansville-based helicopter charter operation. Robards was a maverick with an eagle eye for making a quick buck. In spite of not completing high school, he possessed a gift for dubious, money-making ventures and a barrow boy's talent for presenting them. His younger sister remembers him as someone 'who always had an angle'. Even when his father lay dying his first thought was how his mother could benefit through an insurance scam. For him, the unfolding Biafran crisis presented a heaven-sent opportunity to cash in. He lost no time putting together the ambitious scheme for the helicopter airlift that UNICEF eventually sponsored.

After winning tacit US State Department approval for his plan, Robards set about selling and promoting it. He touted it to the American Red Cross, various church groups and then UNICEF, which in early August 1968 finally agreed to award him the contract to deliver some of the food aid then being shipped to Calabar. Under the terms of the deal, he was to receive $150 per relief flight for a minimum of twenty flights a week, plus $1,500 a week to cover additional expenses.[1] His convincing performance on a late-night television chat show promoting the cause moved viewers to tears and brought a flood of people eager to help. He hastily acquired the two ex-US Army H-19s, assembled his team from among the many volunteers and arrived in Lagos, leading to the chance meeting with Terry at the airport. By then he had already started looking around for more helicopters to expand the programme. His subsequent discussions to buy five H-34s from the Israeli military immediately attracted State Department scrutiny. The US Embassy in Lagos took a special interest. Long before Terry was taken in by him, the smooth-talking, self-proclaimed aviator from Dansville – he was never a pilot himself – was described by embassy officials as 'not the most reliable reporter, given to exaggeration and on occasion displays of deviousness'. His first team leader in Calabar, a husky twenty-seven-year-old volunteer from *The New Yorker* named Shepard Spink, complained of 'too many loose ends' in most of what he promised.

When UNICEF decided to terminate the Calabar-based relief contract, Terry knew from Robards that he was desperate to find an alternative sponsor. However, although Terry had by then developed his own misgivings about Robards, he seriously underestimated the lengths to which his boss would go to maintain the lucrative income generated by the operation. The first gambit on Robards's part was to try and get the US Government to step in and pay him to maintain the relief operation. With this objective he called on the US Embassy in Lagos, disingenuously claiming that UNICEF had not given him the required thirty days' notice and seeking embassy backing for government intervention. However, as a result of his earlier dealings over the Israeli helicopters and on-off attempts to acquire up to three helicopters from the NAF, the embassy already had him branded as 'a slippery operator'. Not surprisingly, he was informed that the US Government had no interest in taking on his contract.

Unabashed by this setback, Robards boasted to embassy officials that he had an even more ambitious scheme to open a relief corridor into Biafran territory using a giant Sikorsky crane helicopter. During the course of the meeting he also hinted at having received Biafran interest in buying his Calabar-based helicopters. Then, to raised eyebrows, he announced that he intended to visit Biafra to assess the feasibility of setting up the new operation and determining 'the need for helicopters in Biafra', despite the fact that his permit to enter the breakaway territory had expired. His plan was to travel on a flight from Cotonou and he claimed to have agreed a code word with the NAF's mercenary pilots to secure safe passage. When challenged over any UNICEF involvement, he insisted that he would be making the trip on a purely private basis. This was an extremely dangerous ploy. He must have known that if any hint of what he was attempting reached the FMG the consequences could be dire. Given their mood at the time, the Nigerians were very likely to treat any discussion with the Biafrans as subversive. They could reasonably argue that even if Robards's intentions were that aircraft supplied by him should be utilized for relief work, the reality was that they would most likely be pressed into military use. When embassy officials pointed out this risk to Robards, he insisted that he would not be holding discussions 'directly with the rebel leadership'.

Understandably, Robards was less than forthcoming with Terry about his Biafran proposals. Whether he ever pursued them and travelled into Biafra is unclear, although Terry did hear that he was seen in Cotonou. What eventually transpired was that Robards was negotiating to sell the surviving H-34 and H-19 to a Lagos-based, general goods trader named Afun, who also had offices in Brooklyn, New York. At the time, both these helicopters were unserviceable. The H-34 needed a new engine and the H-19 a new tail rotor. Robards explained that the FH-1100 – the aircraft flown to Calabar from Lusaka by Terry three months earlier and the only one then worth saving – would need to be flown out of Nigeria to Douala, the capital of Cameroon, as soon as the UNICEF contract ended. He told Terry that he had already booked shipping space from Douala to New York. What he failed to mention was that he intended to remove the helicopter from Nigeria illegally, making Terry an unwitting accomplice. The problem was that it had never been formally imported by Robards, an omission that itself potentially exposed him and the entire UNICEF operation to accusations of being involved in subversive activity given the on-going civil war. Worse still, there were suggestions that its purchase may have involved an illegal currency deal.

The Lagos businessman involved in the purchase of the two unserviceable helicopters was an Ibo descendant of Biafra's predominant tribe. His precise role in the transaction is obscure. One possibility is that he was acting as an intermediary with the breakaway regime. If so, how he planned to deliver the helicopters is difficult to imagine unless the whole thing was an audacious confidence trick. Another more plausible scenario is that he was setting Robards up so that he could steal the helicopters from him. Whatever the truth, early in the afternoon of 12 June, Terry went to see Afun in his Lagos office at Robards's request. He took with him a briefcase containing photographs and specifications of the helicopters and details of the relief effort. After the meeting he was supposed to rendezvous with Robards and two of the remaining members of the UNICEF relief team back at the *Federal Palace Hotel*. 'I was sitting in Afun's office with my briefcase open on the floor when two or three Nigerian secret policemen burst in. Afun jumped up and started protesting but they told him to sit down and keep quiet and then started questioning me.'

'Who are you? What are you doing here?' the policeman in charge demanded.

'My name's Terry Peet. I'm discussing the sale of some helicopters with this gentleman,' Terry answered calmly.

'Well, we've come to arrest this man and we'd like to see what you have in your briefcase,' his interrogator responded.

'Why? Why do you want to do that?' Terry queried.

'Never mind why, we just want to,' he was told firmly.

The policeman looked through the documents and photographs. He seemed particularly interested in some pictures of refugee children.

'Where did you get these?' he wanted to know.

'That's the job I'm doing. I'm working down in Calabar for UNICEF. I see sights like that every day,' he replied.

'Where are you staying in Lagos?' the policeman asked.

'At the *Federal Palace Hotel.*'

'What room number?' he demanded. Terry told him.

'Well, we need all these photographs,' the policeman continued. After handing Terry a receipt for them, he told him that he was free to go.

Terry picked up his briefcase with the remaining contents and went downstairs. The taxi that he had arrived in was still waiting, as instructed. He told the driver, who he used regularly when he was in Lagos, to take him back to the *Federal Palace Hotel* as quickly as possible.

As I walked into the main lobby, I was greeted by the sight of Timms and a chap called Thomas Marinkovich, who was our Lagos representative, sitting side by side with their heads down and surrounded by policemen. Karl looked up towards me and shook his head, so I walked straight past them to the reception desk to call Robards. Before I could do this I saw him being led towards the lift by three policemen. He and the others were all obviously under arrest and I didn't intend to hang around and find out why.

Terry walked quickly out of the lobby and found his faithful taxi driver standing by.

'Those men, they're the secret police,' the driver confirmed as he accelerated away.

One of the precautions Terry took soon after arriving in Nigeria was to establish a 'safe house' in Lagos. 'I thought it was a prudent thing to do in a country like Nigeria.' This was a routine he had learned with the CIA in the Congo. The idea quite simply, was to have a place with no apparent connections where an agent could seek refuge if his cover was blown. Terry's bolthole was the home of Seija Tikannen, a tall, blonde Finnish Red Cross volunteer, with whom he had become friendly while instructing for the NAF. She habitually wore black, knee-length boots and had rather an officious air about her. Nonetheless, Terry found her 'delightful and sexy'. His good friend Crawley, the Calabar Red Cross co-ordinator who also knew her, was less enamoured and referred to her disdainfully as 'Jackboots'.

As soon as he reached Seija Tikannen's house, Terry telephoned the US Embassy. He asked to be put through to the military attaché, Major Richard Russell, whom he knew.

'Look, I'm calling to let you know that three of your citizens with the UNICEF mission in Calabar have just been arrested at the *Federal Palace Hotel* by the secret police. I don't know why but I think they're probably after me as well, so I'm lying low,' he told him. After giving Russell the men's names, Terry also recounted what had happened at Afun's office earlier in the afternoon.

'Okay, thanks for letting me know. Leave it with us. We'll see what we can do,' Russell said. Immediately afterwards an embassy official went to the hotel. He was informed that Timms and Marinkovich had been taken to the police station but found Robards upstairs with three policemen who were searching his room. The official was allowed to speak to Robards privately while the policemen continued to rifle through piles of papers. Robards confirmed that he was being held on suspicion of 'subversive activities'. He said that he had not been mistreated.

Terry laid low for a couple of hours and then went back to the hotel to see if the dust had settled. By then Robards had also been taken to the police station. Terry went upstairs to Robards's room and found the door open and the room ransacked. 'It was still full of cigarette smoke and had been turned upside down. There were papers everywhere. The wardrobe was empty and his clothes strewn all over the floor.' Downstairs, the concierge confirmed that the police had enquired about Terry's whereabouts and also searched his room. It seemed that he had only escaped being arrested in Afun's office by chance. He concluded that the police must have been expecting to find Robards there.

Robards, Timms and Marinkovich were interrogated until ten-thirty that night. After a meal and a few hours' sleep the interrogations continued early the next day. Eventually, they were allowed to return to the hotel under guard and told to report back for further questioning at eight-thirty the following morning. Both Timms and Marinkovich were relieved of small sums of money they were carrying, although, oddly, Robards was allowed to keep the considerable amount in his possession.

Meanwhile, Terry had returned to Seija Tikannen's house to plan his escape.

> Terry Crawley happened to be in Lagos and he turned up unexpectedly after hearing about the arrests. I asked him to get a message to Hooper in Calabar warning him to get out to Cameroon before he was picked up as well. McLaughlin and Nastau had already gone home because we were winding the whole operation down.

With Crawley's help, Terry then went to the airport at Ikeja and with characteristic charm and confidence bluffed his way into the UTA mechanics' changing room. He donned a pair of white overalls, mixed with a group of mechanics and strode out to an aircraft that was due to leave shortly for Douala. 'Once aboard I locked myself in the lavatory, took off the overalls then came out and sat down in an empty seat. The next I knew I was in Cameroon.'

After receiving Terry's urgent warning from Crawley, Hooper also made it safely to Douala. Without Terry or Timms in Calabar to fly it, the FH-1100 remained behind with the two unserviceable aircraft. A few days later, Seija Tikannen flew down to Douala to let Terry know that Robards, Timms and Marinkovich were still in custody and that the helicopters in Calabar had been impounded. The UNICEF operation was over and there was nothing more that he could do. Terry was furious with Robards for getting them all into such a mess.

> In the end I don't know who was double-crossing whom or who tipped off the police. Even if he didn't actually talk to the Biafrans, Robards was playing a dangerous game and it was a sad way for him to end what had been a worthwhile operation, whatever his motives for doing it in the first place.

From Douala, Terry flew to Washington DC, where he had arranged to stay briefly with his former CIA field boss, Leighton Mishou. 'I'd contacted him when I knew the UNICEF operation was coming to an end and he suggested getting together to discuss possibilities for me in Laos. He was already involved in the CIA operation there, working out of Bangkok.'

After seeing Mishou, Terry intended to rejoin Joan in Montreal. She had left Nigeria several weeks earlier to seek treatment for a chronic ear infection that flared up nastily as a consequence of swimming in the

Calabar River. Most of Terry's old Congo comrades had gone to the airport in Lagos to give her a fitting send off. She had said farewell to Africa with mixed feelings after the immigration officer threatened to detain her on some trumped up charge unless she agreed to go out with him when she returned. However, at least she had been able to leave with all her personal possessions. All that Terry was able to take was a change of clothes he kept at Seija Tikannen's for use in the event of just such an emergency and his precious flight log that he guarded with his life. During the course of the Calabar airlift he had added 370 hours to the grand total of almost 2,500 hours he had then logged flying helicopters.

Much later he and Joan heard that a CIA agent was sent from Lagos in the aftermath of the UNICEF men's arrests to check on the situation at the operational base in Calabar. At what had been Terry and Joan's home, the agent found Sparky, the parrot. He decided to take the bird back to Lagos with him but was arrested at the airport. According to Terry, his briefcase was crammed with detailed maps of the Cross River Delta that he had recovered from 'the palace' and he was accused of being a spy.

> Well, of course, he was, although not the sort they thought. Anyway, he talked his way out but the police refused to let him take Sparky. They thought the bird might have overhead something valuable and would repeat it! I know it sounds far-fetched but it's absolutely true.

The investigation into Robards's connection with Afun and his alleged dealings with the Biafrans continued for more than three weeks. On 3 July, he was finally released, along with Timms and Marinkovich, after agreeing to hand over all his Nigerian assets and pay a hire charge of $14,000 for the two helicopters he had procured from the NAF. These were the unserviceable machines cannibalized by the UNICEF team for spares. However, what Terry and his comrades did not know was that neither of them had ever been paid for by Robards. The intervention of Michael Ogun, a leading Calabar politician with a strong vested interest in seeing the UNICEF operation continue, appears to have been instrumental in securing the men's release. Ogun, who was also the commissioner responsible for rehabilitation in the south-east region, argued vehemently that Robards had a genuine interest in relieving suffering in the country and that he had been framed by Afun in an elaborate plot to steal the helicopters. He was fiercely critical of UNICEF for ending the Calabar airlift, which he claimed was of far more value than what he described as the ICRC's 'dubious relief effort'. Back in Calabar, he arranged for features and editorials to appear in the local press extolling the virtue of the Robards operation and condemning UNICEF for its 'cold- hearted action' in withdrawing his contract and leaving the people in the Cross River Delta to face 'the agony of slow death'. He also arranged street protests.

Terry knew Ogun well. 'He used to tell the local population that the yams we were distributing were coming from him personally and that to keep them coming they had to vote for him. It was very much in his personal interest to keep us there.' Nevertheless, Ogun's vigorous publicity campaign forced both the ICRC and UNICEF onto the defensive. They were anxious to see the back of Robards in Nigeria and the whole sorry affair forgotten as quickly as possible. This may explain the apparent absence of detailed records about the Calabar operation in UNICEF's archives. It certainly ensured that Robards would be shunned by both relief organizations subsequently. After his release he returned to the US and abandoned any further attempts to capitalize on the Biafran crisis. He eventually moved to Florida, where he ran a run-down motel among other things. Constantly beset by marital, money and drink problems, he died suddenly of a heart attack in 1998 alone, rejected by his siblings, ex-wives and only child.

In a strange sequel to Terry's Nigerian adventure, his friend Crawley was arrested soon afterwards when he was trying to leave Lagos. 'They falsely accused him of looting a museum in Biafra.' Crawley confirms this.

> It was across the river from where we were but I'd never been anywhere near it. Of course that didn't make any difference to the police chief in Calabar, who was totally corrupt. His wife was involved in all sorts of dodgy import-export deals and she was unofficially using my Red Cross trucks, something I had no choice about. In the end I had to do a deal – she could keep the trucks if I was allowed to leave.

Another, more significant consequence of the Biafran crisis was a reappraisal by established aid agencies of the way they approached disaster relief. In this sense it was a defining moment in humanitarian aid operations, leading directly to the founding of Médecins Sans Frontières,[2] one of the world's leading relief organizations.

Notes

1 Around $900 and $9,000 at today's prices.
2 Founded in 1971 by Bernard Kouchner and a small group of fellow French doctors and journalists who witnessed the suffering in Biafra during the civil war. Kouchner went on to become a leading French politician and Foreign Minister in President Nicholas Sarkozy's government until 2010.

Chapter Twenty-four
Call to Laos

Mishou was waiting for Terry at Dulles International – then still a showcase, modern airport with revolutionary mobile lounges conveying passengers effortlessly between the terminal and aircraft. He greeted him effusively, talking non-stop on the drive back to his modest suburban home in Vienna, one of Washington DC's dormitory towns in Fairfax County, Virginia. The welcome from Mishou's wife, Jane, could not have been more affectionate if Terry had been a returning son. She had adopted him as if he were her own progeny back in Leopoldville, convinced that he was an orphan, a misconception shared by her husband. Mishou knew only that Terry was a former RAF officer whose employment by the CIA had been cleared through the appropriate channels. He knew nothing about the manner of his recruitment and faked drowning. However, in working so closely with him in the Congo, he had developed a high regard for him personally and professionally and, like his wife, treated him with the warmth of a family member. Terry did nothing to correct their mistaken belief about his lack of parents and family. It neatly sidestepped the awkward business of having to tell the truth about how he had severed all connections with his past. Moreover, in a Machiavellian sense it suited him to have such an intimate relationship with a CIA operative who clearly had his welfare at heart. Terry may have been a gentleman and loyal friend but he could also be manipulative and opportunistic.

Over the next few days, Terry enjoyed the Mishous' undisguised pleasure at having him in their home. They caught up with each other's news and reminisced at length about the Congo. Jane Mishou was busy packing in preparation for their return to Bangkok and onward posting to Vientiane in Laos, where her husband was to take over as the local operations manager of Continental Air Services, Inc (CASI).[1] He told Terry that this was one of the outwardly civilian airlines providing transport for the CIA's major covert paramilitary operation supporting a resistance army of Hmong tribesmen against communist Pathet Lao insurgents aided by North Vietnamese regular troops.

'I don't think I'll have any choppers: they're all with Air America and Bird Air. But we need good pilots in Laos and I know you're one of the best. I'm sure we can use you,' he volunteered encouragingly.

'That's great Mish. I'll fly whatever you can fix, with or without wings,' Terry enthused, confident that his friend had just solved his next job quest. He needed the money. Although contract flying had brought him an income he could only have dreamed about in the RAF, he had developed expensive tastes to match and he was notoriously generous. When he had money, Terry always bought the first round and usually the last as well. He saved little.

After agreeing with Mishou that he would make plans to join him in Bangkok, Terry flew to New York to rendezvous with Joan. His mood was exuberant, in sharp contrast to the downcast man she had left behind in Calabar. Terry had retreated into himself when he first heard that UNICEF was not going to continue with the relief effort. The news was a major blow. Performing humanitarian work gave him a genuine sense of self worth and kept his conscience clear about the fraudulent aspect of his secret life. Ending the airlift was not only going to deprive him of this but also throw him back into the job market, a prospect that worried him. Most civilian employers would ask too many questions. For this reason he had tentatively reached out to Mishou in the hope of renewing the CIA's interest in him. When the debacle over Robards's arrest forced his premature departure from Nigeria, this was his only lifeline. By intimating as strongly as he did that there would be a role for Terry in Laos, Mishou sent him off to New York for his reunion with Joan full of confidence.

Terry and Joan's memories vary over exactly what transpired in that last weekend in June in the run up to Terry's thirty-fourth birthday. They agree that he arrived in New York ahead of her and had already planned how they would spend the next couple of days doing the sights before hiring a car to drive back up to Montreal. They both recall enjoying a lavish picnic at Orchard Beach on Long Island, the 'Riviera of New York', seeing a show at Radio City Music Hall and then doing the usual round of museums and galleries. However, they diverge about what then happened on Terry's birthday, when they left for Montreal. Joan's recollection is that they stopped to eat at a bowling alley en route and Terry sprang a surprise. 'He asked me to marry him. He told me, "The diamond's in Brussels: *Madame* Troger's looking after it for you." He'd first talked about marriage back in February and then not mentioned it again. Now, on his birthday we were engaged.' Terry insists that he did not formally propose to Joan until much later because he did 'not feel that it was appropriate until I was divorced'. He agrees, however, that he told her that if she went to Brussels, *Madame* Troger would have something for her and that it was a diamond. Francine Troger was Dr Close's chief nursing assistant in Leopoldville. Joan had stayed with her when she visited the Congo. She was close to Mobutu's wife and often instrumental in buying jewellery for her. Terry had contacted her, asking her to obtain a diamond for Joan. 'She found this absolute beauty, just like a perfect tear drop and I paid $1,800 for it and asked her to give it to Joan with a note saying, 'Do whatever you want to with this'. From that Joan sort of got the message that she was engaged.' Whichever version is true, the eventual outcome was the same.

Back in Montreal, Terry resisted a tempting offer of $500 from the city's leading newspaper to tell the story of his Congo and Nigeria exploits. He was astute enough to recognize that courting publicity would not endear him to the men upstairs at Langley and sabotage any chance for Mishou to deliver a CIA-sponsored job for him in Laos. That was a risk he was not prepared to take. Over the next few days he planned his trip to Southeast Asia. He included a detour to Tijuana in Mexico to secure a divorce and took the precaution of having it notarized at the US Embassy during a stopover in Sydney on the way from Los Angeles to Bangkok. (At that time it was possible for one party of a marriage to secure a divorce in Mexico without having the agreement of the other.) 'I suppose I was trying to tidy up my affairs. I wanted to make a clean breast of everything to Joan and start afresh with her.' Towards the end of July he arrived in Vientiane with the Mishous.

The US was spending more dollars per head of local population in Laos than anywhere else in the world in its bid to prevent the land-locked, former French Indo China kingdom falling into communist hands.[2] Most of the money was going on covert military support for the huge tribal army trained and equipped by the CIA with Air America, Continental Air Services and Bird Air providing the necessary transport for arms and munitions, as well as food supplies and undercover military personnel. Hotel bars and restaurants in Vientiane hummed to American voices, most of them supposedly civilians working on aid projects but many of them covertly engaged in the war effort. The impoverished kingdom's dusty, run-down administrative capital, on the Mekong River in the centre of the country, oozed faded, colonial grandeur. Wide, Parisian-like boulevards lined by dilapidated mansions enclosed narrow side roads and alleyways hosting a chaotic mix of small shops and stalls offering everything from electric rice cookers to canned wine. The main street was a small-scale copy of the Champs Élysées, right down to an incomplete mock of the Arc de Triomphe. This was actually a war memorial built with US funds originally designated for a new airport and was commonly referred to by expatriates as the 'vertical runway'. Throughout the city, ramshackle cars competed for room with taxi tricycles, pedalled by sweat-soaked riders.

To begin with, Terry joined Mishou and his wife living in a large bungalow set in half an acre of garden planted with mango and papaya trees amid swathes of bougainvillea and poinsettias. Over drinks one evening in the spacious, open-plan living room, one corner of which was devoted to a large, tropical fish tank and bar, Mishou told Terry that he was to join Laos Air Charter, a small contract company working for the CIA.

> To do this I had to have a Laotian flying licence. The drill was to be checked out on a DC-3 by Royal Air Lao's senior pilot – a very colourful character called Babal. He was a white-haired mulatto from Mauritius who was a first-rate cook when he wasn't drunk. He must have been sixty and always flew with a bottle of Johnny Walker between the seats from which he took copious swigs every so often.

Terry joined Babal in the cockpit for a flight to Pakse, following the course of the Mekong River southwards along the border with Thailand. 'The aircraft was full of people, pigs, goats and bags of rice – everything you can imagine. I'm sure it was overloaded but that didn't seem to bother Babal.'

About halfway into the flight, Babal banked steeply to the right and headed across the Mekong into Thailand.

'Hey, are we supposed go over the border?' Terry challenged.

'Ah, I have a little personal mission,' answered Babal, as he pointed the aircraft's nose down and started losing height rapidly before levelling off and opening the cockpit side window. Then, asking Terry to take the controls, he scooped up twelve packages of opium bundled in silver foil, each attached to a small parachute, and tossed them out of the window.

'Just a little business deal; no problem, no problem,' he grinned mischievously.

Pakse was one of the most dangerous destinations in Laos at the time because of its proximity to the Ho Chi Minh trail. Landing there required a right-hand approach rather than the usual left-hand circuit to avoid flying over communist-held territory and being shot down. When they arrived, Babal took Terry to a small banana-leaf shack near the airport. 'It turned out to be a bar run by a girlfriend of his and we had a couple of drinks. When he offered me another, I said, no thanks, not when I'm flying.'

'Ah, no problem, no problem, the DC-3 flies itself,' laughed Babal, swallowing another beer. Back at Wattay airport, two miles outside Vientiane, where the entire right-hand corner of the airfield was devoted to the CIA air support programme, Babal cheerfully signed Terry off for his local licence. Immediately afterwards he started flying for Laos Air Charter, carrying cargoes north to Luang Prabang and south to Pakse and Savannakhet. The work was routine and Terry quickly tired of it, notwithstanding the spectacular terrain of heavily forested mountains and massive limestone, sheer-sided karsts projecting into the clouds. Laos Air Charter was owned by a former French soldier named Georges Mercier, a veteran of the Indochina campaign. He operated three DC-3s but paid poorly and rarely on time. Terry liked him all the same and they became firm friends.

On most weekends Mercier liked to go bird hunting in the countryside outside Vientiane. Americans were generally restricted to an area within two or three miles of the capital but Mercier regularly ventured much further afield. He often invited Terry to join him. On one foray, well to the north of Vientiane with several other friends and a pack of hunting dogs, they were picnicking on wine and cheese when half a dozen Pathet Lao guerrillas appeared.

They came towards us across this rice paddy , all wearing what looked like black pyjamas and carrying Kalishnikovs. Georges told me not to open my mouth under any circumstances because my French wasn't good enough. Then he stood up to greet our visitors.

'*Bonjour, bonjour,*' he called out.
'*Bonjour, bonjour, bonjour,*' the Pathet Lao returned.
The leader of the group then addressed Mercier directly, referring to him as '*Mon Colonel*' and asking if he remembered Dien Bien Phu.
'*Oui, bien sûr Corporal,*' Mercier answered, pointing to a tattoo on his arm signifying his old regiment and similar to one the Pathet Lao man then revealed by rolling up his sleeve. Mercier invited the guerrillas to share the hunting party's picnic and at the end of the meal they all shook

hands and parted company. Terry recalls that when he told his American friends 'they were speechless'.

One night shortly after the hunting excursion encounter with the enemy, Terry was sitting in the bar at the *Hotel Lang Xang*, where he was then living, when two American men in dark suits approached him.

'Are you Terry Peet?' one of them asked.

'Yes, that's me,' Terry nodded.

'You fly a DC-3 with Laos Air Charter. Is that right?' the same man continued.

'Yes, that's right,' Terry confirmed.

'Well, we'd like you to accompany us to our room upstairs. We need to talk to you about something in private,' the man said. Put on his guard, Terry reacted warily.

'Oh really, why would I want to do that?' he challenged. 'And who are you anyway?'

'We're representatives of Pacific Architects and Engineers[3] and we've got a proposition to put to you,' the second man volunteered.

'Pacific Architects and Engineers? Wonderful, now that really rings a bell with me,' Terry chortled sarcastically.

'No, no, we're serious. Trust us,' one of the men assured.

'Look, not trusting people like you is how I stay alive,' answered Terry.

The two men persisted and eventually Terry agreed to accompany them upstairs. 'I arrived in this smoke-filled room where two or three more of these suits were sitting like a meeting of Mafia bosses. They offered me a Scotch and then got straight to the point: they wanted me to steal one of Mercier's DC-3s and fly it to Bangkok.'

According to the men, Mercier had leased the aircraft from PAE and not paid a cent of the agreed charge. They wanted Terry to repossess it for them and offered to pay him $2,000.

'Everything in Bangkok is fine, the customs and police are in the picture and the American Embassy here knows all about it. You've nothing to worry about,' they assured him.

'You're telling me that Mac Godley[4] and Devlin have approved this?' Terry demanded.

'Yes, yes. It's all kosher. We just need the job done quickly. What do you say?'

'I'll think about it but I can't make any promises,' replied Terry.

Later he tracked down Mishou and reported the whole conversation. It quickly transpired that the men's claim that the 'theft' had embassy approval was completely bogus. The DC-3 stayed in Mercier's fleet but

Terry grew increasingly restless making mundane fixed-wing, supply flights. He yearned to get back to flying helicopters and angled for a contract with Bird Air. 'This was owned by the Bird brothers who also ran hotels in California. They had Bell-47s, like the one I flew in the Congo, doing secret work ferrying CIA personnel all over the country. That was much more my kind of scene.' Terry knew that another of his good CIA friends from the Congo, Ken Weber, was working undercover out of Pakse and he hoped that they might work together again if he was flying with Bird Air. 'Ken was a great guy, a genuine hero. Sadly I never did see him again. He died of a heart attack on a commercial airliner when he was on an assignment.' However, by relentlessly badgering Bird Air's operations manager, Terry finally managed to get as far as being checked out by him on one of the helicopters and then accompanying him on a flight to Udorn, the hub for CIA air operations in Laos, just across the border in Thailand. 'It was a huge base crammed with aircraft, like Butterworth when I first went there.' In the end Bird Air, like Air America, would only hire American pilots and although there were no qualms about Terry's ability or experience, he was eventually told that he could not be taken on. It seemed the ultimate irony after the Congo, where anyone but Americans could fly operationally.

Joan arrived to join Terry towards the end of the year after travelling to Brussels to collect her diamond and have it set in a ring.

> *Madame* Troger handed me a plain white envelope and inside I found this lovely 1.28 carat diamond – like a bright droplet of water. I remember going back to the cheap hotel where I was staying, locking the windows and putting a chair under the door handle and then lying awake all night worrying that I'd be robbed.

In Vientiane, she and Terry moved to a bungalow near the airport. By then Mishou had introduced Terry to a hulking, naturalized German-American named Haas, who masqueraded as an electronics and computer engineer at the US Embassy but was obviously a CIA agent. Haas was clean-shaven with a handsome, square face and typically Germanic, blue eyes. He sported a Marine-style crew cut and looked every inch a tough guy. 'We met in the bar at the *Lang Xang* and he suggested that I might be interested in doing the odd assignment for him. I would be paid $500 a month, not much but a start and more than Mercier was paying me.' Terry readily agreed. He would be spying as well as flying and that suited him fine because it appealed to his thirst for a niche role rather than being one of the crowd. DC-3 pilots were two a penny. As it happened, so were spies in Vientiane.

Haas started by introducing Terry to all his contacts, 'a strange assortment of Russians, Frenchmen, Poles and women in bars all over town', and suggested that he should get to know them. Terry's role was to distance Haas from them by acting as a go-between. He decided to begin the process by hosting a party at his bungalow and inviting the new contacts, along with a lot of the suspected spooks in Vientiane. 'Most of them turned up. Of course, they all knew each other and it was hilarious to watch them all keeping an eye on who was talking to whom.' For Terry though, the CIA party was over. As soon as he started working with Haas, the CIA followed the standard protocol of consulting with London. This time the response was an emphatic no: under no circumstances would his employment in Laos be sanctioned. The news was conveyed to Terry by Mishou, who showed him a copy of a heavily censored internal CIA memorandum.

> Whole bits of the note had been razor-bladed out but the gist of what was left said that I was illegally absent from the RAF, had a wife and two children called Erica and Nicola who I'd abandoned in the UK, and that I should not be used as an intelligence asset in the Laotian or Vietnam theatres, end of story.

Initially, Mishou was understandably angry and felt betrayed. However, he and his wife were quickly forgiving when Terry explained why he had done what he did. They gamely agreed to say nothing to Joan. Nonetheless, despite their clemency, Terry was then *persona non grata* in Vientiane. He had to plan what to do next. 'The CIA dropped me like a hot potato and you don't hang around in that sort of situation if you know what's good for you.'

With Jane Mishou's help at the US Embassy, where she was working, Terry compiled a mailing list of most of the world's registered, private helicopter operators. He then prepared a résumé of his flying qualifications and experience with accompanying photographs, had two hundred copies printed in booklet form and posted them off with personalized covering letters. He received one reply.

> It came from a man named Jack Harter who'd started the first ever helicopter tours in Hawaii. He wrote saying that I could have as much sand as I could eat and as much sunshine as I could take and he'd pay me $800 a month so long as I didn't weigh more than 180

pounds. I wrote back saying that I weighed 185 pounds but I'd take five off on my way.

A few days later Terry and Joan left for Honolulu, where they arrived in the middle of December 1969. Terry told Joan nothing about what had prompted their abrupt departure from Vientiane but this came as no surprise to her. By then she was used to him suddenly announcing that he had a new job in a far-flung corner of the world. Terry, of course, knew that even if he had been 'cleared all the way' with the British authorities in the Congo and then ignored by them in Nigeria, the official blind-eye was not being turned to his presence in Laos. What he did not know was that MI5 suspected him of espionage. Even so, for the first time since leaving Tern Hill he felt like a fugitive.

Notes

1 CASI was formed in April 1965 by Continental Airlines at the suggestion of the US Government to provide a 'less visible' air transport alternative to the CIA-operated Air America. It started operations with 22 aircraft and 350 employees acquired from Bird & Sons, Inc (Bird Air), another significant CIA contractor, and maintained offices in Bangkok, Vientiane and Saigon. CASI operated in Laos as Air Continental.

2 Military support began openly in the mid 1950s and increased in the early 1960s with the training of the mountainous Hmong tribesmen militia by US Special Forces with air support by Air America in Operation *Hotfoot*. Following the Geneva Accord guaranteeing Laotian neutrality and requiring the withdrawal of all foreign military personnel, the support became increasingly covert, making it the CIA's largest ever paramilitary operation. The Soviet Union and Great Britain co-chaired the Geneva Accord and each turned a blind eye to transgressions by its own ally while protesting loudly about those by the other. By the height of the campaign in 1971 the North Vietnamese Army had nearly 70,000 regular troops in Laos and had won the upper hand. The so-called CIA 'Secret War' ended in 1973 with the agreement of a ceasefire following the Paris treaty to end the Vietnam War. In his memoir *A Look Over My Shoulder*, late CIA Director Richard Helms insists it was the 'war we won' and debunks the idea that it was secret since it had full presidential approval and at least two committees of Congress were briefed on it.

3 PAE, now a Lockheed Martin subsidiary, was a major construction contractor for the US Government in Vietnam. It built the interrogation centres for the CIA's notorious Phoenix Program and also supplied Caribou short-landing aircraft, as well as operating a small fleet of air transports.

4   G McMurtrie 'Mac' Godley was the US Ambassador. He had been posted to Vientiane from Leopoldville and was joined there by Congo compatriot Larry Devlin as the CIA station chief.

Chapter Twenty-five
Paradise Found...

Kauai is the northernmost of the Hawaiian Islands, geologically the oldest and the most verdant. Known as the 'Garden Isle', it has captivated visitors ever since Captain James Cook became the first outsider to set eyes on it in 1778. There are few places on earth where such an array of stunning scenery is compressed into five hundred square miles with the ocean as an ever-present backdrop. For Jack Harter, a quiet, gentle veteran of the Korean War, Kauai represented nothing less than the Garden of Eden. Enraptured by the island's beauty and mythical legends, he recognized the opportunity for helicopter tourism. When Terry arrived to join him, Harter had been enthralling visitors for six years with hour-long, sightseeing helicopter rides from his base at the *Kauai Surf Hotel* in Lihue on the island's south shore. He owned two helicopters – a Bell-J2 and Fairchild Hiller FH-1100 – but was struggling against a new competitor equipped with more modern Bell Jet Rangers, much better suited to the task.

Terry and Joan moved into a small flat in Lihue overlooking the limpid water of Nawililiwili Harbour. A short walk past a giant banyan tree brought them to the *Kauai Surf Hotel*. While Terry settled into flying the tourist circuit, Joan helped with bookings in the office. They quickly made friends and relaxed into the easy-going routine of island life. Terry's debonair charm and dry humour made him a natural tour guide. He beguiled passengers with his version of Harter's captivating commentary, liberally laced with facts and folklore and memorable one-liners. The usual circuit started by going northwards from Lihue. It then followed the rugged contours of the north shore, skirting golden, sandy beaches bathed in dazzling-white surf. One of these was where Mitzi Gaynor immortally 'washed that man right out of my hair' in Hollywood's version of *South Pacific*. Continuing westward, the flight hugged 4,000-feet-high cliffs whose faces plunged vertically into the aquamarine ocean at Na Pali. If they were not already gasping with awe, the return journey was guaranteed to leave most passengers wowed. It swooped southwards for ten miles between the 3,600-feet-high bluffs of Waimea Canyon, a breathtaking defile aptly described by Mark Twain as the Grand Canyon of the Pacific, before a giddying climb over the rain-soaked slopes of Waialeale peak, the second wettest place on earth. Even Terry found it exhilarating.

> Borneo and Thailand could be very beautiful from a helicopter but Kauai had to be one of the most spectacular circuits in the world. When you flew into Waimea people simply couldn't believe their eyes. I remember one little old lady who asked me in all sincerity if it was real. I think she thought Disney had laid it on.

Terry rather mischievously teased her.

'Well, actually, we scooped it all out with bulldozers and dumped the earth over there,' he told her, pointing across to the neighbouring island of Nihau. 'She just said, 'Wow, imagine that'.'

On another occasion, Terry and Joan went hiking in Waimea Canyon with friends and arranged with Joe Healey, one of the other Harter Tours' pilots, to drop them some cold beer on his way through with visitors.

> Joe spun the tourists some yarn about occasionally having to drop things to a long lost tribe of people deep in the canyon, who were possibly related to the *menehunes*, the little people who come out at night and do great feats according to island legend. When he landed, we emerged dirty and very dusty from the undergrowth, unaware of his story. The tourists started clicking away at us with their cameras. Then one of them asked if we spoke American but before we could say anything Joe revved up and whisked them away. I expect there's an old granny in Minnesota or somewhere telling her grandchildren about the lost tribe of Kauai to this day.

Sending visitors away struggling for superlatives to describe their experience became Terry's new mission. The job may have lacked the sense of purpose, risks and adrenaline-driven excitement of search and rescue work, but it had many compensations. Besides, he was ready to settle down with Joan and could not believe his luck in finding somewhere so idyllic to make a new life with her. His discovery in Vientiane that the British authorities had not lost interest in him was an unpleasant surprise. Hidden in faraway Kauai, he felt secure and abandoned any notions of reconnecting with his past. He told Joan that he wanted to get married, suggesting 28 March for their wedding day. In a rare confession, he finally admitted to her that he had been married before and that he had just staged his death when they met on the cross-Channel ferry five years earlier. He assured her that he had obtained a divorce in Mexico on his way to Laos and that she had nothing to worry about. Joan accepted the revelations with characteristic composure, although by her own admission she was 'stunned that he could do such a thing' when he told her about his faked drowning. Given his candour on this occasion, Terry strangely stopped short of getting all the bad news out in one go. He said nothing about the existence of his daughters. He also omitted to mention that 28 March happened to be the anniversary of his first marriage.

Shortly after joining Harter Tours, Terry calculated that the company was losing $300 a day.

> When I pointed this out to Harter's investors they asked me to take over managing the business as vice-president, much to Jack's displeasure. We bought out our rival with the Jet Rangers, got rid of our old Bell and then started bidding for fire fighting, search and rescue and crop spraying contracts to boost our sightseeing revenue. After a while we had quite a large fleet of aircraft, with contracts on Hawaii and Mauai, as well as our established tourist circuit in Kauai.

In a sense, Terry had found his new stimulus – building a successful business. The hours he had spent reading the business guide on 'how to make a million' in the Congo were finally going to pay off. He invested his own small savings in the venture to become a joint owner. Meanwhile, he and Joan moved to a larger apartment on the beach at Poipu, at the southern extreme of the island. They acquired a parrot to replace the abandoned Sparky and a Great Dane that they christened Goris.

As Terry set about restoring the fortunes of Harter Tours, Joan started a job as a rehabilitation specialist at the Waimea Hospital and took on voluntary work for the American Cancer Society. In between these commitments she made preparations for their wedding. Life for them both had rarely been so good. Terry faced each day with the same zest as he had when confronted by the challenges of casevacs and medivacs. He was ebullient; fun to be with and uncommonly willing to share his inner thoughts. Joan was as transported by him as she had been during their heady week together in Brussels just after meeting when she confided in her diary that he was 'way out of my league'.

They were married in a pretty, stone church in the centre of Lihue. Joan wore a simple, white dress that she made herself. Her father was there from Canada to give her away. Terry's best man was Bob Billings, the

United Airlines pilot who accompanied him on the epic delivery of H-34
from Tel Aviv to Calabar and who had accepted an invitation from him
to join Harter Tours during a lay-off period. A small gathering of their
new friends joined them for a boisterous reception at JJ's Broiler, one of
Lihue's most popular restaurants owned by Jim and Mary Jasper, with
whom they had become especially close. They posed happily for
customary photographs as they cut the traditional, three-tiered wedding
cake that Joan had also made herself with help from the cook at the *Kauai
Surf Hotel*. Terry recalls that from JJ's they went downtown to the Lihue
Athletic Club to continue the celebrations.

> We eventually left to go to a hotel for a honeymoon break and ended
> up at the wrong end of the island well after midnight with all the ice
> melted in the complimentary champagne bucket and too tired to
> drink the champagne anyway. Otherwise, it was just another day in
> paradise.

Three months later, Terry was sitting behind his desk in the Harter Tours
office when a stranger arrived, flashing a US Immigration and
Naturalization Service (INS) identity card. 'Apparently he'd already been
to see just about everybody else in the company, asking questions about
me before eventually showing up in my office.'

'Are you Mr Terence Peet?' he wanted to know.

'Yes, I am,' Terry answered.

'You're from England, I believe,' the immigration official said.

'Yes, that's right, I am,' Terry agreed.

'Well, we'd like to talk to you about your family and what you're doing
here illegally,' the official continued. 'You need to come to Honolulu and
sort things out with my boss.' Terry cheerfully volunteered to go as soon
as he could spare the time a few days later. However, his broad smile and
friendly handshake as he saw the man out disguised a deep sense of
foreboding. Instinctively, he knew that the British authorities had caught
up with him. His mood changed with chameleon-like speed to reflect his
sense of apprehension and he characteristically retreated into himself.

At the meeting with the head of the INS in Honolulu, a man named
O'Shea, Terry's worst fear was confirmed. The first hint of a possible hitch
over his immigration status had occurred a few weeks beforehand when
he re-entered the US after going back to Nigeria on a business trip. He
had been to Lagos to try and win a lucrative contract for harbour clearance
using a giant helicopter crane. At the time, he treated the query over his
status on his return as nothing more ominous than a paperwork

irregularity. However, what he learned at the meeting with O'Shea was that the interest in him had been triggered by information received from the British Government through diplomatic channels and the news was not good.

> He told me that I was wanted by the British authorities for various charges, including desertion from the RAF. Stupidly, when I left Laos I'd made no secret about where I was going and it hadn't taken London long to start raising questions about my application for immigration. O'Shea couldn't be specific about the accusations, although I was supposed to be a bigamist and a security threat. Basically, they'd done a pretty good job of painting the blackest possible picture of me.

Being portrayed as a criminal and traitor angered Terry. In staging his death he had been careful to eliminate any potential for fraud. Similarly, he felt that by obtaining a Mexican divorce he had done what he could to avoid the serious accusation of bigamy. Even more worrying was the suggestion that he had done something to betray his country. 'Okay, I was a deserter but I couldn't accept any of the other stuff and if O'Shea did, to put it bluntly, I was in deep shit.'

Terry decided that the only thing to do in the circumstances was to tell O'Shea the whole story and appeal to his American sense of fair play. 'After all, the British had shown no interest in getting me back when I was working with the CIA in the Congo or when I was heading up an American relief team in Nigeria, so why the sudden change now that I was leading a civilian life in Hawaii?'

To his credit, O'Shea was sympathetic but firm. He told Terry that he would give him a four-month visa extension to resolve the questions that had been raised over his immigration application. But he also advised him that he should probably start looking for somewhere else to live in case his application was refused. This came as a real body blow. Just as his life seemed to be back on track, he was confronted by having to contemplate another kind of disappearing act. Back in Kauai he broke the news to Joan, playing down his real fear and insisting that everything would be all right.

When Terry told his director colleagues of his immigration setback, they rallied to support him. They acknowledged that he was key to the continuing growth of their million-dollar business.[1] With their help, he began what became a year-long fight against the looming threat of deportation, enlisting the influential help of Senator Daniel Inouye and hiring a combative lawyer named Clarence Fong, whose brother Hiram Fong was also a Hawaiian senator. A heavily decorated Japanese–American war hero,[2] who lost his right arm during the Italian campaign, Senator Inouye had represented Hawaii in Congress since the islands achieved statehood in 1959. He was elected to the Senate in 1963 and is now the third most senior Democratic senator. Although his encounter with Terry came early in his senate career, he was still a formidable ally.

> He was the one-armed warrior and I couldn't have had anyone better on my side. At one stage, we all trooped off to Washington to get the CIA to vouch for me. I wasn't allowed to attend any of the meetings but the others told me afterwards that they got nowhere. I didn't exist so far as the men at Langley were concerned. To be honest I never really expected anything else. The only person we found who admitted to knowing me, was Major Russell from the US Embassy in Nigeria.

Terry was not surprised by the CIA's unwillingness to acknowledge his role with WIGMO. Operation *WITHRUSH* was still classified and, anyway, he was only ever a contract employee and as such a complete non-entity in CIA terms – what it refers to as a 'deniable asset'. The same was true of Mishou, who could not provide any official help either. Letters written by Terry to Devlin, Weber and Johnson appealing for recognition, went unanswered. He was hung out to dry.

Nevertheless, according to Terry, Inouye and Fong stalled for time while he made monthly trips to Honolulu, pleading successfully with O'Shea for a series of visa extensions. While all this was going on, another stranger arrived at Harter Tours looking for Terry.

> He was a youngish guy who claimed that his name was Warwick and that he worked at the British Embassy in Tokyo. I was pretty sure that he was a spook who'd been sent to check me out – remember Tokyo's a lot closer to Hawaii than Washington – but decided to treat him just like any other tourist and give him a good time. I took him for a ride round the island with a young Japanese woman who he said was his girlfriend and afterwards they invited me for dinner. I realized then that if London was prepared to go to that much trouble to find me, they'd probably stop at nothing to block my immigration.

At this juncture, Terry decided to test the temperature by writing to the RAF Air Council asking how he would be treated if he surrendered himself.

In October 1970 he posted a lengthy letter pleading for mercy. He confessed to faking his drowning, explaining that he was driven to it by his matrimonial breakdown and his determination to take personal action to help save lives in the Congo, where Europeans 'were being slaughtered daily'. He also claimed that he was afraid of being grounded following a private medical check revealing that he suffered from high blood pressure. He lived for flying, he wrote, adding that he had done what he did in a state of 'complete dilemma and mental turmoil'. Without referring to the CIA or the manner of his recruitment to WIGMO, since he thought doing so would prejudice his case, he then gave details of his rescue work in the Congo and subsequent involvement in the UNICEF airlift in Nigeria.

Although sticking to the facts would have been compelling enough, Terry resorted to embellishing them to strengthen his case. Given the seriousness of his predicament, it is easy to understand why he was driven to this by his persistent lack of self-belief. Yet it was foolhardy to risk undermining the validity of his entire case if the RAF had tried to verify his claims.

The assertion that he was afraid of being grounded at the time of his desertion was stretching the truth. His chronic hypertension was first diagnosed by Dr Close in Leopoldville almost a year after he left Tern Hill. However, it would have been uncovered soon enough by his RAF medicals and may well have curtailed his career, so including it in mitigation can be forgiven. Similarly, he might be excused for feeling the need to exaggerate his humanitarian efforts, even though the truth was undeniably impressive. For example, he claimed to have *personally* saved 570 lives in the Congo and to have delivered 200,000 tons of food aid in Nigeria. In the absence of official records, Terry's flight log is the most reliable guide to his life-saving exploits in the war-torn jungle of equatorial Africa, where personally saving scores rather than hundreds of lives was nearer the reality, although he may also have participated with others in saving many more. Similarly, his Calabar-based helicopter relief flights delivered a fraction of the tonnage he claimed – which may have been nearer the total for the entire relief agency airlift – although it undoubtedly contributed to saving many thousands of starving refugees in the Cross River Delta. In the end the figures themselves are not really that important since only the very churlish would quarrel with the contention that much of what Terry had done was heroic.

His letter ended with an ardent appeal. 'I request clemency and amnesty,' he wrote. 'I remain a loyal subject and a patriot and I have always tried to uphold the values taught to me in fourteen years of Service life.' Unmoved, the RAF responded bluntly. An internal memorandum circulated by Air Commodore J A G Jackson of the Special Investigations Branch set the tone for an uncompromising stance. He wrote: 'Peet's letter raises no new issues other than the fact that he now knows we know where he is'. It confirmed that there was no chance of securing his extradition and instructed 'a curt acknowledgement, exactly as you would to any other deserter' adding 'it would be better not to answer any of his questions or give any hint of our attitude'. The reply, when it eventually arrived in Kauai, was unequivocal. Terry was told that there were 'no procedures for pardoning deserters'.

Faced with the RAF's forthright rejection of his appeal, Terry resolved to redouble his efforts to persuade the US authorities that he should be allowed to remain in Hawaii. Both Daniel Inouye and Clarence Fong pressed the political and legal campaign on his behalf. Apart from the accusation that Terry was a deserter, what none of them knew was the nature of the other allegations that the British had hinted at. However, a single loose minute dated June 1970 in Terry's service records, confirms that he was by then under investigation by the intelligence services and that his security clearance had been withdrawn. Sometime later that year, two MI5 officers paid a visit to Wing Commander Derek Eley, Terry's former commanding officer in Malaya. Eley was then the chief flying instructor for the School of Army Aviation at Middle Wallop in Hampshire, near the south coast of England. He recalls being questioned at length about Terry by his MI5 visitors.

> They wanted to know everything I knew about him but refused to tell me why. From their questioning I got the impression they thought he'd been working for the Russians or one of the Soviet satellite states. At any rate, I couldn't believe it; I wouldn't believe it. I told them quite plainly that they were barking up the wrong tree. Terry may have gone about doing what he did the wrong way but he was no traitor.

As the uncertainty over his future grew with each passing month, Terry relied increasingly on Joan's support to bolster his flagging morale. Much of the time he was withdrawn and reticent, leaving her to guess at the depth of his anxiety. She drew on every ounce of her professional training, above all what occupational therapists define as 'the inner maturity that governs self control', to remain cheerful and raise his spirits. Conscious of how much he owed her, Terry finally decided to share the last important secret about his past and tell her about his daughters, although he feared the consequence of doing so and needed to summon all his emotional courage. His intention was laudable but his timing terrible. They were in the car on the way to a restaurant for lunch with friends when he rather clumsily made the admission out of the blue. Joan was dumbfounded. 'I remember having to go into the restaurant and pretend everything was all right but I was shocked and angry. I just didn't understand why he'd kept it from me.' Afterwards, Terry showed enough remorse to win her round and their relationship survived.

By late summer 1971, it was quite obvious that Terry would have to leave Hawaii voluntarily or risk deportation. O'Shea advised him that if he left and resubmitted his immigration application, he had a reasonable chance of having it approved. On the other hand, if he forced the authorities to deport him he would never be allowed to return. It was a stark choice. Terry opted to leave, in the hope that with continuing help from Inouye and Fong, his exile would not be for too long. He wrote to Bob Brannon, his old compatriot from the Congo, explaining the problem. 'Bob replied immediately offering me a job flying fishery protection patrols with him along the south-west African coast. He offered to put Joan and me up until we could find a place of our own.' Filled with new-found optimism by Brannon's generosity, Terry prepared to leave Kauai temporarily. As an adjunct to the helicopter business, he was part owner of a small travel firm. The company had just won a contract from the Kauai-based University of Contemplative Arts to send 110 monks on a worldwide meditation tour taking in Japan, China, India and Russia. Terry thought that it would be a good idea for him and Joan to go ahead of the monks to prepare the venues and check the hotels. They would then go to South Africa and stay with Brannon until the immigration issue was resolved.

In early October, they left for Tokyo on the first stage of the trip. The plan was then to go to Hong Kong and Vientiane en route to Delhi, where they would collect their visas for Moscow. Before leaving, Terry contacted Warwick, the Tokyo-based British agent who had shown up months earlier in Kauai for a helicopter ride with his Japanese girlfriend, and arranged to meet him for dinner. 'We didn't talk about me or my situation at all when he came to Kauai but I was curious to see if he'd let anything slip if we met again.' Whatever Warwick's role, he appears to have succumbed to Terry's charm offensive in Tokyo.

Again we didn't talk about me or my problem at all but towards the end of the evening I had the feeling he was trying to warn me not to go to Hong Kong. He didn't say it in so many words but he talked in general terms about some people having problems trying to pass through.

At the time, of course, Hong Kong was still a British Crown Colony.

The next day Terry thought seriously about re-routeing their flight. 'I could have changed our tickets so that in Hong Kong we went through the transit lounge from one flight to another without going through passport control and nobody would have known I'd been there. But I didn't.'

Notes

1 $5.6 million in today's values.
2 Inouye enlisted in the US Army in 1943 when it lifted a ban on Japanese–American servicemen. He served with the 442nd Regimental Combat Team and was awarded the Bronze Star, Purple Heart and Medal of Honor.

Chapter Twenty-six
...And Lost Again

Reclining in his seat in the first-class cabin of the Japan Airlines flight from Tokyo, Terry could not help speculating about what sort of reception he might find in Hong Kong. Nevertheless, he was resigned to whatever awaited him rather than consumed with apprehension.

> I'd come to the conclusion that the game was up. We were due to fly to London from Moscow and I was pretty sure that if the RAF didn't get me in Hong Kong they'd probably get me there. Anyway, I felt it was time to sort this thing out and clear the air so I could get on with life without being on the run. That's why I decided not to change our tickets. I was going to take my chances and see what happened.

As the aircraft dropped over the skyscrapers of Hong Kong to make its final approach to Kai Tak International Airport, he smiled at Joan and took her hand for the landing. They were due to spend three days luxuriating in one of Hong Kong's finest hotels before flying on to Vientiane and then Delhi. Terry had promised Joan that it would be a memorable experience. However, as he approached the immigration desk with their passports in hand, he took a deep breath fully expecting to find that, for him at least, the journey would be over.

'Thank you. Enjoy your stay,' the immigration officer said routinely, after stamping their passports and handing them back.

'Oh, I'm sure we will,' grinned Terry, as he led Joan away to find their baggage.

Early on the morning of 7 October, after a whirlwind few days shopping, sightseeing and checking on arrangements for the forthcoming monks' meditation tour, they arrived back at Kai Tak to catch a Royal Air Laos flight for the next stage of their trip. This time Terry was not expecting any problem.

> I reasoned that if they were going to get me in Hong Kong they'd do it on my way in, not my way out. I'd actually thought about going to the RAF station and handing myself in but decided to finish the trip

and do it in the UK. To be honest, I'd reached the stage where I knew they were going to catch up with me; it was just a question of time. The powers that be were bigger than I was. They'd succeeded in making me *persona non grata* in Hawaii, where my livelihood was, and they'd probably try to do the same wherever else I went.

When he handed over their passports and tickets at the check-in desk, the young female clerk glanced sideways towards two RAF military policemen standing out of sight nearby. They immediately came across.

'Flight Lieutenant Peet?' one of them asked.

'Yes, that's me,' Terry acknowledged.

'Come with us please, sir,' the policeman commanded.

Terry was led away to a small room where an RAF officer was waiting. After being told that he was under arrest for being illegally absent since September 1965, one of the two MPs handcuffed him.

'Look, is this really necessary?' Terry protested. 'I'm not going anywhere.' The officer nodded his agreement and ordered the removal of the handcuffs. Terry then explained that he was travelling with his wife. He said that he would like an opportunity to see her and sort out their belongings, which were mixed up in their numerous bags. The officer nodded again. A few moments later, Joan was brought into the room with the baggage. She was left alone with Terry while the officer and MPs stood guard outside.

> It was nice of them but quite ridiculous really. We were left unsupervised for half an hour or so to repack our clothes in separate bags. If I'd been a spy I could've got rid of any incriminating documents by transferring them to Joan's bags without anyone being any the wiser.

He and Joan agreed that she should complete the organizational trip for the monks' tour and then find out where Terry was being held once she reached the UK. He knew from the arresting officer that he was being flown back to the RAF base at Brize Norton in Oxfordshire, some fifty miles west of London later the same day.

'Don't worry about me. Everything's going to be fine,' he assured her after a tearful goodbye.

While Terry was being held under close arrest in the RAF Kai Tak guardroom, a former sergeant pilot named Tug Wilson, who had flown Sycamores with him in Malaya, paid him a visit. 'By then he was a wing commander. I was glad to have somebody to talk to and he was very supportive.' Meanwhile, a cable confirming Terry's arrest reached the Ministry of Defence in London. His first wife and parents were telephoned with the news, the first official communication to them about him since they were informed of his death by drowning almost six years earlier. The RAF had maintained its silence despite knowing full well that he was alive after being sighted in December 1968 and then corresponding with him in October 1970, but lost no time announcing his capture. News of his arrest was also released to the wire services the same day, leading to a flurry of 'back-from-the-dead airman' newspaper reports, including mine in *The Birmingham Post*. In South Africa, Bob Brannon read of Terry's arrest in utter disbelief. 'I'd swallowed all that stuff about his wife and kids tragically dying in an air accident and the truth was that he'd faked his death and left them. But Terry is Terry and I couldn't help myself forgiving him.'

The RAF VC-10 returning Terry to England landed at Brize Norton in the late morning on 8 October 1971. He remembers feeling 'very criminal' as he was driven to RAF Innsworth in Gloucestershire in the company of three armed escorts. Once there, he was installed in an air commodore's suite with hastily barred windows and guarded day and night by three RAF police sergeants. 'I questioned why I wasn't simply under close arrest with an officer of my own rank to watch over me as provided under RAF law. The answer I got was that the rules had been changed in my case.' Immediately after arriving at Innsworth, Terry was subjected to a round of intense interrogation by officers of the Special Investigations Branch. From their questioning, he quickly realized that he was suspected of a lot more than desertion.

> They were particularly interested in my association with Haas in Laos. I got the feeling they thought he was an East German agent and that I was in league with him. The fact that I had an Aeroflot ticket to Moscow in my possession when they arrested me didn't exactly help. You can imagine their reaction when I told them I was organizing a meditation tour for 110 monks! Anyway, I just kept insisting that I'd never been disloyal to my country.

In spite of being closely guarded most of the time, Terry was able to tape record one of the questioning sessions. He smuggled the tape out when Joan eventually visited him. Although the recording is of poor quality, his interrogators' references to Haas and Terry's persistent denials of any treachery on his part are clearly audible above a background din of slamming doors, scraping chairs and ringing telephones. After several sessions, the interrogation stopped abruptly. 'Apparently they'd confirmed from their sources that Haas was not a Soviet agent and there was indeed a University of Contemplative Arts in Kauai. So then I was just a deserter not a spy and they lost interest in me.'

Terry was informed that he was to face a court martial for desertion. He was allocated a civilian lawyer from a firm in Gloucester who Terry claims 'knew absolutely nothing about military law or procedures' to prepare his case. Meanwhile, he faced questions from detectives investigating the legality of his Mexican divorce. 'They went away satisfied that I was not a bigamist provided my lawyer regularized the divorce in the UK at a later date if that were necessary.' With his court martial set for Thursday 28 October, Terry was allowed some visitors and to make telephone calls. Among the first to see him was an old buddy from his flight training days named Curly Dawson, who was by then a wing commander piloting RAF VC-10s. Terry asked Dawson to arrange for Dave Tennyson, who had been his closest compatriot in Malaya and Borneo, to be appointed as his 'officer friend'. However, to Terry's great disappointment, Tennyson turned down the request. 'I suppose he must have had his reasons but I remember being very upset at the time because we'd been through a lot together and I could've done with some moral support.'

One of his other early visitors was his father. The reunion was warm but awkward as Ernie Peet recounted how much anguish Terry's mother had suffered.

> He told me that she'd been heartbroken when she heard that I'd drowned. That had been bad enough. Even worse though had been the discovery later that I might be alive and then wondering whether she'd ever see me again. She'd spent years hoping that every telephone call or knock on the door would be 'our Terry'. Did I have any idea how difficult that had been for her?'

'When they told us that tha'd been arrested she didn't know whether to cry with joy because you're alive or cry with worry because you're in trouble. She wanted to come with me today, son, but she were just in too much of a state,' Ernie Peet told him. 'When I've gone, give her a call. There's no need to explain owt. It'll just do her a world o' good to hear your voice again.'

Later, Terry steeled himself for what he sensed would be the most difficult conversation of his life. 'I told her that I was sorry for what I'd done, that I'd never stopped loving her and that I hoped she'd forgive me.

She was wonderful: she didn't say a cross word. All she wanted to know was that I was okay. And when would I be home?'

Terry's defence options on the charge of desertion were limited. His letter to the Air Council was a complete confession. He was tempted to use the way he had been recruited to WIGMO to mitigate his action. However, that would have meant betraying the confidence of the officer who gave him the CIA-front's telephone number, which he had sworn never to do. At any rate, even if he did, it would be that officer's word against his. At the same time, he was strongly advised against implicating the CIA since there was no hope of getting any corroborating evidence. The CIA had already disowned him in the context of his immigration appeal in Hawaii and was hardly likely to change this stance for a public trial in the UK.

Basically, I felt under a lot of pressure to plead guilty and hope for the best. I was repeatedly told that things would go a lot more easily for me if I didn't make a fuss and cost the RAF a lot of time and money flying in witnesses and that sort of thing. In the end I decided that I had no choice really.

Shortly before his trial, Joan visited him. He told her that he intended to plead guilty and rely on his unblemished naval service, his exemplary flying record with the RAF and his subsequent life-saving work to keep him out of prison. They would then go to South Africa and stay with Brannon as planned, in the hope of eventually being allowed back to Hawaii to pick up the pieces of their shattered life in Kauai. Before Joan left, Terry explained that he had heard nothing from his first wife but was anxious to know how his daughters were. He asked her to visit them on his behalf. Although she wanted to do everything she could to support him, she found this request too much. 'I simply couldn't face it and told him so.' He shrugged and beamed an understanding smile.

Joan could not face being present at his court martial either, although his first wife attended and sat at the back of the small, packed courtroom. Terry was marched in flanked by two MPs. He wore the air force-blue, flight lieutenant's uniform that he had last donned six years earlier. It looked and felt a little tighter on him but he still cut a dashing figure. After smartly saluting the presiding tribunal he turned to face the courtroom and took a seat alongside his defending counsel immediately in front of the crowded Press benches. Apart from entering his plea of 'guilty' he remained silent throughout the short hearing, his face impassive to the end.

Presenting the facts for the prosecution, Flight Lieutenant John Le

Mesurier-Hurley relied almost entirely on Terry's letter to the Air Council, quoting at length from it. Until the RAF's receipt of the letter, he claimed that nothing had been seen or heard of Terry by the RAF since his disappearance. He also claimed that when arrested he was in possession of two passports, the clear implication being that he used an alias. Both these misleading statements went unchallenged. Terry may not have been in touch with the RAF until late 1970 but he had been positively identified and his whereabouts reported almost two years earlier. The RAF had made no attempt to pursue him but the court was not told this. The so-called second passport was a UN identity document in Terry's correct name. Throughout his absence, Terry only ever travelled on his British passport, including the occasion when he visited London after leaving the Congo.

Pleading mitigation, Terry's counsel, Michael Russell, argued that: 'at no time in the six years (of his absence) did Peet engage in any activities with which the RAF itself could not have been proud. His desertion was in no way associated with defection and no security element was involved in the case.' He insisted that Terry had never been a mercenary and never been involved in combat operations. These claims, of course, were not entirely true either. The CIA may have used the terminology 'contract pilot' but as Brook-Fox had pointed out, however the Americans dressed it up, WIGMO was a mercenary air force. Moreover, although Terry's motivation had always been humanitarian he had been drawn into combat operations in the Congo, albeit reluctantly. In Nigeria he resisted that temptation when the UNICEF relief effort collapsed, even though the reality was that at the time Britain was unofficially happy to see former RAF pilots bolstering the Nigerian Air Force and the High Commission in Nigeria was actively encouraging it.

Pointing to Terry's life-saving accomplishments in the Congo and Nigeria, Russell pleaded for him to be allowed his freedom to continue doing similar humanitarian work. He asserted that at the time of his arrest, Terry was on his way to Pakistan to help with a refugee crisis then unfolding there, adding that he had 'contacts all over the free world geared to mount relief operations anywhere at a moment's notice'. The latter claims were as disinguous as the RAF's pretence that it had not seen or heard of Terry until his letter from Hawaii. In a sort of tit-for-tat way, they too went unchallenged by Le Mesurier-Hurley. In retrospect, it seems that the evidence on both sides fell short of what might be expected in court proceedings. The case had been assembled in three weeks and on close examination has more the appearance of a show trial than a serious judicial process.

The verdict, of course, was a foregone conclusion. Terry knew perfectly well that the least he could expect was to be cashiered.[1] What was really at stake was his liberty. The tribunal did not take long to reach its decision. Group Captain V S Duclos, presiding, confirmed the sentence of cashiering with the addition of a year's imprisonment. In doing so, he said that the twenty-two days Terry had spent under close arrest had been taken into consideration. The outcome was much worse than Terry had hoped. However, he showed no emotion and marched out between his guards as smartly as he had arrived. At the back of the court his ex-wife hissed 'you bastard' as he left but he did not hear her. He had not even seen her.

Banner headlines in the next day's national newspapers portrayed Terry sympathetically as a renegade hero. The two biggest-selling tabloids set the tone with the *Daily Mirror* proclaiming: 'AMAZING DOUBLE LIFE OF A FLYING PIMPERNEL' in two bold decks dominating a page. Not to be outdone, its arch-rival *The Sun*, carried an equally fulsome report under the heading: 'THE PILOT WHO DESERTED TO BECOME A HERO'. However, Terry felt nothing heroic about being incarcerated in Her Majesty's Prison Gloucester with a serial thief as his mentor. 'I had to learn to survive inside and they gave me this old hand, who was always in and out of jail, to show me the ropes and make sure I stayed out of trouble.'

By today's standards the length of the prison sentence seems harsh although it was in line with sentencing guidelines issued by the Judge Advocate General's office. The Air Force Act 1955 did not set any minimum or upper limits on the length of sentence but for comparison, a flight lieutenant who refused to serve in Iraq in 2006 was dismissed with eight months' imprisonment.[2] There is an argument that Terry's peacetime disappearance was less serious. Indeed, the Air Force Act 2006, which came into force in January 2009, sets an upper limit of two years' imprisonment for cases of desertion like Terry's with life imprisonment for cases involving desertion to avoid 'active service'. The Courts Martial Registers at the National Archives are incomplete and some remain closed. As a result it is impossible to determine how many RAF officers faced courts martial for deserting during the period 1950 to 1975 or what sentences they received. In response to a Freedom of Information request, the RAF claimed that it holds no centralized data on officer desertions and sentences for the period involved. So no useful comparisons can be made.

Unfortunately, the records of Terry's court martial have been destroyed. This is normal procedure after seven years except in cases involving murder, manslaughter, treason or sedition; trials ending in custodial sentences of five years or more; cases of mutiny and insubordination with sentences of two years or more; cases involving terrorist activities, and cases considered to be of historical interest. It could be argued that Terry's case was sufficiently out of the ordinary for the record to merit retention on historical grounds, not least because he was almost certainly the last RAF officer to be 'cashiered'.[3] Moreover, the 'unusual' nature of his case was highlighted by the Judge Advocate General's office in a letter to the officer responsible for reviewing his sentence on 2 November 1971, the only surviving document relating to his court martial. Significantly, it ends with the comment that 'while you might find it difficult to relieve the accused completely of imprisonment, the case does appear to contain many features justifying clemency'. As a result Terry's prison term was reduced to one of nine months. In practical terms that made little difference.

The most troubling feature of the destruction of Terry's court martial records are that there is now no way of knowing whether they might have shed any light on what triggered the curious MI5 investigation that undoubtedly led to his arrest. Nor is there any way of knowing whether evidence that might have explained why it took the RAF six years to apprehend him was suppressed. Needless to say, the security services refuse to discuss the case. There is nothing enlightening in Terry's service records. Only a handful of documents relate to his disappearance, the sightings of him and his subsequent arrest and court martial. With stunning bureaucratic efficiency, however, there are pages and pages of correspondence concerning the requirement to recover from him the sum of £112 13s 7d for RAF clothing, equipment and books that he took when he staged his drowning. Freedom of Information requests for any other documents relating to his case yielded nothing. This means that whatever it was that changed the official attitude from one of turning a blind eye to one of active pursuit will remain a mystery.

One of the first people to visit Terry in prison was Wing Commander Eley, accompanied by his wife.

'How are you?' asked Terry's former CO with obvious sincerity.

'I'm fine, thanks,' answered Terry.

'Well, I must say you look very well,' observed Eley.

'That's because I've had to give up drinking,' quipped Terry with characteristic joviality. At the end of the visit, Eley exhibited genuine compassion for his one-time 'go anywhere, do anything in a Sycamore' pilot.

'Is there anything at all I can do for you?' he wanted to know before he left.

'Yes, as a matter of fact there is: you can get me out of here,' Terry replied seriously.

Eley remembers his plaintive appeal. 'I wanted to help but it was impossible really. Frankly, I took my hat off to Terry for going off to save lives. Unfortunately, he just didn't go about doing it in the proper way.'

After a couple of months, Terry was moved to the high security prison at Bristol where he shared a cell with three hardened convicts. 'That place was like something out of the Middle Ages. I was eventually made the governor's valet and given a red badge entitling me to certain privileges but, believe me, I counted the days to my release.' Joan was staying with a cousin in nearby Swansea, Wales. She visited him whenever she could. She recalls one visit towards the end of February when she was allowed a 'generous three-quarters of an hour' with him. Afterwards she wrote in her diary that he was 'very thin and nervous-looking but receiving privileges'. The separation and waiting were an ordeal. However, she remained resolutely loyal and supportive. At Terry's request she flew to Spain and sold his apartment in Fuengirola. She also wrote countless letters of support to friends and contacts, often at his bidding.

> When I visited Terry he would have instructions that he had planned during the previous days and weeks. I'd go home and carry them out, making 'phone calls, writing letters, keeping alive relationships with his friends, of whom he had many. He didn't want to be forgotten.

She even wrote to his parents and received a 'kind and well-meaning' reply from his mother. 'I guess it can't have been any fun not knowing where your son was for so many years,' she confided in her diary.

Joan remembers there being some confusion about Terry's release date.

> I'd been thinking he would be released on 14 March but when I heard nothing from his solicitor I rang the prison and they confirmed that he was still there and nothing else. Eventually, we heard that the date would be 27 April. The day before, I went to Bristol and picked up a hire car and then had my hair done.

At 7:15 the next morning she drove to the prison gate in Cambridge Road, arriving just as Terry walked out, a little over five months after being imprisoned. Their reunion was marred by the unwelcome and uninvited presence of two men who claimed to be freelance journalists. They talked Terry into letting them take photographs and accompany them to a local hotel for a lengthy interview. Afterwards, he and Joan left for Swansea and a couple of days in the protective custody of her cousin before facing the test of making amends with Terry's family.

On 30 April, Terry telephoned his parents in Farnham to say that he was on his way with Joan. He knew that facing his mother was going to be difficult, even though she had forgiven him. He was deeply ashamed of what he had put her through. The worst of it was that he had allowed her to go on not knowing the truth for more than a year after writing to the RAF. That had been unforgivable. Even he was at a loss about how he could explain it. The truth, of course, was that as usual Terry had waited for fate to take its course rather than facing up to making a painful admission of his own volition. That had always been his nature. But he really need not have worried.

Nance Peet greeted him at the door of the cottage at Woodlarks School in Farnham, where she had last said goodbye to him at the end of a visit more than six years earlier, with tear-filled eyes. She took him in her arms without a moment's hesitation.

'Welcome home son, welcome home,' she sobbed repeatedly. Terry hugged her, mute with emotion. He wept openly on her shoulder. While they remained locked in embrace, Ernie Peet looked on, saying: 'Nobody could ever convince me that tha wa dead, lad.'

'I'm sorry, Mum,' Terry eventually croaked. 'I'm sorry.'

'It's all right, son. You're home now; that's all that matters,' Nance replied wiping the tears from her eyes. 'Now, come on in. You'll catch a death standing here. The kettle's on.'

Terry's homecoming was an uncanny replay of his sorrowful return after running away from bullying at school more than twenty years earlier. On that occasion, of course, his father had had to go and collect him and bring him back to his distraught mother as she lay in a hospital bed.

'I'm sorry. It's not you or me Dad,' Terry had said. 'You wait. I'll show them who's the best.' He was forgiven then without a word of reproach and the same would be true again. In his mother's eyes he was never anything less than the best and he did not have to prove anything to her. Her profound relief and happiness at seeing him by her hospital bed after his schoolboy disappearance was matched by her intense gratification at having him home again then. Terry remembers his homecoming being nothing like the ordeal he might have expected.

It was as though I'd never been away, my mother fussing and loving, my father listening to what I had to say and not making any comment either way apart from repeating what he'd said when I first arrived – nobody could convince me that tha wa dead. That evening we all went out for drinks and dinner and the whole episode was like a distant memory. I was back and that's all that mattered.

Joan recalls that 'after a few emotional moments, little was ever mentioned again of Terry's other life'.

Not long afterwards Terry made contact with his ex-wife.

I left it a little while to let all the malicious gossip subside and then called and said that I'd like to see the girls. She agreed and we all went out for a meal together. I felt like crying when I first saw the girls again. They were very pretty and had grown up so much compared to the little bundles I'd kissed goodbye when I left. As you can imagine though, they were shy and apprehensive at first, not quite sure what to think. Not surprisingly I suppose, they'd heard a lot of bad things about me from their mother. But there I was being kind and nice to them and to her too.

In the weeks to follow Terry made several more visits to the small house in Farnham where his daughters lived with their mother. He was never allowed by her to take them out alone and her attitude was often understandably 'cool and clinical'.

Over time our meetings warmed up, especially when this monster turned out to be rather a nice guy who'd done good things for poor people in Africa. The first time they hugged me I knew that nothing would ever make me give them up again.

*   *   *

In the autumn of 1977, Nance Peet appealed to The Queen to pardon her son. Her petition was referred to the Secretary of State for Defence. A one-paragraph letter informed Terry that his mother's plea had been given 'careful consideration' and that its contents had been 'formally noted and placed with your personal records'. However, the petition, like Terry's letter to the Air Council, is not with his records, omissions the RAF cannot explain. In February 2008, Terry received an envelope from the Ministry of Defence addressed to Flight Lieutenant T J Peet. Inside, he found a medal and clasp for his service in Malaya and Borneo. This irony amuses him. 'Amazing, isn't it? They've obviously forgotten that they cashiered me!'

Notes

1 A sentence used by the Army and RAF to dismiss officers with ignominy, depriving them of their pensions and preventing any further Government employment.
2 Flt Lt Malcolm Kendall-Smith who argued that the war in Iraq was illegal.
3 Under the Armed Forces Act 1971, which came into effect shortly after his trial, the sentence of cashiering was changed to one of 'dismissed with disgrace', bringing the three armed services into line.

Postscript

Inevitably, a man like Terry was never going to lead an ordinary life. He and Joan eventually left for South Africa to take up Brannon's offer of a job and somewhere to live. A few months later, Terry received his American 'Green Card', apparently much to the disgust of the consul charged with issuing it. 'He made no secret of the fact that he disapproved and was acting under orders. I think it must have been a reward for keeping my trap shut.' However, back in Kauai, Terry and Joan found it difficult to recreate the life they had left. He sold his interest in the helicopter business and they returned to South Africa, where Terry was asked to manage a growing helicopter charter operation near Cape Town. This turned out to be another false start, ending in an uncomfortable brush with the law over the repossession of an aircraft. Terry was cleared of any wrongdoing but the investigation exposed alleged precious stone smuggling on the part of the owner of the business, leading to the company's downfall. Faced with this setback, Terry jumped at an offer to fly patrols monitoring Russian naval movements in Arctic waters for the Norwegian Government. He and Joan moved to Spitsbergen with their baby son, Roger, who had been born in March 1975.

In Europe it was easier for Terry to follow the progress of his daughters through school. He saw them as often as he could. His divorce had long-since been ratified under UK law and he had paid a lump-sum settlement to compensate his ex-wife for the costs of bringing up the girls. On one of his regular visits to Britain to see them, he was headhunted to fly helicopters in support of United States Geological Survey field trips in Saudi Arabia. 'The money was good and the weather warm, so I said "yes" and we went to live in Jeddah.' A year later, Terry accepted a position flying Gulfstream Jets with the special flights unit of Saudi Airlines. This launched a series of adventures flying Yasser Arafat, then the leader of the Palestinian Liberation Front, on fundraising trips around Arab countries.

He came into the cockpit once after taking off from Beirut and asked me to fly the wrong way round Israel. I said it was absolutely impossible because of air traffic control. He pulled out his nine-millimetre pistol, so I told him that the aircraft was pressurized and if he fired it we'd all *end up in Israel*. He laughed and showed me the empty cartridge. He said he had silver bullets but he kept them in his belt because they were too expensive to fire. Then he said, 'Here have one' and I gave it to my mother as a memento.

On another occasion, Arafat presented Terry with a bottle of Scotch on the approach to Jeddah.

He knew this was an absolute no-no going into Saudi. But as it happened the VIP drop off was a long way from our own dispersal, so I told the stewardess to pour three large glasses, which my crew and I drank as we taxied at a crawl. Air traffic asked us why we were going so slowly and I told them the brakes were overheating. Anyway, we managed to finish half the bottle and poured the rest down the sink.

While he worked for Saudi Airlines, Terry's daughters joined him in Jeddah. With his help, they both became air hostesses with Saudi and occasionally they flew together. Meanwhile, Joan had fallen in love with one of the geophysicists who Terry had flown on desert field trips in the early days after their arrival in the Arabian kingdom. She asked him for a divorce, finally ending their eventful life together.

Terry returned to the UK and began a hair-raising episode ferrying single-engine, light aircraft across the Atlantic from the United States. This involved flying a northerly arc with fuel stops in Iceland and the Faeroe Islands, often in extreme weather. He persuaded his former Congo co-pilot, Eugenio Papotti, to accompany him on one delivery, an experience that almost ended their friendship.

We ran into terrible weather and almost ran out of fuel. Eugenio thought he was going to die and refused to speak to me for ages afterwards. The crazy thing is, he now goes hang gliding every weekend. There's no way you'd catch me doing anything so dangerous.

After a spell flying helicopters to oil rigs in the Arabian Gulf, Terry joined Sheik Mohammed's Dubai Air Wing. Ten years later, aged sixty-two, he retired as a captain and settled in France with his third wife, Marie, whom he had married on 29 March 1986 – a day later than his previous wedding anniversaries. He reluctantly sold up in the Dordogne and moved back to England in early 2007 after undergoing major heart surgery at the end of the previous year.

Terry's complete reconciliation with his daughters is something he cherishes. He proudly gave them both away when they married and enjoys being a grandfather. Although his relationship with their mother has never thawed, he remains on affectionate terms with Joan and Roger, who live in Arizona. Many of the other people who featured in his extraordinary double life, also remain loyal friends. Few, if any of the people who knew him then, spurned him after discovering the truth. Separated by distance and time, they do not see each other often but they speak on the telephone, swap e-mails and exchange Christmas cards. They include Terry One in Texas, Ares Klootwyk in South Africa, Bob Brannon in Australia, Jane Mishou in Maine, Bob Billings in California, Eugenio Papotti in Italy, Pelle Ornas in Denmark, Terry Crawley in France and *Madame* Francine Troger in Belgium.

Events in Africa and particularly the Democratic Republic of Congo deeply sadden Terry. He cannot help feeling that his own efforts at saving lives over forty years ago were largely in vain. During thirty years of Mobutu's despotic rule the country was economically plundered and then in 1998 plunged into another civil war. Although a peace agreement was supposed to end the war in 2002, at the time of writing fighting continues in the east of the country. A mortality survey by the International Rescue Committee estimates the death toll attributable to this war and its humanitarian consequences at 5,400,000, making it one of the deadliest conflicts since the Second World War. Every month, as many as 45,000 people are estimated to die as a result of fighting, starvation and preventable diseases associated with the conflict. Much of the terrible violence, including the widespread, systematic rape of women and girls and brutal killings of whole families, is the work of Rwandan rebel militias – the Interahamwe – who fled over the border after being responsible for the genocide there in 1994.

Exactly fifty years after Congo's independence, the UN once again has its largest peacekeeping force there with a contingent of over 17,000 troops. Although they have helped contain the fighting, they stand accused of arming militias and trading illegally in stolen gold. Corruption continues on a massive scale. Meanwhile, the Chinese, who the CIA succeeded in keeping out of the Congo in the aftermath of independence, now have a powerful economic presence in the country – along with much of the rest of Africa – in pursuit of its vast mineral wealth. Under a $9 billion 'infrastructure for minerals' deal signed in January 2008, China is rebuilding 2,050 miles of roads left to rot in the jungle after Belgium's departure; restoring over 2,000 miles of railway track; building 32 hospitals and 145 health centres; installing two hydro-electric power plants with electricity distribution networks and constructing two new airports. In return, they have secured the rights to five copper and cobalt mines in the mineral-rich Katanga Province. US concern over China's growing presence in Africa was recently highlighted in the Wikileaks cables with one senior diplomat referring to Beijing's role as 'aggressive and pernicious'.

Flying in the Congo was dangerous in Terry's time. His friend, Henry Laurent, returned there to fly commercially after leaving Nigeria and died shortly afterwards in a fatal crash in spite of being an outstanding pilot. Today the country has the distinction of having the worst air safety record in the world.

Africa now provides another proxy battleground, this time in the West's so-called 'war on terror'. In Somalia American-backed Ethiopian forces have confronted Islamic insurgents with CIA black operations heavily involved behind the scenes. At the same time the concept of contracting out war to private enterprise with men who would have been called mercenaries, except by the CIA, has reached new heights. Contractors in the form of large corporations such as the former Blackwater Worldwide, renamed Xe Worldwide in 2009 in an attempt to distance itself from the controversial killing of seventeen Iraqi civilians in Baghdad in 2007, openly employ soldiers and airmen alike and enjoy lucrative security contracts in the war zones of Iraq, Afghanistan and elsewhere. They undertake duties that would normally have been seen as properly the role of regular forces, including the guarding of diplomats. Early in 2011 there were reports that Blackwater's founder was involved in trying to secure a contract for Saracen – a South Africa-based security company – to win a major contract in Somalia. The use of the term 'security' is intended to obscure paramilitary activity and circumvent the UN and OAU ban on the use of mercenaries in Africa. What the CIA began by sponsoring contract companies like Air America and WIGMO has spawned an industry making vast sums from conflicts today.

Sources

In addition to the first-hand accounts of those interviewed for this book – as set out in the acknowledgements – the events described are based on extensive research of official archives as well as other unpublished and published material. The principal sources are as follows:

The National Archives (UK)
AIR 27/2966 Operational Record Book 110 Squadron

AIR 28/1649 Operational Record Book RAF Tern Hill

AIR 2/15786 and AIR 28/1651 – files applicable to Tern Hill

AIR 29/3506, 3507 & 3795 Operational Record Books for RAF Valley

AIR 2/18396 RAF Courts Martial – policy

Key files relating to Congo
DO 183/710 Congo (formerly Belgian Congo)

FO 1104 Foreign Office, Embassy, Democratic Republic of the Congo, registered files 1965

PREM 11/4602 Constitutional Development in Africa, situation in Belgian Congo

FO 1100/10 Mercenaries in Congo

FO 1100/19 British missionaries in Congo

FO 1100/31 Military operations & behaviour

FO 1100/32 & 33 Military operations – Kisangani mutiny

FO 1100/34 Congo – Military Situation and uprising

FO 1100/35 New constitution and referendum

FO 1100/36 – 38 Civil War

FO 1100/42 Mercenary activity & recruitment 1967

FO 1100/44 British military aid to Congo 1966

FO 1100/50 & 53 Alleged murder of Bottomley by Cassidy

FO 1100/51–52 Arrest of John Latz, AP correspondent & mercenary

FO 1100/55 Counter subversion and aid 66 & 67

FO 953/2409 Press & Journalists, Leopoldville

FCO 47/146 Evacuation of Congo

FCO 47/4 British subjects in Congo

FO 1100/20 Hijacking of aircraft with Tshombe

FCO 36/126 Rhodesian mercenaries

FCO 36/266–268 War & Belligerency: Evacuation of mercenaries

FCO 47/170–172 Trevor Bottomley murder in the Congo by Major Cassidy

FCO 47/178 Death of Winifred Davies, missionary

FO 369/5843 Action in detention of Martin Leonard

Key files relating to Nigeria

FCO 25/232 Secession of E Nigeria (Biafra) from Nigeria

FCO 23/182 Nigeria & Biafra

FCO 25/189, 190, 200 Nigeria & Biafra

FCO 25/ 251–252 Arms sales to Nigeria

FCO 25/253 Military assistance to peace-keeping force

FCO 38/270–273 Supply of arms from UK to Nigeria

FCO 38/276 Emergency planning on evacuation of UK citizens 67–68

FCO 38/298–299 Relief operations & financial aid for Nigeria

FCO 38/312 Possible air drops with ICRC

FCO 65/253–255 Soviet involvement with Nigeria

FCO 65/278 Congo desire to assist Nigeria

FCO 65 345–346 Arms shipments to Nigeria

FCO 65/349 Soviet arms sales to Nigeria

FCO 65/384 Food situation in Biafra

FCO 65/376 Relations of ICRC & Nigeria

FCO 65/380 Discussions on relief flights & donations

FCO 30/293 Nigeria 68–69

FCO 16/4, 5, 14, 81, 118 Nigeria 68–69

FCO 61/497 Emergency aid to Nigeria 1968

FCO 14/123 Nigeria 67–68

FCO 26/299–302 Publicity & propaganda about Biafra & civil war

FCO 19/ 98, 129 Nigeria 68–69

FCO 79/200 Expulsion of UK defence adviser

DEFE 31/27 Intelligence general: Nigeria

FCO 65/266–273 French military support for Biafra & effect on relations with UK

FCO 65/288–290 Relief supplies & Van Rosen's activities

FCO 65/324 Food supplies for Biafra

FCO 65/327 Nigerian Air Force – request to train pilots

FCO 65/343 Arms purchases by Biafra

FCO 65/344–346 Arms shipments to Nigeria

FCO 65/347 French arms supplies to Biafra

FCO 65/362 Mercenaries in Biafra

FCO 65/363 Interception of relief flights

FCO 65/370 Policy on relief ops

FCO 65/378–382 Talks on relief flights '69

FCO 65/384 Food situation in Biafra

FCO 65/385 Surveys on food situation

FCO 65/390 UN relief policy

FCO 65/395–396 Air drops & possible RAF involvement

FC O 65/425–429 Daylight relief flights

FCO 65/488–489 RAF fact-finding visit

FCO 65/792 Involvement of ICRC in relief in Nigeria

FCO 26/365 Prime Minister Wilson's visit to Nigeria

PREM 13 2818/1, 2819/1 & 2820 Prime Minister Wilson's visit to Nigeria

Key files relating to Laos

FCO 15/892 Military situation report 1969

FCO 15/1263 Military activity by USA in Laos

FCO 15/131 – 133 US military involvement & counter-subversion activity 1967 – 1968

National Archives & Records Administration (USA)

Key files relating to Congo

General Records of the Department of State Bureau of African Affairs 1958 –
1966 (RG 59 Box 27)

General Record of the Department of State, Central Foreign Policy Files 1964
– 66

> Consular Protective Services (RG 59 Box 303)
> POL 27-4 Use of International Forces The Congo – UN to POL 1
> Internal Security The Congo – Zombia (sic) (RG 59 Box 2740)
> POL 23-9 Rebellion Coups The Congo to POL 23-9 Rebellion Coups
> The Congo (RG 59 Boxes 2734, 273 and 2737)
> DEF 19 BEL – The Congo 1/1/64 to DEF BER 1/1/64 (RG 59 Box 1610)
> DEF 9 The Congo 1/1/64 to DEF TRIN & TOB – US (RG 59 Box 1687)

Key files relating to Nigeria

Nixon Presidential Materials Staff, White House Special Files & White
House Central files – CO 135 Republic of South Africa (1969–1970) to
CO164 Venezuela (1971 – 1974) (Box 9)

General Records of the Department of State, Central Foreign Policy files 1967–
1969

> DEF 19 US-NIC to DEF US-PAN (RG 59 Box 1700)
> DEF BEL-GER W to DEF 6-5 Biafra (RG 59 Box 1522)
> POL 27-9 Biafra – Nigeria 9/1/68 to POL 27-9 Biafra-Nigeria 11/1/68
> (RG 59 Box 1882)
> POL 27-9 Biafra-Nigeria 6/1/69 to POL 27-9 Biafra-Nigeria 7/4/69 (RG
> 59 Box 1886)

General Records of the State Department, Consular PS 7-6 Nigeria to PS 10-4 US-PAN (RG 59 Box 291)

Key files relating to Laos

Nixon Presidential Materials Staff, National Security Council (NSC) Files

> Vietnam Security Files, Advance warning of US air strikes to Air
> Activity in Southeast Asia Vol III Jan–Aug 1972 (Box 96)
> Country Files – Europe, United Kingdom through May 1964 – Vol I
> to United Kingdom – June 1969 – 30 Aug 1970 Vol II (Box 726)
> Country Files – Europe, United Kingdom – 1 Jan 71 – Mar 71 Vol V
> to United Kingdom – 1 Apr – 31 Aug – Vol VI (Box 728)

General Records of the Department of State, Central Foreign Policy Files 1967–1969,
Political & Defense
DEF Laos to DEF Laos-A (RG 59 Box 1572)
DEF 19 US-Laos to DEF 15-4 US-Libya (RG 59 Box 1698)

General Records of the Department of State, Bureau of Asia & Pacific Affairs, Office
Laotian & Cambodian Affairs, Subject Files 1961 – 1975 (RG 59 Box 11

UNICEF Records

CF/RAD/USAA/DB01/1996-0012PDF (Interview Edmond Bridgewater by Dan Jacobs Nigeria Biafra; Red Cross; airlifts)

CF/RA/BX/PD/1975/TO54 (Programme Division – Africa Section Correspondence Background Material, Food Supply, Airlift, Nigeria)

CF/RAF/ZW/H0917-1975-539035705 (Nigeria Emergency Background 01-Jan-1968

14-Oct-1999 & Air Lift General 01-Jan-1969)

CF/RA/BX/ED/X/1979/T002 (Nigerian and Biafran Relief)

CF/RAF/ZW/A017 – 1979-000000028 (Airlifting of Supplies to Nigeria/Biafra)

Key unpublished sources

Terry Peet's Flight Log

Terry Peet's Service Records

Joan Peet née Milner's diary recordings and correspondence between Terry Peet and herself

Operation *WITHRUSH* – the detailed memoir of Leighton Mishou

Published sources

A Look Over My Shoulder, Richard Helms, Random House

Beyond the Storm, William T Close, Medowlark Springs Productions

Captive in the Congo: A Consul's Return to the Heart of Drakness, Michael P E Hoyt, Naval Institute Press

Chief of Station, Congo, Larry Devlin, Perseus Books Group

Confrontation, the War with Indonesia 1962–1966, Nick Van Der Bijl, Pen & Sword Books

Congo Warriors, Mike Hoare, Robert Hale Ltd

Conway's All the World's Fighting Ships 1947–1982, Robert Gardiner, Conway Maritime Press

Dragon Operations: Hostage Rescues in the Congo, 1964–1965, Thomas P Odom, Combat Studies Institute, US Army Command and General Staff College

Dragon Rouge: The Rescue of Hostages in the Congo, Fred E Wagoner, National Defense University, Research Directorate

Drop Zone Borneo, The RAF Campaign 1963–65, Roger Annett, Pen & Sword Books

Foreign Invaders, The Douglas Invader in foreign military and US clandestine services, Dan Hagedorn and Lief Hellström, Midland Publishing Ltd

Heart of Darkness, Joseph Conrad, Penguin Books

In Search of Enemies, John Stockwell, W W Norton & Company Inc

Instruments of Statecraft: US Guerilla Warfare, Counterinsurgency and Counterterrorism, 1940–1990, Michael McClintock, Pantheon Books

In the Footsteps of Mr Kurtz, Michela Wrong, HarperCollins

Jane's All The World's Aircraft, Paul A Jackson, Jane's Information Group

Killing Hope: US Military and CIA Interventions since World War II, William Blum, Zed Books Ltd

King Leopold's Ghost, Adam Hochschild, Macmillan Publishers Ltd

Legacy of Ashes, The History of the CIA, Tim Weiner, Allen Lane

RAF Helicopters, Wing Commander John Dowling, HMSO

Shadows, Airlift and Airwar In Biafra and Nigeria 1967–70, Michael I Draper, Hikoki Publications

Shadow War: The CIA's Secret War in Laos, Kenneth Conboy & James Morrison, Paladin Press

The American Agent: My Life in the CIA, Richard L Holm, St Ermin's Press

The Malayan Emergency and Indonesian Confrontation: The Commonwealth's Wars 1948–1966, Robert Jackson, Pen & Sword Books

The War of the Running Dogs: Malaya 1948–1960, Noel Barber, Cassell Military Paperbacks

War of Numbers, An Intelligence Memoir, Sam Adams, Steerforth Press

Newspapers and periodicals

UK and US newspaper and periodical reports too numerous to list.

Index